Famous British Columbia Fly-Fishing Waters

Art Lingren

Famous British Columbia

Fly-Fishing Waters

Art Lingren

Frank Amato
PORTLAND

Dedication

To the fly fishermen who came before and
provided the roots for future generations of fly fishers.

Frank Amato Publications, Inc.
P.O. Box 82112, Portland, Oregon 97282
503•653•8108 • www.amatobooks.com

All photographs by the author unless otherwise noted.
Map illustration by Kathy Johnson

Book & Cover Design: Kathy Johnson

Printed in Singapore

Softbound ISBN: 1-57188-226-X   UPC: 0-66066-00464-2
Hardbound ISBN: 1-57188-227-8   UPC: 0-66066-00465-9

1 3 5 7 9 10 8 6 4 2

Contents

Acknowledgments

Many fly-fishing friends have provided information that appears in the following pages and others have read parts of or the entire text and provided valuable comments that have made the book better. My sincere thanks to all who gave a hand and especially to:

- Robert Taylor, Peter Broomhall, Michael Uehara and Ron Schiefke for reading the manuscript and providing helpful comments.
- James Craig for his information on the Ministry of Environment's Vancouver Island swim counts on the Campbell, Cowichan and Stamp rivers.
- Jim Fisher for his comments and input to the Adams and Little River chapter.
- Van Egan for his comments on the Campbell and Stamp rivers chapters and for letting me use some of his photographs.
- Paul Dorien Smith for giving me so much information on his father Paul Moody Smith and the Capilano River.
- Tom Heath of the Greater Vancouver Regional District for the copies of H. B. Smith's report and other GVWD information.
- Bill Westover, Ron Grantham and Jeff Mironuck for comments and input on the Columbia, the Kootenay and tributary rivers chapter.
- Peter Caverhill for his comments on the Harrison and Coquihalla rivers.
- David Anderson, Joe Saysell and Charlie Stroulger for information included in the Cowichan River chapter.
- Many Totem Flyfishers and guests who have shared days on the Dean River with me and indirectly provided me with information for that river's chapter.
- Brian Chan for his comments on the Bill Nation Kamloops lakes.
- Gil Sage and Peter Caverhill for comments on the Skagit River.
- Rob Brown, Bob Clay, Jim Adams, Ray Makowichuk, Bob Hooton, Mark Beere, Jim Yardley, Gwen Rawlins for providing information for and or comments on all or sections of the Skeena chapter.
- Greg Gordon for sharing with me some of his Thompson River trout fly-fishing spots.
- Bob Crooks, Doug Richardson and Bill Nelson for providing information for the Tlell chapter.

KATHY JOHNSON

British Columbia Map

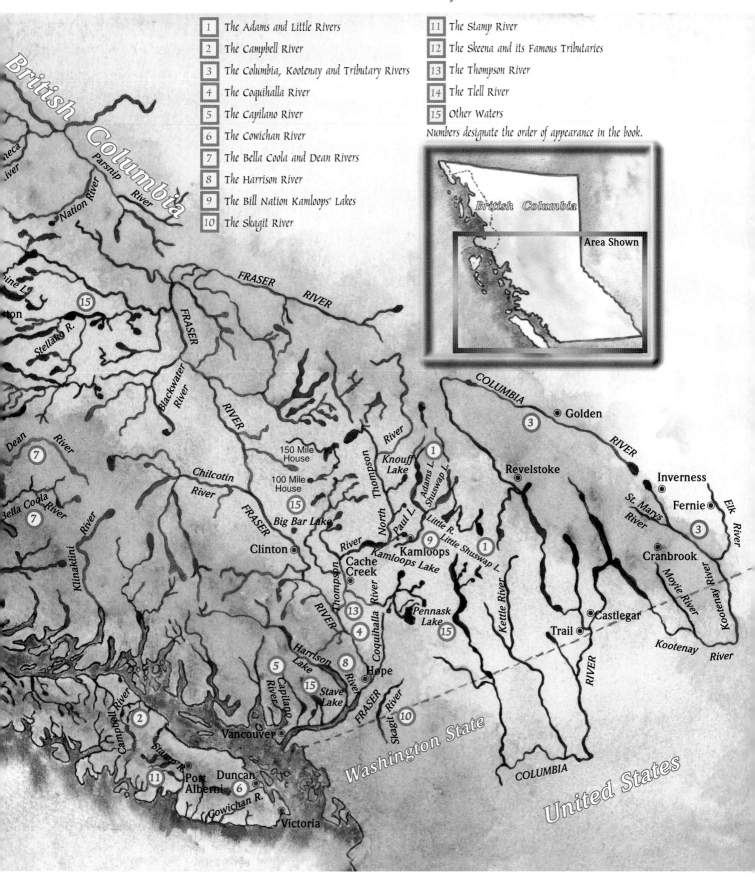

1 The Adams and Little Rivers
2 The Campbell River
3 The Columbia, Kootenay and Tributary Rivers
4 The Coquihalla River
5 The Capilano River
6 The Cowichan River
7 The Bella Coola and Dean Rivers
8 The Harrison River
9 The Bill Nation Kamloops' Lakes
10 The Skagit River
11 The Stamp River
12 The Skeena and its Famous Tributaries
13 The Thompson River
14 The Tlell River
15 Other Waters

Numbers designate the order of appearance in the book.

Introduction

Natural history illustrator, conservationist, fly-tyer and ardent fly-fisher, Loucas Raptis searching for a Kispiox River steelhead.

IN 1998, WHEN CANADA POST ISSUED ITS COMMEMORATIVE, fly-fishing flies stamp series, of the six flies featured three were of British Columbian origin. British Columbia's fly-fishing heritage is rich with roots that penetrate deep into the origins of the sport. This book is about the origins of fly-fishing in British Columbia, those special waters where fly-fishing developed, and the fly-fishers who laid the foundation for the fly-fishers who came after.

Some of British Columbia's waters became so well known, they attracted fly-fishers from England, America and other parts of the globe. Some waters have suffered seriously from man's presence while others have been less affected and remain world-class fisheries. But make no mistake about it, man's global footprints have affected even the best and most wilderness of waters. Access to many waters was entwined with the development of the province. In the paths laid by the explorers and trappers, came wagon roads then railways. The railways were followed by roads and highways

suitable for driving cars and trucks, and they eventually ribboned the countryside, providing easy access to many of the waters. Later fishermen in float planes and helicopters traveled to the most remote waters.

For nearly 150 years, fly-fishers have been plying British Columbia's water with rod, reel and fly. Save for the past 25 years, for most of that time, a caught fish was a dead fish. Old fishing pictures help illustrate the abundance of the land and the sport fly-fishers experienced. I have included a number of old photographs in this book, some with many dead fish. I make no apology for them: in the old days; the kill was considered part of sport.

I have a fascination with fly-fishing history and fly-fishing books. They are just two things that enhance my passion for fly-fishing that make it, for me, an all-consuming sport. Almost 20 years ago I assembled a list of British Columbia sportfishing books, which I sent to two wise fishermen well versed in angling literature. They filled some gaps, but notable was the lack of pre-1900 books. Visits to the University of British Columbia's and Vancouver Public libraries to see their sportfishing sections added no new titles to my list. At the Vancouver Public Library a librarian directed me to the Northwest History section. The books there are for the most part rare ones and can be viewed only one at a time, but because of their condition they could not be opened wide and copied. If you wanted information you had to take notes.

When I explained to the librarian what I was looking for she suggested I might have better luck if I used Barbara J. Lowther's book *A Bibliography of British Columbia: Laying the Foundations 1849-1899*. With over 2000 entries, the bibliography helped eliminate many days' toil. With each entry—of which many were

important papers and reports and only some were books—Lowther included a brief description of what a book, report or letter contained, as well as author and, if a book, publishing details. Rarely did the brief description include a reference to fishing, but if the

description or title indicated that the author was travelling, hunting or exploring British Columbia, I scanned the book's table of contents and then, if further hints about fishing were there, I reviewed specific pages or chapters. I did find a number of books published

between 1865 and 1900 that had reference to fish, fishing, or fly-fishing. I made notes from which I compiled *British Columbia Angling and Fishing Literature*. By looking through used book stores and antiquarian book dealers' catalogues, I have managed to acquire some titles over the years.

Often the titles were deceiving. For example, John Keast Lord's *The Naturalist in British Columbia* published in 1866, Lowther describes as:

> *Written for the general reader from the author's observations and experiences while he was the naturalist for the British North American Boundary Commission. It contains extensive general descriptive information, and offers some information about the work on the commission.* (p. 33)

On closer examination I found that Lord devoted about 60 pages to fish and fishing and, in those pages, he described trying to catch salmon on the fly, the dressing of British Columbia's first trout fly, and one of the earliest reports of fly-fishing for trout. The book is an absolute gem for the fly-fishing history buff but extremely hard to find. I have seen two for sale in 20 years. My copy, with its repaired spine, cost $350 in the mid-1980s.

In the pages that follow you will find the first fly dressed for British Columbia trout; the first recorded use of the dry fly on still waters and rivers in British Columbia, Canada and North America; the first records of fly-fishing for salmon and the development of the sport called bucktailing; as well as British Columbia's first stillwater dry flies, Chironomid and dragonfly nymph patterns; and the introduction in North America of the dry-fly, waked-fly and greased-line techniques to steelhead fly-fishing. You will read about the revival of the double-handed rod in the mid-1980s and about Spey casting with sinktip experiments on British Columbia rivers that revolutionized Pacific Northwest steelhead fly-fishing.

You will read about early fly-fishers and the contribution to the sport by Dr. Thomas Wilson Lambert, Arthur Bryan Williams, General Noel Money, Bill Nation, Roderick Haig-Brown, Paul Moody Smith, Frank Darling, Francis Whitehouse, Tommy Brayshaw and many others.

I have tried to avoid second-hand anecdotal information, relying wherever possible on the best available written references to document past events. If a reader has other information that contradicts what I have scribed, please drop me a note citing book title, author and date of publication or send me copies of letters, diaries or magazine articles. My home address is 3588 West 38th Avenue, Vancouver, British Columbia, V6N 2Y1.

Fly-fishing is a deep-rooted sport based on tradition with those fly-fishers that came before providing an ever-lasting heritage. This book is a look back at the past 150 years of fly-fishing heritage in British Columbia and the wonderful experiences that fly-fishers found on our waters. Our environmental stewardship record has not been a good one and man's presence with its local and global ramifications will effect what future generations of fly-fishers may experience fly-fishing in the third millennium.

Art Lingren
February 2001

1

The Adams and Little Rivers

A good catch from the Adams, circa 1900.

NEAR THE TOWN OF CHASE ON THE SOUTH THOMPSON River system are two rivers where trout grow large and, if you hit it right, the fishing superb. Little River is a three-mile-long stretch of the South Thompson River joining Shuswap and Little Shuswap lakes. Adams River flows into Shuswap Lake just a hop, skip and a jump from the lake's outlet. The Adams is home to the famous sockeye salmon run, where every fourth year the cycle peaks. On the peak year, the sockeye return to spawn in the millions and visitors flock to the Adams' banks to view this wonder of nature. For the fly-fisher it is a beautiful trout stream with trails along both banks between Shuswap and Adams lakes, a distance of about seven miles.

The Canadian Pacific Railway was constructed along the south bank of Little Shuswap Lake and Little River, providing easy access to Little River and a jumping-off spot for the Adams River. After spending time trout fishing at Spences Bridge, H. W. Seton-Karr "took a leap in the dark, not having any reliable advice," and he chose the Shuswap area as his next stopping point. There he hired a Native guide and with camping gear rode on horseback to the outlet of Adams Lake. About his July, 1890 journey along the river to the lake, in *Bear-Hunting in the White Mountains* (1891), he writes:

> *Adams River is a very swift stream, only available for canoe navigation at lowest water.... There are good pack trails on both banks between Adams and Shushwap [sic] lakes, that on the east side being rather the better but the less used of the two; the route along the west or right bank being the one I employed. The way at first rises gradually and mostly keeps along terraces, high above Adams River, which can be heard thundering below, but is not approached until the lake is almost in sight....*

> *The path descends and Adams Lake bursts suddenly upon the view. This body of water probably took its name from some more ordinary person than our common ancestor; but the Garden of Eden might well have been situated in a less pleasing spot.*

After putting up camp on a grassy promontory at the lake's outlet and crossing the outlet with a canoe stashed by his guide, about the spot and the fishing, he writes:

> The surface was of glassy smoothness, reflecting the wooded hills and high bare bank upon the opposite side; but upon the breast of the rapids, where the water toppled over and sank rushing away with gradually increasing speed, the surface seemed elongated and furrowed with changing lines as though drawn and sucked downwards with the growing velocity. Collected by the concentration of the waters from all parts of the lake, were floating to destruction myriads of large and small moths and flies, unable to rise from the surface. The smoothness of the water above this point was constantly being broken by the splash of the great trout as they fed greedily upon the plentiful harvest of the air....
>
> The canoe was as cranky and dangerous as any of those on the lower lake, and if someone were to build a boat on this lake it would prove a great convenience, as the trout fishing here is undoubtedly the best in the district, and future anglers would then be able to ply their craft in safety, because the best fishing is on the very brink of the rapids, where any delay or accident might result in one's being carried down a mile in five minutes.
>
> On landing I immediately set to work, with a fine cast and moderate-sized brown flies, and enjoyed the best sport I have met with since I fished the Shellefto River in North Sweden, the Vouksa in Finland, or the Sardinian Fluemendosa, or the Umeo, or the Saquenay, or other of the best pleasure-grounds of the enthusiastic angler. (pp. 123-126)

The largest trout taken by Seton-Karr and his guide pulled the scale needle down to four and a half pounds. Seton-Karr's account

In the spring, wildflowers add beauty to the landscape.

is one of the earliest fly-fishing records for the Adams. Early in the 20th century, both the Adams and Little rivers would draw fly-fishers from all over in pursuit of its voracious sockeye fry- and fingerling-eating trout.

Dr. T. W. Lambert, in his *Fishing in British Columbia* (1907), describes the good sport with rod and reel in Shuswap Lake and at the mouths of the salmon bearing creeks. Lambert also provided, perhaps, the first Little River fly-fishing testimonial. He was passing Little River one July morning and noticed in a back eddy at Sullivan's Pool that the "water was alive with large trout chasing the small fry on the surface" and "mergansers attacked them from above (p. 25)." It was a sight he had never witnessed before or since. When he returned in the evening, he requested they stop and Lambert was put into a small boat where on his first cast he caught "a beautiful 4 1/2 lb. rainbow, which was promptly cooked for dinner (p. 26)." He knew that first light is often the best time to take fish in this sun-baked, desert-type setting and wished that he could have stayed and fished the pool in the morning.

A regular visitor spanning many decades, Arthur Bryan Williams was one of the first of the Little River fly-fishers. He is probably the river's most famous devotee.

Williams was born in Lismany, Ireland on December 9, 1866. When he was 22 years old he emmigrated to Canada and arrived in Vancouver in the spring of 1888. He fished the Capilano frequently and a pool near the downstream end of the canyon bears his name to this day. He mentions in one of his books that for the next five years after 1898 he spent most of his time on the Skeena River hunting and fishing. An extremely knowledgeable man about fish and game, he became British Columbia's first game and forest warden in 1905. With little support from members in the Government, his new job proved trying and difficult at first. With limited funds to work with, Williams implemented a firearm's license program, realizing $80,000 in its first year, quite a sum in those days. With funding secured through the licensing program, as well as through perseverance and hard work, he won support from Government members. As the head of the Game Department, he was one of the first to realize the value of British Columbia's hunting and fishing resource by displaying game trophies in some European cities in 1910. During his term, which ended with his retirement in 1918 "due to the rigid economy," came fish and game laws as well as licenses and fees. The new game act emphasized, among many things, the concept of providing recreation from hunting and fishing based on fair rules of the chase.

After his first retirement he became a guide outfitter, but was coaxed out of retirement and appointed Provincial Game Commissioner, a post he held from 1929 until his final retirement in 1934.

Williams, by his own words, said he never intended to stay permanently in British Columbia, but go south. He found that "the glories of this wonderland and the magnificent sport that can be obtained here appealed to me and have held me ever since." We are fortunate that he did stay. In his new land he sampled the sport unlike few others could and he wrote three books all of which are

As the sun sets at the mouth of the Adams River, the trout become more receptive.

classics. *Rod and Creel in British Columbia* was published in 1919, *Fish and Game in British Columbia* came out in 1935 and are of most interest to fisherman. In between, in 1925, *Game Trails in British Columbia* was released. As the title suggests it is a hunting book, but he included some fishing sketches. *Fish and Game in British Columbia* became the prototype from which all later British Columbian fishing and hunting guide books evolved.

He did not tie flies but he is responsible for the development of British Columbia's first dry flies. When Rod Haig-Brown was writing *The Western Angler* in 1938 he asked Harkley and Haywood for the particulars of Williams Grey-Bodied Sedge pattern. But they considered it a trade secret and refused. Haig-Brown then wrote Williams asking him for the dressing of Williams' Grey-Bodied Sedge. In his 26 April 1938 response to Haig-Brown, Williams writes:

> While I have never made any secret of any of my flies or for a matter of fact of any little success I have had in the way of any sort of sport, I am afraid it is out of my power to help you about the dressing of the dry sedge. I have had three different sedges tied, grey, green and yellow bodied. The first two I brought from the Kamloops district. The latter from Vancouver Island.
>
> It is a good many years since I discovered that there were hatches of sedges in the interior and that when a hatch was on trout would hardly look at a wet fly. So I caught some of them, brought them to town and got Harkley and Haywood to make some for me. After several trials they produced a very good imitation. Now while I went several times to give advice to the woman who ties their flies I still could not give you the particulars of the actual materials used. However, as far as I know, there is nothing to prevent you giving your idea of the dressing. At any rate I have not the slightest objection.

> I may also say that while it is absolutely no matter of interest to me I can quite understand their feelings with regard to their flies. That woman went to a lot of trouble in getting the right material and experimenting and I imagine she has done and is still doing well as a result. Incidentally I may tell you that a good many gross of this fly have been sent to New Brunswick where they are very deadly with salmon at low water. I may also say that I believe that dry fly-fishing in this country was hardly ever practiced, at any rate to any extent, until I started it with the grey sedge. Later on I originated the green bodied which is also even more deadly on the waters where they hatch.

Later a fourth dry fly, Williams' Dark-Bodied Sedge, was added for coastal waters. Williams was not the first to use dry flies on British Columbia waters, but he certainly is due credit for British Columbia's first dry flies and popularizing dry-fly fishing, particularly on lakes in the Kamloops area.

Lee Richardson fished Little River for 19 seasons, starting in 1934. During his spring 1935 trip, he met Williams and asked the "great man" who "had angled these waters more than any other… about his most memorable day:" The story Williams told took place on a June 1913 morning and Richardson reported it verbatim in *Lee Richardson's B.C.* (1978). Williams says:

> So next morning I dropped anchor above the rip just as it began to get light. I had the place to myself. Of course, there were no resorts; and, in any event, few people had ever heard of Little River in those days and those that had were not disposed to undertake such a long and arduous journey when there was good sport nearer home. The fingerlings were running, and I began fishing about 4:00 a.m. and quit at 8:00. During that time I had ten strikes and boated eight trout, the

largest twelve and three-quarter pounds, the smallest about four pounds. All the rest were from seven to nine pounds. Every one of those fish went into the backing before I could scramble forward to free the anchor, holding the rod with one hand while tugging at the rope with the other. Usually I was a quarter of a mile into the lake before I netted them. (p. 7 - 8)

An amazing four hours of fishing considering those were the days before outboard motors and after each fish was landed Williams had a good row into the current back to his anchor. He must have been either playing trout or rowing most of the time.

Williams was one of the first to praise the fishing in and around Shuswap Lake. In *Rod & Creel in British Columbia* he says:

Fly fishing is at its best in June and some wonderful sport is generally to be had. The average weight of the fish would be somewhere about two pounds, but fish of five or six pounds are more or less common. (p. 118)

Later in the book, when he describes the fishing around Chase, he mentions that the Silver Doctor, Jock Scott, Dusty Miller, Montreal, Butcher, Red Palmer, March Brown, Black Gnat, Brown Hackle, Professor and Cow Dung are the popular flies for the area.

In *Fish & Game in British Columbia*, Williams gives a glowing report for Little River and its fly-fishing where it flows into Little Shuswap Lake and, as well, he reported on the fishing to be had in the Adams River. He also provides a list of flies to use and writes:

At this point the current is swift for about a quarter of a mile into the lake, and at times the fly-fishing there is marvelous. Kamloops trout up to 12 1/2 lbs. have been caught on the fly...A short row from this camp will take you to the mouth of Adams River, where the fishing somewhat similar to that at Little River is to be obtained. At Adams River, the spring months are usually the best, when a hatch of Stone Flies occurs. Excellent sport is always to be had when the hatch is on if you use a Stone Fly Nymph. It is often extremely good in September and October.

From this point you can drive by car up to Adams Lake and fish the river down. There are some good pools in it, which occasionally are full of fish running from 1 to 3 pounds...

The best flies for Little River are the Big Bertha, tied on a No. 2 hook; the Bucktail, tied on a No. 2/0; and a Silver and Light Mallard, without any hackle, also on a No. 2. (p. 110-111)

Noteworthy is the evolution in flies between Williams' two fishing books. In Williams' 1919 book he recommends British patterns, but by 1935 all the flies had a distinctive British Columbian flavour and all had the tell-tale silver body representative of the small sockeye fry the trout were crazy for.

Tommy Brayshaw, another famous British Columbia fly-fisher, put down roots in Vernon in the 1920s and he too would add to the

On a cycle year, the sockeye return to the Adams in the hundreds of thousands.

There are good trails along both banks of the Adams.

Little River and Adams fly-fishing lore. Brayshaw kept meticulous records of his fishing and a review of his diaries shows he fished the Adams and Little rivers often. He made his last trip on May 15, 1943. Brayshaw, the masterful fly designer and tyer, developed a number of patterns for the Adams and Little rivers. Rod Haig-Brown included Brayshaw's Little River No. 1 and Little River No. 2 flies in *The Western Angler*, published in 1939. Brayshaw used minnow imitations dressed on single hooks when the sockeye fry were newly emerged from their gravelly bed. When the sockeye fingerlings started their migration to the ocean, he used flies dressed on hooks in tandem to better represent the fingerlings. Another silver-bodied, mallard-winged pattern he named the Yolk Sac, which he later referred to as the Alevin, was dressed with a red throat, to represent newly emerged fry with yolk sac not fully absorbed. The Egg 'n' I is the current rendition and remains a popular salmon-fry pattern, not just for Little and Adams rivers, but on many coastal rivers when salmon-fry emerge.

For many years there were no accommodations close to the Little River and Adams River fishing spots and Bryan Williams and others camped. Sometime in the 1920s, A. C. M. Danielson built Little River Fishing Camp "situated at Shuswap Lake and Little River, opposite mouth of Adams River." In *Fish and Game in British*

Columbia Danielson advertised:

- *Fly-fishing continuously from April to late fall.*
- *Fish up to 12 pounds caught on fly in swift water.*
- *Five and six-pound fish plentiful.*
- *Cabins, per day $1.25 and up; Furnished, per day $1.50 and up; Bungalows, per day $2.50-$3.00*
- *Dining-room service; Meals, 50 cents and 60 cents; and Lunches put up.*

Danielson's camp became the Little and Adams rivers' fly-fishing headquarters and, at any given time when the fishing was good, guests would rub shoulders with the great fly-fishers of the day such as Bryan Williams, Tommy Brayshaw, Lee Richardson, and Francis Whitehouse to name a few.

Whitehouse, a regular at Little River, describes in his book *Sport Fishes of Western Canada* (1945) the four distinct phases of the art of fly-fishing for Little and Adams river trout. The April fishing begins with the stonefly hatch. For his stonefly nymph he recommends a yellow, white, and red body with a brown back dressed on number eight or six hooks cast across and brought across fished on a line oiled to within nine inches of the fly. Sometime in April the salmon fry emerge and later the sockeye fingerling migration takes place. Whitehouse recommends silver-bodied flies such as Teal and Silver, Mallard and Silver, Cumming's Fancy, Bucktails dressed on hooks as large a number two. The fry and fingerlings move down river in a bunch and the fish follow and attack the schools as they move downstream. The fly is cast beyond and below the fry and brought through as the small salmon pass. From mid-July through mid-September, he describes it as the difficult season. The large trout have moved away from the mouths of the river. Because the current in Little River is not as strong for the river trout, he recommends using the standard wet- or dry-fly methods with smaller flies such as Sedges, Alders, Black Gnats, Seth Greens, Montreal, etcetera, dressed on number eight and ten hooks. Lastly, from mid-September the mature salmon start to arrive and the large trout move in to gorge on salmon eggs. Because salmon eggs are pink or reddish, Whitehouse recommends flies of red-and-white construction such as the Parmachene Belle, Red Ibis, Montreal and Royal Coachman. The Royal Coachman dressed on a number six hook was the best killer, he claims.

Few fly-fishers cast Royal Coachmans or Red Ibis' into the waters today, but favour more representative salmon-egg patterns. As well, the Sedges, Alders and Black Gnats have been replaced by patterns more representative of the natural insects. No fly-fisher gets to cast stonefly nymphs or salmon fry to hungry trout in April through the end of May. It is trout spawning time and both the Adams and Little rivers are closed to fishing between March 15 and May 31 inclusive.

For parts of the 1920s and 1930s the legendary Bill Nation guided clients at Little River. Nation believed it was a superb fishery and in an 8 August 1939 letter he stated that next year the fingerling migration would be from the cycle year of 1938 and invited Haig-Brown to come up if he could:

It is perhaps the most interesting fly-fishing in the world when the trout are coming down in quantities. You see all your fish, as they are a quarter of their depth out of water, and [you] can tell the size, condition and sex. The problem being to spot the fly just in front of their nose. Use a line greased to the end, and a twelve or fourteen foot leader greased half way, and a light mallard and silver #2 fly. Fish that are upstream from you, cast just below them, about nine inches, and let the fly come down stream unchecked about three feet, lift and recast, strike at the splash; the least drag is fatal. Fish that are abreast of the anchored boat, strip with a rather gentle flowing strip; fish well down on the quarter, cast four feet below and four feet beyond, and strip as fast as humanly possible; it is impossible to tear the line through the rings too fast. The fish are travelling down stream faster than the

current, and the fly must be kept below them; both speed and accuracy are needed.

Nation told Haig-Brown in an earlier letter that there is a run of 12- to 19-pound rainbows that appear around April 25th and then disappear in early May. However, as more people settled in the Shuswap area and a new highway provided easier access to the area, more came to fish, many not for the sport but to fill their freezers. In the early 1950s, Lee Richardson stopped his annual trips to Little River. He forsook the fishing and tossed in the towel when he:

saw a man trolling a wire coat hanger, to which he had attached two lengths of monofilament and a rather large number of worms. I knew then that I had seen everything, and that in the future I would have to search farther afield for the incomparable sport I had known at Shuswap. (Lee Richardson's B.C., p. 16)

About the time Richardson stopped going to Little River Camp a young wide-eyed Peter Broomhall made his first trip. He has fond, ever-lasting memories of Little River, Big Bertha, and his years there and in recent e-mail correspondence to me, Pete writes:

Incidentally, in 1952, I worked for Doug Robertson at Little River Lodge, across from the mouth of the Adams and near the outlet of Big Shuswap Lake. Someone there told me that Little River was so-named because it was so short. My first glimpse of the river told me that "small" didn't refer to water volume. I can't remember whether it was stern- or side-wheelers, or both, that once navigated the South Thompson, Little Shuswap, Little River and Shuswap Lake, but I remember feeling somewhat deprived for not having witnessed such a marvel.

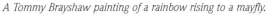

A Tommy Brayshaw painting of a rainbow rising to a mayfly.

Mr. Dick Underwood and friend with a catch of 'speckled trout" (rainbows) from the Adams River, circa 1900.

While I'm reminiscing, I should add not only that I favored the Big Bertha at the mouth of Little River, but why. In narrative terms, the explanation dates back to a day in mid-July (of '52), when Robertson took me on a fish-finding expedition to the mouth of Little River. We anchored right where the juvenile sockeye entered Little Shuswap. The pods of small fish shimmered in the surface film as they came downstream. When they reached the drop off, the rainbows greeted them in a fast and furious burst of activity.

During a quiet spell, Robertson gave me a quick lesson in fly-casting (up until then I was primarily a steelhead float- and spin-fisher). Robertson's teaching technique was simplicity itself. He stood behind me, ordered me to hold onto his fly rod above the handle, to "feel" but not "resist" his movements, and then made a few casts. He then told me to demonstrate what I'd learned. He observed, commented on my efforts, repeated the backcast "lift" and the forward cast "snap"—to emphasize their importance—and then declared that I was on my own.

A week later, a camp guest told Robertson that I had helped him with his fly-casting, and the next day Robertson sent me out guiding for the first time—a

welcome relief from shore-based work. Soon after, I bought a fly reel (J.W. Young Beaudex), and some flies (including a Big Bertha) from the lodge's modest fishing tackle "store". For a line, I used a discarded and much-worn silk King Eider, and for a casting instrument, I made do with my homemade, nine-foot, light-weight fibreglass steelhead float-fishing rod. Since I'd been catching steelhead on float-fished "gob" flies for a few years, and since I'd learned from Haig-Brown that Kamloops rainbows weren't always selective, I figured that the Big Bertha—which looked like a steelhead-tempter to me—would be a good alternative for minnow imitations.

Because my age (17) and my nature (timid) prevented me from claiming a place in the "hot" zone when two or more boats were already anchored there, I usually had to settle for second-choice water whenever I visited the mouth of Little River. It was in such a spot, just where Little River emptied into Little Shuswap Lake, that I first met one of area's legendary trout—and almost lost my fly-gear in the process. The fish grabbed my trailing Big Bertha while I was setting anchor. The reel ratchet alerted me. I turned backward, and somehow grabbed the rod on its way overboard. I'd like to report that the trout was 10 *pounds, but it wasn't. I know it was half that size because it made several leaps before throwing the hook. It nevertheless remains the most memorable Shuswap rainbow I've ever hooked.*

Although I've read no definitive literature on the subject of diminished Adams-Little River trout stocks, I suspect not only that anglers played a role, but that salmon-eggers were disproportionately responsible. I've witnessed the consequences of the bait fishing there-in September and October of '52 and in the autumn of subsequent years. You'll recall that, in those halcyon days, fisheries biologists believed anglers incapable of over-fishing salmon or trout. That a present-day fisheries biologist endorses bait fishing for mainstem Thompson steelhead attests to a couple of truths that anglers should never forget: that some people who should know better, don't, and that ignorance can be remarkably durable.

It takes a number of years to grow large trout even for those fish whose diet consists for the large part of other fish. Those huge trout weighing in the teens fed on the Little and Adams river sockeye fry and fingerlings and were probably six-year-olds, perhaps older. From the early days when Seton-Karr and Williams first fished these waters and for many decades thereafter, a caught fish was a dead fish. From the early 1950s on through to late 1980s, the human population increased and access became easier, the fishing showed steady decline, even though limits were reduced. Some caring anglers released some of their catch, but the voluntary catch and release was not enough to save the superb Little and Adams river fishery. Just too many anglers killing too many fish and, around 1990, the Adams and Little rivers became catch-and-release only.

The sockeye still return and on a cycle year they spawn in the many hundreds of thousands, providing food for trout. Both the Adams and Little rivers flow through provincial parks providing some protection from development. The Roderick Haig-Brown Provincial Park provides a buffer strip for the Adams River from its outlet at Adams Lake down to Shuswap Lake. Little River too enjoys land-use protection: abutting portions of Shuswap and Little Shuswap lakes are protected by Shuswap Lake Provincial Park. The water quality remains good, the insects are still hatching and providing food for trout when they are not feeding on salmon eggs, fry, fingerlings or decaying flesh from dead sockeye. Because of catch and release, the trout populations have rebounded.

Over his twenty years fly-fishing the Adams, Jim Fisher, fly-fishing and fly tying instructor, ardent fly-fisher, fly-fishing writer and a charter member of the Kalamalka fly-fishers' Society in Vernon, has witnessed first hand that river's trout fly-fishing recovery. About the Adams and Little river fishery, Jim in a 22 August 2000 letter to me writes:

Like you undoubtedly have done, I've read many accounts of A. Bryan Williams, Pochin, and Lee Richardson about fishing the Adams and Little rivers in the early days. Williams' accounts are particularly

interesting, as they are so detailed, usually giving precise weights and numbers of trout taken.

It is my strong opinion [that] the quality of Adams River during the dominant-year sockeye run now eclipses that experienced by Williams and his contemporaries. How is this possible? Well, I've never intentionally killed an Adams River trout, and the fact it is currently not legal to do so, has enabled this fishery to rebound magnificently.

Jim provided me a couple of extracts from his diary and his catches are impressive indeed. Fisher's fly of choice is his own Adams River Spuddler, which is dressed on size four to eight long-shanked hooks, with a body of gold Mylar, rib of oval gold wire, wing of two matching badger hackles and a clipped deer-hair head. Sometimes Jim adds lead wire to the hook shank, covering it with nylon floss before wrapping the Mylar body. Jim says that other anglers do well in the fall with Egg patterns and that an Egg 'n' I works well in the late winter.

The sockeye salmon runs that sustained Natives for millennia are also responsible for the bounty of trout. As long as the sockeye return and the catch-and-release fishery remains, the trout will grow large and fly-fishers will experience the ferocious take of large trout from Bill Nation's "most interesting fly-fishing in the world."

References

Fisher, Jim. *Tying Flies for B.C. Game Fish.* Vernon: Wetfeather Publications and Yellow Dog Press, 1996.

Hume, Mark. *Adam's River.* Vancouver: New Star Books, 1994.

Lambert, T. W. *Fishing in British Columbia.* London: Horace Cox, 1907.

Murray, Allan (Editor). *Our Wildlife Heritage.* Victoria: The Centennial Wildlife Society of British Columbia, 1987.

Raymond, Steve. *Kamloops.* Portland: Frank Amato Publications, Revised 1980 edition.

Read, Stanley E. *Tommy Brayshaw: The Ardent Angler-Artist.* Vancouver: University of British Columbia, 1977.

Richardson, Lee. *Lee Richardson's B.C.* Forest Grove: Champeog Press, 1978.

Seton-Karr, H. W. *Bear Hunting in the White Mountains or Alaska and British Columbia Revisited.* London: Chapman and Hall, 1891.

Whitehouse, Francis C. *Sport Fishing in Canada.* Vancouver: Privately printed, 1945.

Williams, A. Bryan. *Rod and Creel in British Columbia.* Vancouver: Progress Publishing Company, 1919.

___. *Game Trails in British Columbia.* New York: Charles Scribner's Sons, 1925.

___. *Fish and Game in British Columbia.* Vancouver: Sun Directories Ltd., 1935.

2

The Campbell River

This 32-inch summer-run took the author's Claret & Black.

THE CAMPBELL RIVER IS RODERICK HAIG-BROWN'S RIVER, just as the Lea is Izaak Walton's, the Dove is Charles Cotton's, and the Stamp is General Money's. Yet, the Campbell was a popular sport fishery for nearly half a century before Haig-Brown came to live there. Sometime in the 1860s, the salmon attracted the first sport fishers to the area. The Campbell River, however, became a destination sport fishery for those with time and money in 1896 when Sir Richard Musgrove caught his 70-pound tyee, the largest ever caught on rod and line up to that time. Ever after, the chinook salmon fishing off the mouth of the river would have its devotees and eventually the Tyee Club of British Columbia was formed to govern that world-class fishery. But, it was not fly-fishing.

Some who came seeking the monster tyees also brought along their fly rods and wandered up the river. H. W. Gordon of the Royal

Engineers was with Musgrove on his 1896 trip and in Musgrove's *Field* article he says that, "Gordon got four of about 3 pounds apiece with a fly."

Another tyee fisherman J. H. Wrigley, wrote an article that appeared in a 1906 issue of the *The Field*. About the river and its trout, he says:

The trout fishing higher up the river is excellent, and one or two remarkable baskets were brought in by American anglers, who combined a day of exploration work with a few hours' use of the fly rod. One catch in particular excited the admiration of the many fishermen who turned up at Campbell River during the first week in August. This catch included fish of 5 lb., several 3 and 4 pounders, a score of 2 pounders, and

Seven-year old Charles Lingren bringing one of his first salmon to the boat. Rob Bell-Irving assists with the net.

many smaller ones, all taken with the fly...In very truth this fine river is practically a virgin stream to fishermen...Nearly all these big trout were rainbows, with the brilliant purple flash along their broad silvery sides that is so characteristic of this particular species. (Edge of Discovery, pp. 250-251.)

The larger "rainbows" were probably small summer-run steelhead. Perhaps, it was the river's good trout fishing that prompted Haig-Brown to plant roots in Campbell River.

Nonetheless, it was the salmon fishing that drew most sport-fishers to the area. In recent years, saltwater coho salmon fly-fishing has become the in thing to do. Many neophytes think they are breaking new ground and few know that the sport was in its infancy 100 years ago. It was on the waters fronting Campbell River that fly-fishers in the early 20th century developed fly-fishing techniques for the scrappy coho. Dr. T. W. Lambert did not fish Campbell River, but he included a Mr. A. Duncan's saltwater coho fly-fishing testimonial in *Fishing in British Columbia* (1907). About the sport Mr. Duncan says:

The cohoe salmon will take a fly: white with silver tinsel, I found best. They take in the sea at sunrise and sunset when they are jumping—in fact, more could be got in this way while they are actually jumping than by trolling, only they must be jumping and also fairly plentiful. I have got an odd one casting, but nearly all by trailing the fly. They give splendid sport on a light trout rod. The largest I got last year (1903) was 12 lb. But they were not "running" this year, and I only got two of 7 lb. each on the fly. (p. 99)

Casting to showing fish and trailing the fly, later to become known as bucktailing, both popular techniques today, owe their origins to those early Campbell River fly-fishermen. Sir John Rogers too came to fish tyee, but he did find good sport casting to coho and reported in his 1912 book that, "the cohoe took a 2-inch Silver Doctor and rose steadily to the fly. (*Sport in Vancouver and Newfoundland*, p. 69)"

The alarm sounded early and getting my son Charles (C.T.) out of bed was a chore. We were going bucktailing with Rob Bell-Irving and early morning with a tide change was prime time. The tide waits for no man. Off Cape Mudge you could see the coho rise, taking very small almost translucent herring.

C.T. likes the outdoors and was enjoying the sights when a lone killer whale surfaced along a kelp bed not too far away. Of course the active mind of a seven-year old wondered if it would bother us.

This was mid-May and the fish, three- to four-pound bluebacks, were not large but were active when hooked. Rob insisted that we hold the fly rods and when the coho hit the bucktail it almost ripped it from C.T.'s grip. He was a proud kid when we netted the 4-pound fish. We didn't get many fish during our two days with Rob, but the two that C.T. caught that first morning were his first salmon and first fishes are memorable ones.

The River Dove in Great Britain has special meaning to anglers and particularly for fly-fishers. The Dove was where Izaak Walton's

friend Charles Cotton practiced his craft. Izaak Walton is the father of sport fishing and his *The Compleat Angler*, first published in 1653, is about rural life, nature and angling. With well over 300 editions it is one of the most popular books in the English language. It is the fifth edition though that is of special interest to fly-fishers. That edition contains Charles Cotton's treatise on fly-fishing and fly making. If Walton was the father of sport fishing then Cotton can be considered the father of fly-fishing. In 1674, Cotton built a fishing house on the Dove, decorated it with fishing scenes and had Walton's and Cotton's entwined initials engraved over the entrance. That hut is still standing and many fly-fishers who visit England drop by and look onto the privately owned property to see the sacred tribute to anglers and friendship.

Roderick Haig-Brown has had a profound influence on many North American fly-fishers and I am one. A city-dweller and not familiar with river terminology I remember dwelling over Haig-Browns' words in *The Western Angler*. Through his writings he taught me so much and in my early years when I tried anything to

Left: Located above the tidal influence on the Campbell, Rod and Ann Haig-Brown called their home "Above Tide."

Below: Haig-Brown playing a Gold River steelhead.

catch a fish, Haig-Brown's writings planted the seed that led me to fly-fishing. To me and many others he is the father of steelhead fly-fishing, and many fly-fishers visiting Vancouver Island make the pilgrimage to Campbell River to see where the master wrote his great works and to cast a line into the waters he fished.

In 1927, aged 18, Roderick Haig-Brown came across the great pond from England to North America. He worked in the USA for a Washington State forest company for some months. Unable to get an extension on his visa, he left the US and went to work in the Nimpkish Valley located on Vancouver Island north of Campbell River. I remember a trip in the 1980s to the Nimpkish with Haig-Brown's friend Van Egan, where we visited some of Haig-Brown's Nimpkish haunts and fished some of the waters Haig-Brown fished so many years ago. I joke about the Americans throwing Haig-Brown out of the USA when giving talks to fly-fishing clubs. British Columbians are fortunate that the Americans didn't extend his visa and that he came to British Columbia, settling permanently in Campbell River in 1933, marrying Ann Elmore in 1934 and purchasing the 20-acre property fronting the river in 1935. Their new home, located just above the sea's tidal influence, they named "Above Tide." Here Rod and Ann raised a family and lived there for the rest of their lives. Haig-Brown died unexpectedly from a massive heart attack in 1976, but he left fly-fishers a rich legacy.

That gift he gave fly-fishers is his writing. Haig-Brown described himself as a writer who liked to fish and not a fisherman who liked to write. There is a profound difference. A prolific pen did he possess. Between 1931 and 1976 Haig-Brown wrote 25 books, contributed to many more and wrote scores of magazine articles. Many of his books have had numerous printings, some in foreign languages. A monumental task taking years of research and work, it took 332 pages for Robert Cave to detail in *Roderick Haig-Brown: A Descriptive Bibliography*, Haig-Brown's productive pen and the numerous printings of his books. The books about fish, fishing or rivers that he wrote during his 40 years in Campbell River are of most interest to anglers and include:

The Western Angler—many a beginning angler cut their teeth reading this western classic; *Return to the River*—a story about the Columbia River chinook salmon; *A River Never Sleeps*—perhaps Haig-Brown's finest angling work; the four season's books

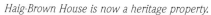
Haig-Brown House is now a heritage property.

Rod Haig-Brown in 1927.

COURTESY OF VALERIE HAIG-BROWN

Fisherman's Spring, Fisherman's Summer, and *Fisherman's Fall* include essays on fly-fishing Pacific Northwest waters while *Fisherman's Winter* is about fly-fishing in South America; *A Primer of Fly-Fishing, The Salmon of Canada;* and *Bright Waters, Bright Fish*, published posthumously in 1980 complete the list. Valerie Haig-Brown who manages her father's writings edited two more Haig-Brown fly-fishing books: *The Master and His Fish* is a series of essays on fly-fishing and, the latest, *To Know a River* is a selection of writings from those works he penned over 40 years.

No other writer has influenced more fly-fishers to take up steelhead fly-fishing than has Haig-Brown. Dry-fly fishing for steelhead started on the Capilano River. Aware of the Capilano fly-fishers earlier dry-fly use, but because that fishery had little publicity, Haig-Brown experimented with dry flies for summer-runs first on the Campbell and then later on other Vancouver Island streams. In *Fisherman's Summer* and *Fisherman's Fall,* he wrote about his exploits fishing the dry fly for Vancouver Island summer-run steelhead. His successes influenced many to try this appealing technique and his Steelhead Bee is probably North America's most famous

Van Egan and the author talk with Kevin Brown the proprietor of the Haig-Brown bed and breakfast.

steelhead dry fly. I used his Bee as a model when I put together the Skeena Steelhead Bee, which steelhead have found an appetizing dish on the Zymoetz and Bulkley rivers. Haig-Brown developed a number of fly patterns for the trout of Vancouver Island, some of which were the first ever British Columbian imitations of forage fishes and insects.

However, we owe him much more because he was a conservationist, educating many young environmentalists about our roles as stewards. He raised the ire of the Provincial Social Credit government many times when he criticized the blatant forestry, mining and other land uses where the destruction of fish habitat was a matter of fact.

After he died, the Haig-Brown place became a Heritage Property. Visitors are welcome to walk the trails along Kingfisher Creek, flowing through the property. The house is operated as a bed and breakfast and access to the house or the fenced lands surrounding the house is for guests or by permission only.

In early September 1988, I slipped over to the Island for a couple of days' fly-fishing. With the kids back at school, usually after Labour Day, the influx of summer vacationers was mostly gone and those that remain, as well as the local fishers, were after salmon in the ocean. Few would be on the river as I searched it for Tsitika summer-run steelhead plants.

I do enjoy catching steelhead from waters that Haig-Brown fished. When I arrived in Campbell River I went first to the Line Fence Pool and quickly hooked a fish on a Claret & Black fly, but it threw the fly during the fight. Through that day and the next, I managed to get many steelhead to rise to size sixes and fours Claret & Black and As Specifieds fished just under the surface on a floating line and a Stacked Deerhair skater waked over the surface. Before I left for home I went back to the Line Fence Pool and very close to the lie where I had hooked the first fish of the trip I was into another. This time the hook held. Fifteen minutes later I slid a lovely 29 1/2-inch male steelhead onto the beach. With slightly tinged pink cheeks and well spotted, it was a fine specimen of a summer-run steelhead. What a pity those fish are gone and few fly-fishers can now experience a tight line and jumping summer-run steelhead from the river Haig-Brown made so famous.

Campbell River fly-fishers, no matter how accomplished, will always be overshadowed by Roderick Haig-Brown. Nonetheless, Van Egan and Bruce Gerhart are famous but for different reasons: Van is the scholar, fly-fisherman, writer and Bruce was the consummate steelheader.

Van made his first trip to British Columbia in 1947 after steelhead, but it was good angling literature and specifically Haig-Brown's writings—*A River Never Sleeps* and *The Western Angler*—that drew him back to the west coast again in 1954 where he met Haig-Brown for the first time. While fishing the Campbell's Sandy Pool with a Silver Lady fly, Van noticed someone watching him from the Elk Falls logging bridge. After a while Van heard a

"I walked along the River Bank Trail to the Line Fence Pool."

voice behind him asking him if he had lost something. Van turned around and there was Haig-Brown holding a Van Egan-tied Silver Lady. Van did not know he had lost a fly and was casting an "empty" line and was surprised that anyone could find a single fly along the bank of such a large pool. With pleasantries exchanged, Haig-Brown invited Van to dinner and a game of croquet. Van was thoroughly trounced in croquet by Haig-Brown's daughter, Mary. This chance meeting on the banks of the Campbell River with Haig-Brown started a life-long friendship.

A concerned environmentalist most of his life, Egan believes "sound conservation solutions must be based on the highest environmental principles. Without the latter, resource stocks and general environmental quality are all downhill." Egan is one of the founders of the Haig-Brown Kingfisher Creek Society. After Haig-Brown died in 1976, Van said that he was:

> ...*prompted by having become good friends of Rod and the Haig-Brown family and what I thought was a need in Campbell River to honour our most famous citizen.*
>
> *The Haig-Brown farm was destined to be part of the "Green Belt" in B.C., but Green Belt lands were later often transferred to other government agencies. The land needs more protection than that. The Haig-Brown Kingfisher Creek Society obtained a "License of Occupation" to carry out a program of stream restoration plus creating a natural park on 17 acres of the farm. Two acres, including the house, garden &*

> *orchard, were turned over to the B.C. Heritage Properties Branch.*
>
> *Our success in bringing back the coho runs in Kingfisher Creek has been reasonably good, given the near total destruction of that creek by logging and development sources over an 80-year period.*

Influenced by Haig-Brown, Van is also skilled with the pen and has had numerous articles published in *The Fly Fisher, British Columbia Sport Fishing,* and *Fly Fishing Heritage* and is the author of three published books, *Tyee: The Story of the Tyee Club of British Columbia, Waterside Reflections* and *Rivers on My Mind.* He stands tall beside Haig-Brown as a writer, conservationist and is a masterful fly tyer and fly-fisher.

A founding member of the Kingfisher Rod & Gun Club, Bruce Gerhart's life revolved around steelhead. A log scaler by profession, the Island rivers lush with steelhead in the 1970s drew him to Campbell River. A masterful gear fisherman, Gerhart turned to the fly in the late 1960s. His enthusiasm for the sport was infectious and as a remarkably skilled technician, he influenced many Campbell River steelheaders to take up fly-fishing, especially during the mid to late 1980s when the Tsitika summer-run plants were at their peak.

I remember my first encounter with Bruce on the Chilliwack River way back in the 1960s. New to the sport myself, I was fishing a run above Tamahi Creek that required wading a back channel. While I was merrily fishing a spot near the bottom of the

The Tsitika transplants provided great sport in the Campbell.

island I noticed a tall lanky fisher come round the bend moving down river wading deep and casting to the far side of river. Nearing me, he caught a steelhead of about 12 pounds. That was one of first steelhead I had seen anyone catch. Bruce said, "If you want to catch steelhead on heavily fished water like the Chilliwack you need to wade boldly and fish pockets others miss."

On my next trip on a cold, freezing day I found the river high from rain, but I was determined to fish the water where Gerhart had taken that steelhead. In those days, rubber-soled waders were the norm and as I edged my way across downstream in the higher water, I slipped. I didn't get too wet but I did dunk my Silex reel and when I arrived at the run I found the reel frozen solid. I couldn't cast but it didn't matter anyway because the river was way too high. I did have a problem though. I couldn't find a safe spot to re-cross the river.

My friends, a little wiser than I, had not crossed and when I saw them wandering the other shore I told them I would need help getting back. I had a 200-foot anchor rope in my car trunk. They cast a fishing line across the river and I attached my car keys so they could get the rope. I was able to wade far enough out and caught the rope they threw me and tying it around my waist I started across. As soon as I edged my way into the main current I lost my foot purchase and away I went into the river. But with two friends anchoring the rope around them I swung across like the pendulum of a clock. With waders filled with icy water I started back to the car. The air was so cold my hair froze and part way there I couldn't move until I removed the icy water filling my waders. The warm air radiating from the car heater felt oh, so good.

Some lessons are learned the hard way. Bold wading may be necessary to catch some fish, but I learned from that experience that a steelheader needs to use sound judgment when wading fast-flowing rivers.

Bruce Gerhart, an enthusiastic master steelheader and the boldest wader to fill a pair of waders in Campbell River, died a young man of only 59 years old on November 9, 1997. He lighted the steelhead fly-fishing spark in many young anglers.

Through this century the Campbell has suffered by man's presence. The watershed was clear-cut when there was little regard for the fish. Then it was dammed in 1947. The John Hart Hydro-electric dam was good and bad. It provided a more stable flow through the low-water months of summer and early fall, but long term much of the salmon's spawning gravel was washed away and the runs have suffered. Considerable stream enhancement as well as spawning channels have been built in recent years to mitigate some of the dam's and Elk Falls pulp mill water extraction. But the Campbell is fortunate that the Quinsam River was a main spawning tributary and home to most of the fish that once lived in the Campbell proper. During the 1970s heavy metal leachate from a mine on Buttle Lake wiped out the Campbell's fish stocks. The copper and zinc pollution was not directly poisonous to adult salmon, but caused the fins in embryos not to form, thus hatching alevins with no fins, leaving their chances of survival as fry at zero. At the same time, the sea-run cutthroat and land-locked cutthroat below La Dore dam

disappeared entirely for years, and haven't caught up yet, and these were adult fish. The leachate also poisoned Campbell River's water supply. I know of residents who, to this day, travel miles up the Island Highway to natural springs to get water rather than drink water from the municipal system. The British Columbia mining industry has always had a poor environmental record and the mine owners escaped prosecution through a legal technicality. The toxic tailings remain an unexploded bomb just waiting for some man-made or natural phenomena to light the wick.

It has taken considerable effort to rebuild Campbell River salmon stocks, most coming from the Quinsam. The Campbell used to have a small run of summer-steelhead and a good run of winter steelhead, which Haig-Brown made famous through his writing. Both runs have not recovered. In the early 1980s, the Campbell River Chapter of the Steelhead Society working with provincial fishery's staff introduced Tsitika summer-runs to the river. Coincidentally, the Tsitika planting paralleled the years of excellent ocean survival and in the mid to late 1980s fly-fishers enjoyed sport with summer-run steelhead, better than that which Haig-Brown experienced back in his early years on the river.

Unfortunately, the excellent ocean survival years, yielding good runs were followed in the 1990s by terrible ocean survival, yielding few if any summer-run steelhead. Poor runs during the 1990s were common all along the east coast of Vancouver Island and because the Tsitika run was down considerably there was no summer-run brood stock available to carry on the plantings in the

Van Egan and the author at the Line Fence Pool.

DAN WILLARD

Bruce Gerhart: A consummate steelheader and bold wader.

Campbell. Other than the hatchery winter-run steelhead that swam into the Quinsam, Haig-Brown's river is a river devoid of steelhead and what a loss that is. This shrine to British Columbian fly-fishing deserved much better.

Considerable work is being done on the Campbell to restore the river's habitat and fish stocks. Gravel replacement in the main river and back channels, new spawning and rearing channels have been constructed and some industrialized property on the lower estuary has been purchased and is being returned to wetlands important for young fishes' survival. Hopefully, the steelhead will return and fly-fishers, making pilgrimages to see where Haig-Brown lived and wrote, can also wet a line and feel the strong pull of a fish from the river he loved, fished and wrote about.

Van and Maxine Egan and I enjoyed a day on the Nimpkish system but I didn't like to leave Campbell River without throwing a line into Haig-Brown's river. I parked the truck and wandered along the Fisherman's Trail, branching off to the left, taking the River Bank Trail to the Line Fence Pool. In my part of the world, June has long evenings but I had only half an hour to fish before I started my two-hour drive to the Nanaimo ferry terminal for the 10:45 p.m. sailing to Vancouver. A couple of casts later I was rewarded when a rainbow took the waked Skeena Steelhead Bee, followed by a cutthroat then a change of fly produced a cutthroat and a rainbow. The last

fish, measuring 15 inches, was a good trout for the Campbell. I left pleased that I was able to renew my bond with Haig-Brown by fishing his river and spending the day with Van and Maxine Egan, two of Haig-Brown's special friends.

References

Cave, Robert Bruce. *Roderick Haig-Brown: A Descriptive Bibliography.* Citrus Heights: Privately Published, 2000.

Egan, Van Gorman. *Tyee: The Story of the Tyee Club of British Columbia.* Campbell River: Ptarmigan Press, 1989.

Isenor, Dick E., Edith Stephens, Donna Watson. *Edge of Discovery.* Campbell River: Ptarmigan Press, 1989.

Lambert, T. W. *Fishing in British Columbia.* London: Horace Cox, 1907.

Lingren, Arthur James. *Fly Patterns of Roderick Haig-Brown.* Portland: Frank Amato Publications, 1996.

Robertson, Anthony. *Above Tide: Reflections on Roderick Haig-Brown.* Madeira Park: Harbour Publishing, 1984.

Rogers, Sir John. *Sport in Vancouver and Newfoundland.* London: Chapman and Hall, 1912.

3

The Columbia, Kootenay and Tributary Rivers

THE COLUMBIA RIVER AND ITS MIGHTY TRIBUTARY, THE Kootenay River, flow through a land rich in history, natural resources, and beauty as well as fish and game. In 1807, famed Northwest Company astronomer and surveyor, David Thompson travelled through the Rocky Mountains, down the Blaeberry River, ascended the Columbia to Lower Columbia Lake and, about two miles from the lake, constructed Kootenae House, the first trading post in the Columbia Basin. Thompson spent the next two years exploring the Columbia and was the first European to travel to its mouth, arriving at Fort Astoria on July 15, 1810.

The rivers and lakes with their bounty of fish provided the early explorers with food to eat. In 1858, after the colony of British

Columbia was established, the Colonial office sent surveyors to mark the British Columbia/USA border on the ground. John Keast Lord, the botanist attached to the group, besides dressing British Columbia's first fly for these waters, was the first to describe fly-fishing the waters in the Kootenay Region. About the fly-fishing he experienced on the Moyie River in his two-volume *The Naturalist in British Columbia* (1866), he writes:

> There was a stream in which I had better sport
> than in any others, the Mooyee [sic], on the western
> slope of the Rocky Mountains—a small stream, very
> rocky, clear as crystal, ice cold and so densely wood-
> ed on each side that fishing in it, unless by wading,

In the early 1900s, the great pool in the Kootenay River below Bonnington Falls was famous for its May-to-November fly-fishing.

This photograph (circa 1900) caption stated that "in the Rockies of British Columbia the lakes and streams are filled with trout." Photo by John Pease Babcock

was impossible. I remember one pool as being particularly productive—a rock-basin, with a little rivulet dancing into it through a pebbly reach; the water so beautifully clear, that everything in the pool was visible, as though one looked into an aquarium. I could not help standing and feasting my eyes on the trout playing about in it. To say the pool was full of fish is no exaggeration; all, with their heads toward the little stream, where gently sculling their tails to steady themselves. I gazed upon a mass of fish, big and little, from four ounces to three pounds in weight.

Having sufficiently indulged in admiring this host of trout (the like of which I had never seen before), I began the war. Dropping my 'sensation-fly' into the little stream, I let it sink and drift into the pool. Twenty open mouths rushed at it ravenously, and trout after trout was rapidly landed on the shingle. I continued this scheme until a heap of magnificent fish were

piled at my side, and the pool was rapidly thinning. One crafty old fellow, however, defiled all my efforts to tempt him. I let the fly drift over him, under his nose, above his nose; but he scorned it, and, if he could, I felt he would have winked his eye derisively at me. (Vol. 1, p. 81-82)

Lord experimented using different things such as grasshoppers, crayfish, and pieces of fish to catch trout, but he says that his "experiments failed signally in discovering anything that could at all compare with my 'first fly.'" About that fly's birth and name, Lord, when he encountered many rising trout in a stream on the western slopes of the Rocky Mountains, hastily scraped together hooks, thread and red wool from his blanket. Using grouse feathers for the fly's throat-hackle and wing, he put all of these materials together by hand without the aid of tying tools.

Lord did not name his creation but, later, after he tried to make a more representative imitation of the insect that he saw trout

Dressed to kill; fly-fishing the Kootenay River around the turn of the 19th century.

feeding upon, he found that his "poor original was better than a good imitation", and he referred to the original as his old, Red-Shirted Trapper—an appropriate name.

After British Columbia joined Canada in 1871, lured by the promise of a link to the east by rail, surveyors explored the rivers and valleys looking for a route though the Rocky and Selkirk mountain ranges. They relied on the bounty of the land for some of their provisions. With the publicity from Lord's book and later reports from surveyors, trappers and railway builders about the fish and game, others came to explore the area and settle, while some sought sport with rod and gun in the most western part of the British Empire.

James Arthur Lees and Walter Clutterbuck with a third companion, a brother to either Lees or Clutterbuck who was living in the Rocky Mountains, joined their expedition. The journey from England across the Atlantic by steamer and across Canada by train took about a month. They departed the CPR train at Golden on August 16, 1887 and spent more than three months exploring the Upper Columbia, Moyie, and Kootenay valleys. During their travels, they fished many of the lakes and tributary streams of the Upper Columbia and Kootenay area, including the Skookumchuck, St. Mary's, Elk, Wigwam and Moyie rivers. Their book, *B.C. 1887: A*

Ramble in British Columbia, published in 1888, provides many a testimonial to the beauty of the area and the fish and game in the Columbia and Kootenay valleys.

On Windermere Lake they practiced fly casting and caught whitefish with a small dry fly. Later, while camped on the Skookumchuck Creek, one of their party had grand sport with a dry fly for probably cutthroat trout, which they called spotted brown trout. About that day's dry-fly sport, they write:

I put on a fine cast, and my own 'beetle,' which I firmly believe to be the best fly ever invented. (The angling reader already knows so much more than we can tell him, that we feel sure a description of the 'Beetle' would be of no interest for him, and refrain from inserting it.) 'I waited for a rise, and then sent this fly dry to the place, and in an instant was fighting with a good fish, which with fine tackle and heavy water gave plenty of trouble before I could land him. The stone I was on was very awkward, and I lost several fish in trying to gaff them, but it was about the only place where you could get a dry fly out, because of the bushes. I never saw such a pool for fish: they kept rising, and I believe I hooked every one that rose.'... So saying, he turned out a bag of spotted brown trout with a very old-country look about them, as different in colour from the silver beauties of the Kootenay as the water of the clear Scotch-looking creek is from the slightly opaque blue of the river. The smallest was just over a pound, and they were fat and well liking; and well liked when they came out of the frying-pan. (p. 191)

Lees' and Clutterbuck's accounts of dry-fly fishing on the Columbia and Kootenay river systems are noteworthy because this is the first recorded use of the dry fly in British Columbia, Canada and North America. Popularized as a method in the south of England in the 1860s, the dry-fly technique exploded through the latter part of the 19th century after F. M. Halford, with the help of the skillful angler and fly tyer George Marryat, experimented with dry flies on British chalk streams through the early 1880s. In 1886 Halford's book *Floating Flies and How to Dress Them* was published. As a result of Halford's work, the dry fly became the tool to catch surface-feeding trout. Halford's writings influenced many other fly-fishermen to try the dry fly on new waters. After receiving sample flies from Halford in an 1890 letter, Theodore Gordon, the father of American dry-fly fishing, introduced that technique to eastern American streams. From Gordon's experiments in the early 1890s, he developed his famous dry flies, the Quill Gordon is the most reknowned.

However, dry-fly fishing happened first on waters of the Columbia and Kootenay watersheds and to this day remains one of the most popular methods of taking cutthroat and rainbows from its waters.

Lees and Clutterbuck provide ample testimony on the streams in the region abounding in trout and char. On the south fork of the Elk River [Wigwam River], they camped on a small river with a stupendous view of a towering mountain. About the superb fishing, they write:

What fish that river held! Very different from the lazy monsters of Elk: these were bright as silver, game to the last, and in perfect condition. There was only one drawback, which was that after one had fished three or four pools there was nothing for it but to go home, for even our powers of assimilating fish-food have their limits, in spite of its brain-producing qualities. (pp. 268-269)

John Keast Lord's Red-shirted Trapper is British Columbia's first fly.

Needless to say, in those days no one thought about catch and release: a fish caught was a fish killed. Earlier on in their ramble through the Columbia system, at their camp on the Upper Columbia River not too far north of the outlet to Upper Columbia Lake (they called Lake Windermere Lower Columbia Lake), they camped and had excellent bull trout fishing with the largest fish weighing about 20 pounds:

A minnow, or still better a spoon, seemed to be what they chiefly fed upon, though we got a few, and also some lovely silver trout, with a rosy tinge on the belly, with fly. (p. 166)

However, they were told of a tributary, which they wouldn't name, where the fish reached much greater size and where one Englishman reported fish to 80 pounds. It is doubtful that the 80-pounder was a bull trout, but up these waters swam the mighty chinook salmon. When Lees and Clutterbuck travelled up the Columbia from Golden in the steamer *Duchess*, they witnessed first hand the salmon and the difficulty in navigation caused by their huge redds. About their passage through the Columbia just below Windermere Lake, they say:

It soon became a race against time whether we should get to Windermere this day or not. The river for a mile or two below the outlet of the lake is very

Dry flies were first cast onto British Columbia waters in 1887.

shallow, its bottom consisting of huge gravel beds, the spawning ground for most of the Columbia salmon, and at this late period of the year it can only be navigated during daylight. The chief difficulty (and this is not a traveller's tale) is caused by the immense numbers of fish heaping up the gravel in the manner familiar to any one who has watched their habits in the old country, thus constantly making changes in the channel. This, when a few inches more or less are of importance, necessitates the utmost watchfulness and care in making the passage, the course being often altered many yards between one voyage and the next.

And so it was that up to the time of our arrival at

A Tommy Brayshaw painting of a cutthroat rising to a fly.

the salmon beds no one knew whether the captain would attempt to get through. He determined to try it, and with men and poles ready in the bows we began to creep up between the gravel banks which in many places showed above the surface. The river here had at length lost the muddy snow-stained character which had marred its beauty hitherto. It was now quite clear, and through the swirl and ripple of its crystal waters we could see the great salmon in numbers slowly moving away from the disturbing steamboat. (pp. 102-102)

They witnessed spawning salmon again in the Columbia River above Windermere Lake. However, nearly half a century later in the early 1940s, the Grand Coulee Dam blocked the salmon and steelhead's upstream access to the headwaters of the Columbia system. The Columbia salmon were mostly caught by Washington and Oregon commercial fishermen and were considered of little value to Canada. The Canadian government paid little lip service to the loss of those mighty fish that used to migrate to the upper reaches of the Columbia River. Years earlier, not long after Lees and Clutterbuck made their trip, the government dredged a passage through the upper Columbia to clear the river of the troublesome redds.

In *Rod and Creel in British Columbia* (1919), A. Bryan Williams listed some waters in the Columbia Valley. He says that the Columbia River itself is coloured most of the year and "has no great merit from a sporting point of view (p. 130)." But he praises highly the Slocan Pool on Kootenay River and provides a list of flies to be used for it:

This famous pool is part of the Kootenay River, a short distance below Bonnington Falls…Slocan Pool is the most famous piece of water in the Kootenays and for the fly-fisherman it used to be paradise. The fish, mostly of the Rainbow variety, run to all sizes.

Of late years the pool has been very heavily fished as it is within easy reach of the town of Nelson, but it is still worth a visit.

Fish can be caught there from the beginning of May until the freshet in June. The best time, however, is after the water goes down, usually from the middle of July on until the middle of September.

For this water you should use the March Brown, Coachman, Red and Brown Hackles, Zulu, Black Gnat, Jock Scott, Blue Dunn and Stone Fly. (pp. 132-133)

By the time Williams wrote this book, the Canadian Pacific Railway had constructed their Crow's Nest Line, providing better access to the Kootenay River and its tributaries. About the Kootenay's two premier trout fly-fishing streams, the St. Mary's and Elk rivers, he says:

> *St. Mary's River. This is a good big stream with splendid fly-fishing. The fish go anywhere from half a pound to three pounds...August is the best month, September also good.*
>
> *The Elk River. This used to be one of best streams in the country for fly-fishing, but the lower parts near Fernie and Michel, both of which are coal mining centres, are pretty well fished out.*
>
> *Some little distance above Michel (on the Crow's Nest Line) the fishing is still fair. The upper reaches of the river are still as good as ever...It is a splendid place for a camping-out trip. August and September are the best months.* (pp. 135-136)

In Williams' 1935 book, *Fish and Game in British Columbia,* the fervent words such as "splendid," "famous," and "good as ever" disappeared from his descriptions of the waters. The bounty of plenty was on the decline. W. F. Pochin in "The Kootenays" section of *Angling and Hunting in British Columbia* (1946) provides a more glowing picture. The rivers and streams had a rest because many of the men served in World War II. As a war measure on those rivers with power or water supply dams, fishing in the dam catchment area was not permitted. About the Kootenay River and the Slocan Pool, he writes:

> *The Kootenay River, even with its three power dams, closed to fishing during the war years gave up limit baskets of fine Rainbows during the 1946 season. Slocan Pool, some 14 miles from Nelson is a case in point.*
>
> *Here the water fairly boils with eddies and rips, and trout of a pound to two pounds rise to flies freely during May, June and then again in the fall.* (p. 91)

The good fishing enjoyed by the generations before was on the wane. After the war years and through the 1960s, the fly-fishing slowly deteriorated until in the early 1980s a 10-inch trout on the region's prime waters was a nice fish. A number of things were responsible for nearly destroying the famed fly-fishing waters of the Kootenay Region.

During the railway exploration and construction period, the men who came to work and live in the Upper Columbia and Kootenay watersheds—besides the attraction of the area's natural beauty and abundant fish and game—found wealth in them there hills. The Rocky, Selkirk and Gold mountain ranges had rich mineral deposits and mining became the dominant industry. To provide power to the mines, the rivers were dammed. Constructed in 1898, the West Kootenay Power and Light's Bonnington Falls hydro-electric development was the first in the Province. Over the years many

more would follow. The Columbia River system is the most dammed river system in the world. The negatives far outweigh the positives when it comes to dams and fish, but one world-class trout fishery at Trail resulted from the construction of Grand Coulee. In the mid-1980s rainbow trout were introduced to Lake Roosevelt, the massive impoundment behind the dam. Those fish seeking spawning habitat migrated upstream across the border, spawned in and colonized streams around Trail, remained and fed until the fall, supplementing existing trout populations. The end result was that the Columbia around Trail became a world-class trout fishery for rainbows up to ten pounds.

However, most industrial activity has negative effects on fish habitat and during a good part of the 20th century the British Columbian mining industry wreaked havoc on the environment. In the Kootenay region it started in the 19th century. William Baillie-Grohman lived in the Kootenay area for 11 years from 1882 to 1893 and witnessed the first phases of progress that transformed the region's pristine environment. In *Fifteen Years' Sport and Life in the Hunting Grounds of Western America and British Columbia* (1900), he says:

> *To-day one can no longer speak of path-finding in Kootenay. Half a dozen live towns, with a population in some cases of seven thousand, half a hundred mining camps, five railways, with two or three more coming in, a score of river and lake steamers, telephone and telegraph lines that connect the remotest camps, electric lighting and magnificent electric power plants that rank among the largest on the continent, roads and trails up every creek almost, while ladies career through the country on book writing bent, these are the truly wonderful result of ten years of Western activity, in which the Yankee has again given us a lead. Without it Kootenay would probably still be the wilderness in which I found it in 1882-3. True, nature has suffered to a corresponding degree. Vast areas of fine forests have been burnt with the ruthlessly wasteful haste of the pioneer prospector, to whom nothing is sacred. Rivers and creeks no longer flow clear and sparking. The drains of mining camps and sluicing operations on their banks have long turned them into muddy, beautiless waterways, not infrequently reeking with the poisonous stench of putrid animal matter, while huge smelting-work chimneys belch forth noxious fumes. Game and fish, if they have not entirely disappeared, have suffered sore decimation, the one in consequence of the good prices obtainable in the camps, the other by fair and foul persecution, in which the deadly dynamite wreaks wholesale destruction in the deep pools once famous for trout of a size hard to be equalled anywhere in the world.* (pp. 296-298)

Progress and development had its good and bad sides. It provided the jobs that brought people to work in the area and, of course, many liked to fish. Resource exploration and extraction also provided road access that often paralleled the banks of remote streams and tourism promotion attracted others. With far too liberal limits, it became another example of too many people taking too many fish.

The 1935 limit for trout was 15 fish a day, down from the 20 allowed during the 1920s, and there was no possession limit. At this period in time, a steelhead was defined as a trout greater than 5 pounds in weight. In 1942, in the Kootenay Region, an angler could take three steelhead as well as 15 trout per day. In 1943, you could kill either 15 trout a day or in aggregate not more than 25 pounds of trout plus one fish. In 1946, a three-day possession limit was added to the regulations. In 1951, the daily trout limit was reduced to 12 or 25 pounds plus one fish and two day's possession limit. In 1962, the possession limit went up to three days at 12 fish a day. The 25 pounds plus one trout was gone, but a steelhead was now a trout over 20 inches length. From 1961, the daily limit of 12 trout included any steelhead killed. In 1962, the steelhead was redefined as a 20-inch-or-greater sea-going rainbow trout and that category was removed from the Kootenay Region regulations. Throughout the 1960s into the 1970s the daily limits dropped to 8 trout per day, 3 days' possession.

The miners mined the riches in the hills and the sportfishers mined the trout populations in the streams. By the early 1980s, the Elk River trout, for example, averaged 10 inches. In that system trout spawn for the first time when they are about 12 inches long and three years old. The trout were being harvested before they could reproduce and, unless checked, the future looked bleak. To improve the stocks of fish, experimental rotational closures were implemented on the upper St. Mary's and Wigwam rivers. They were closed for two years then opened with a limit of four fish, two days' possession. The rotational closures produced fish large enough to spawn, but with more people fishing the four fish, the two-day possession limit was still too liberal and by the end of the first year there were few catchable fish left. But the experiment showed that the habitat was reasonably good.

To counter the overfishing in 1984 and 1985, new regulations were implemented. The limit was reduced to two fish, 30-inch minimum size, trout and char release in the winter months and single hook, bait ban during the summer fishery. About six years later, after two spawning cycles, the populations had recovered and the fish were much larger.

In 1995, a 100-year flood hit the area during spawning time and as a result two age classes of fish were lost. Catch and release was implemented for the remainder of 1995, 1996 and 1997, resulting from that the populations exploded and the fish grew large. Too, an April 1 through June 14 closed season protected spawning trout. Currently, the East Kootenay part of the the region is single-hook barbless with some streams having sections where it is fly-fishing, catch-and-release only with a bait ban. In the kill sections anglers are allowed to harvest one trout.

Drawing with caption from Lees and Clutterbuck's book BC 1887.

" Two great trout simply whooping with excitement came right out of the water at it."

Ron Grantham with a 17-inch Westslope.

DON ANDERSEN

Andersen, of Rocky Mountain House, Alberta, and spent a wonderful week angling for Westslope cutthroat. Several months earlier, while planning the trip, Don had explained to me that the insects don't start coming off the water until after the sun has warmed the morning air. That was fine with me for it meant no alarm clock, eating an unhurried breakfast, then ambling down to the creek at our leisure.

Using only handmade bamboo rods, floating lines and dry flies we hooked and released a great many of those colourful trout up to 18 inches in length. I was casting a recently-made seven-foot, four-weight rod, while Don mainly used an eight-foot, five-weight which he had built about 15 years ago.

Having fished the area for more than 20 years, Don has discovered many secret spots, a few of which he showed to me. Wading up the riffles on the small creeks, we would pause at each pool, looking for signs of feeding trout. When we spotted a rise, a size 20 Blue Wing Olive or other dry fly was cast and dead-drifted over the spot. Almost invariably, the hungry trout would snatch the tiny feathered hook.

As surely as the trout take the dry fly, I have been bitten by the small-stream bug, and I plan to make many more trips to the southeast corner of BC.

Referring to the restored fishery on the once highly-polluted and devastated St. Mary's River, Cranbrook writer and fly-fisherman Jeff Mironuck, in *Angling in the Shadows of the Rockies,* says that:
> *we are blessed with nature's beauty...let's hope that we will have the knowledge and will to keep it this way... so that our following generations will be able to enjoy our fly-fishing...*(p. 104)

I have not had the opportunity to fish the Kootenay Region. The draw of coastal rivers and steelhead has just been too strong. But those who have ventured and fished waters in the area give glowing reports. Ron Grantham, an old high school chum, and I became reunited in 1983 when I joined the Totem Flyfishers. Grantham is a bamboo-rod builder who has been smitten with the Kootenay's small-stream fly-fishing and closes this chapter with an anecdote about bamboo, dry flies and Westslope cutthroat. Ron writes:
> *No more getting up in the pre-dawn darkness and heading for my favorite steelhead run; no more trying to be the first one on the river. Instead, I have found that going trout fishing after the sun is over the horizon has a certain appeal. That's what awaited me when I made my first trip to the Columbia/Kootenay region of BC.*
>
> *This past September, I met with fellow bamboo rod-builder, superb fly-tyer and great companion Don*

References

Baillie-Grohman. William A. *Fifteen Years' Sport and Life in the Hunting Grounds of Western America and British Columbia.* London: Horace Cox, 1900.

Francis, Daniel (Ed.). *Encyclopedia of British Columbia.* Maderia Park: Harbour Publishing, 2000.

Halford, F. M. *Floating Flies and How to Dress Them.* Glouchester: Barry Shurlock & Co., 1974 reprint of the 1886 edition.

Hills, John Waller. *A History of Fly Fishing for Trout.* New York: Freshet Press, 1971 reprint.

Hume, Mark. *The Run of the River.* Vancouver: New Star Books, 1992.

Lees, James Arthur and Walter J. Clutterbuck. *B.C. 1887: A Ramble in British Columbia.* London: Longmans, Green and Co., 1889 revised edition.

Mironuck, Jeff (Ed). *Angling in the Shadows of the Rockies.* Cranbrook: Privately printed, 1998.

Netboy, Anthony. *The Columbia River Salmon and Steelhead Trout.* Seattle: The University of Washington Press, 1980.

McDonald, John. *The Complete Fly Fisherman: The Notes and Letters of Theodore Gordon.* New York: The Theodore Gordon Flyfishers, 1979.

Williams, Arthur Bryan. *Rod & Creel in British Columbia.* Vancouver: Progress Publishing Co., 1919.

__. *Fish and Game in British Columbia.* Vancouver: Sun Directories Ltd., 1935.

CHAPTER 4

The Capilano River

IF YOU SURVEYED PRESENT-DAY STEELHEAD FLY-FISHERS FOR the river of the 20th century, topping their list would be many of British Columbia's big-name steelhead rivers. The Dean and Thompson would be there and also we would find some of the world-famous tributaries of the Skeena, such as the Kispiox, Bulkley, Morice, Babine, Sustut and Copper. There are a few fly-fishers around who remember the Capilano River's last days of glory and those few, I am sure, would nominate that river. A river that flowed rich with summer-run steelhead and summer-run coho.

In his 1888 book, *Three Years Hunting and Trapping in America and the Great North-West,* J. Turner-Turner provides a very early reference to sport fishing the Capilano. Turner-Turner spent three months camped on the Burrard Inlet's north shore and fished the Capilano, Seymour and other streams. He managed to catch only sea-trout with the fly. But the construction of the Vancouver waterworks in the mid to late 1880s provided anglers with access to the river. By the turn of the century, fly-fishers were taking the ferry from Vancouver to North Vancouver and journeying to the Capilano to fly-fish for coho, cutthroat and summer-run steelhead.

Arthur Bryan Williams in *Rod & Creel in British Columbia* (1919) wrote the first glowing report about the Capilano, its fish and its sport:

> *The Capilano is one of those streams which stands in a class by itself...Apart, however from its merits as a beauty spot, it also stands in a class by itself as a fishing stream. Owing to its close proximity to Vancouver it has been fished and fished, until you might think that fishing in it was a thing of the past. If you go there on a Saturday or Sunday any time after the winter is over, you will likely find a man with a rod every few yards: some will be scientific fishermen casting a fly with considerable dexterity or spinning a minnow or prawn, others will be bait fishermen. Every yard of that stream that can be got at will be fished over and over and yet it is a stream that a good fishermen can be reasonably sure of catching fish, providing conditions are favourable.* (p. 92)

That the Capilano was a fine cutthroat and coho salmon river there is no doubt. From the time of those early explorations, and for

Frank Darling with a catch of cutthroat trout, circa 1925.

*When the salmonberries are ripe, the summer-runs
are in the Upper Capilano.*

over half of the 20th century, the Capilano River reigned supreme as a fly-fisher's dream. But it was the runs of steelhead, particularly the summer-runs, that made it renowned and many anglers were christened into the world of steelhead fly-fishing by Capilano summer-runs. Jerry Wintle is one of the most respected and well-known steelhead fly-fishers in the Pacific Northwest. He cut his teeth on Capilano summer-runs.

Jerry, an east-end Vancouver lad, was born in December 1930. He started to fish for steelhead at the age of 12. He vividly recalls his first encounter with this grand gamefish, and says:

> *I rode my bike over to the Capilano River's Salmon Pool, armed with an old, brittle, greenheart rod my grandfather had found in his attic, and it was with that old, dried-out rod, a poorly lubricated reel and a wooden float and worm that I hooked one of those big summer-runs.*
>
> *When the fish took, I leaned into the rod. The fish took off and this old, unoiled Nottingham reel froze solid. I ended up holding a rod that had shattered into three pieces.*

Wintle took up fly-fishing early in his fishing career and stuck to it, even though he grew up in an era where most fishermen took the easy way and spin- or float-fished. Wintle started fly-fishing in the early 1950s, and caught his first fly-caught steelhead in Campbell River's Line Fence Pool in front of Roderick Haig-Brown's home.

Already adept at finding steelhead with float gear, Jerry didn't take long to hone his fly-fishing skills. The Capilano, Seymour, Vedder and Allouette rivers were his haunts in the early 1950s, then the Thompson in 1959, the Morice and Kispiox in 1961, and the Dean in the early 1970s.

If you ask Jerry for the secret to his success, he gives a modest, casual answer: *"All you need do is chuck the fly out, bring it around properly and you will catch fish."* A simple statement, yes, but to do it with Wintle's proficiency requires skill and much knowledge. You must know steelhead habits, be able to judge the

river's currents, (i.e., "read" water), pick a fly that suits the current speed, water colour and temperature, know the correct presentation technique, and cast and control the fly line so that the current brings the fly across the lie properly.

Not many fly-fishers combine all those things the way Jerry can. He is so skilled at picking just the right spot and presenting his fly so well that far more fish are tempted by his presentations than they are from us mere mortals. Where others might hook one, Jerry hooks several. But, one of the drawbacks of superb presentation skills is that, although many fish are attracted, not all are well hooked and many are lost. Therefore, Jerry talks in terms of fish hooked, rather than landed. Even then, his landed-fish count usually far exceeds those of other "good" fly-fishermen.

Wintle does tie flies, but more from necessity than desire. Rather, over the years, he has developed a technique for getting others to part with their creations. He is a master fly-wheedler. Most of us who know that cunning have become guarded about showing him our fly boxes. However, there still are many unwary victims out there along the river banks.

A man of ideas, Wintle, the innovator, usually inveigles others to do the work. Jerry thinks, for instance, that he may be the first person to design a sink-tip line. In the early 1950s, the Cleveland Dam was being built on the Capilano and the new, plastic-coated, sinking fly-lines had just been introduced. Jerry thought that he could fly-float-fish the deep Salmon Pool if he spliced a section of sinking fly-line onto his floating fly-line.

Paul Moody Smith fly-fishing a favorite run on the Capilano.

*The famous twin peaks called the Lions look down
on the upper reaches of the Capilano.*

Part of the 1871 deal that brought British Columbia into Canadian federation was a link to the east by a trans-continental railway. It took a number of years to build but on November 8, 1885 the Canadian Pacific Railway's first train chugged into the western terminus at Port Moody. Not long after, the railway decided that a terminus 15 miles west in the growing settlement of Granville more appropriate. The Granville settlement was incorporated by a Provincial Act and on April 6th, 1886, birthing the City of Vancouver.

Destined to be a great seaport, the city would need a reliable water supply. On the same day that the city received its charter, the Vancouver Waterworks Company was incorporated to supply that reliable source of water. One year earlier, George Keefer, an engineer, foreseeing that the railway would move its terminus west and that the terminus was the Granville settlement, explored likely water supply sources. He charged a younger colleague, Henry Badeley Smith, with exploring the streams of Burrard Inlet's north shore. Those explorations took place during 1885 and 1886 and about the Capilano River, Mr. Smith wrote:

> *The River Capilano is a mountain stream of considerable magnitude. Prospectors who have penetrated its conons, and claim to have reached its source,*

The gorge with Cleveland Dam in the background.

He took his lines to a local sporting goods store where his friend, Don Traeger, worked and asked Don about joining the lines together. Traeger contacted Bob Taylor, another friend of Jerry's, and asked if he could do the job. Because it was for Jerry, Bob spliced the lines. The Salmon Pool on the "Cap" is deep, but, with his new line Jerry could cast it upstream and let the sinking tip take the fly down to where the fish lay. Jerry proceeded to use the newly developed line with his usual success.

Jerry has spent his lifetime seeking, finding, hooking and landing or losing steelhead, appropriating others' flies, and honing his fishing craft to become the master he is. Rare is the steelhead fly-fisherman who learns to fly an airplane so he can fish; even more rare is one who purchases his own plane to fish. Wintle is one of those rare breeds. Now retired from B.C. Hydro, he can be found with his wife of many years, wherever steelhead are running in the Dean, Thompson, the American Skagit, the Bulkley at Barrett Station and many other rivers. He is a living legend amongst steelhead fly-fishermen in the Pacific Northwest and it all started on the Capilano River.

The fickle hand of fate, however, proved to be the downfall of this once magnificent river. A number of things happened, in the early years of British Columbia and the City of Vancouver, that flowed one after another, each having a further consequence resulting in the damming of the river and the drowning of the prime fly-fishing waters.

A Tommy Brayshaw painting of a scrappy coho leaping clear of the water.

estimate its length at no less than 50 miles. It rises in the snow-covered mountains of the Howe Sound district, and flows almost due south, emptying into Burrard Inlet at the First Narrows.

Although nothing definite is known as to its source, all accounts agree that its origin is not a mountain lake, but the accumulated waters derived from melted snow and ice falling from the mountain summits. For a distance of seven miles from its mouth, the river has been surveyed. Throughout this distance it flows at an average of five feet per second over a bed of granite, basalt and conglomerate boulders. Sand and gravel can be found only in a few sheltered bays. It passes through several canyons of granite and whinstone rock, one of which is 15 feet wide at its base, 94 feet wide at its top, 500 feet long and 218 feet deep. Previous to the creation of this canyon, the whole valley to the north must have been one large lake. The wall of rock through which the stream penetrated ages ago, by some sudden effort of the earth's hidden forces, stands like a huge gate at the south end of the valley, the valley itself being but a strip of flat land from 1000 to 1500 feet wide, lying at

the base of two parallel ranges of mountains, which tower upwards to a height of 3000 feet. The fall that took place when the river flowed over the summit of this rocky wall must have equaled the Niagara of today for depth, if not volume. Should the City of Vancouver increase to the magnitude predicted, it may be that its people at some future day will cause a dam to be constructed across the narrow gorge, and once again convert this valley into a lake. (Vancouver Water Works, p. 318)

It was through Smith's 1885 and 1886 explorations and his proposal of a dam in that narrow 15-foot-wide gorge that ultimately sealed the fate of the Capilano River. Years later other engineers agreed that that gorge was the best place for a dam. In 1954 the Cleveland Dam was completed blocking the access of steelhead and coho to the upper river. However, as part of the fish mitigation, the Greater Vancouver Water District built a fish trap and transported all coho and steelhead above the dam releasing them at the head of Capilano Lake. The runs suffered and in place of the natural migration, spawning and rearing in the valley above the gorge, the Department of Fisheries and Oceans built a hatchery. That the upper Capilano River and its magnificent summer-run steelhead and coho were the sacrificial lambs of progress there is no doubt. The hatchery and the dam are signs of man's presence, altering all.

In 1904, 18-year-old Paul Moody Smith started fishing the Capilano River. Enamoured with the river and its fish, over 40 years later, Smith wrote in a letter to *Field & Stream* magazine about the river and its fish. This is part of what he said:

Above the canyon the river flows through a narrow mountain valley of steep gradient; hemmed in on both sides by heavily wooded steeply rising mountains. Here too, as in the delta, the river bed is in gravel but with a difference. For now there are great boulders and rock fragment that create the scour necessary to the formation of pools. These pools or more properly runs are of ideal depth for fly-fishing—six to eight feet at the head, shoaling to a foot at the tail. Between these pools are long stretches of violent rapids, unfishable and unfordable and in most instances with bank obstructions that do not permit the river to be followed closely from pool to pool. If your steelhead gets into the slick at the tail of the pool and is drawn into the rapids, for the fly-fisherman it is all over. You would lose that fish even if it were dead on the end of your line.

After explaining that the Capilano watershed was owned by the Greater Vancouver Water Board (District) and, that the GVWB permitted bone-fide fishermen to visit the 2 1/2 miles stretch below the domestic water intake, he continues:

I am old now and have found this long walk in gum boots pretty tiring, and particularly so the return journey, with its half mile long hill to the top of the canyon bench if I had a steelhead to carry. But I would not have it changed even should this mean that I can no longer go. A narrow dirt road hidden in an arbor of trees, leads to a region of peace, undefiled natural beauty and solitude. Here are no hot dog stands, no riverside homes and litter, no garages or auto camps and, except for the odd fisherman, no people. Be prepared, however, to make the acquaintance of a goodly number of quite friendly bears. The summer fishing season coincides with the time of ripe salmon berries and the bears come down from the hills. A half hour after you leave Vancouver you are in a land as wild and natural as it was in the days of the Indians.

The Capilano, like most all other steelhead rivers in this part of the world, has two distinct runs of fish—a winter run which starts entering the river in the latter part of December and continues into March, and a summer run commencing in early April and terminating, except for a few belated stragglers, in June. About the first of April fish of both runs may be in the lower river at the same time. They are, however, easily distinguishable, for all winter fish are well

Jerry Wintle, about to release a summer-run, cut his steelheading teeth on the Capilano.

advanced towards spawning condition when they enter the river, whereas fish of the summer run are still months away from spawning. The roe or milt sacs of these fish show no signs of development. Among all the steelhead rivers I am acquainted with, the Capilano is unique in that the summer run is the dominant one. This happy provision has made the river an ideal one for the fly-fisherman.

Due mainly to the high degree of protection that the regulations of the Water Board, not the Game Department, has afforded the Capilano, though in the back yard of a city of 400,000 people, has continued to provide steelhead fishing year after year. Sanctuary waters for fish pay as big a dividend, as has been proven to be the case with game. I would, however, be guilty of misrepresentation should anything I have said give the impression that the Capilano is a river lush with steelhead. Far from it—the palmy days are long since over, but there is some fishing to be had there yet. During the summer of 1949 I took seven fish, including the one I entered in the contest, and all these on the dry fly. I lost an equal or greater number. There are, however, many occasions when I made that long walk with no other reward than the feeling of peace and escape that the beauty and solitude of the Capilano Valley has ever brought me. To a true disciple of old Isaac [Walton] this is all I can promise for sure.

In days long since past, the Whiskey and Soda drifted over summer-run steelhead in once-famous pools with names like Blue Rock, Stovepipe, Blaney's Cribbing, Crown Creek, Upper and Lower Darling, and Snake Ranch (or Whiskey Ranch as some called it).

These names are unfamiliar to most present-day steelhead fishermen. Yet the pools for which they were named were almost within Vancouver's city limits. It's a prime example of simultaneously being near yet far away. All these runs disappeared when the upper Capilano River valley, behind the Cleveland Dam, was flooded in 1954.

There is little left now to remind us of that once-magnificent fishery. Most of those who fly-fished the Upper Capilano's summer-runs in the river's glory days—Frank Darling, Paul Moody Smith, Bill Cunliffe, Cliff Welch, King White, and others—have long since been fishing in Paradise. And the next generation of Capilano anglers—Paul Dorion Smith, son of Paul Moody Smith, Peter Broomhall, Jerry Wintle, Colin McPhail, and others—those who saw and fished the upper river in its dying days have bittersweet memories of the river. Bitter because the river was sacrificed to progress; sweet because they at least knew the river before it was drowned. And their experiences, combined with bits and pieces of Capilano memorabilia left, directly or indirectly, by Paul Moody Smith, Bill Cunliffe, and King White, depict a summer-run river worthy of any steelheader's dream.

That the river was a world contender is attested by its award-winning fish. For many decades through the 20th century, anglers competed for prizes in *Field & Stream* magazine's fishing contests.

Capilano fish often ranked well in those competitions.

Frank Darling regularly submitted his Capilano catches and in a 1934 letter says that,

> *I won two prizes for steelhead fish caught in Capilano—3rd prize $50 and fifth prize $20—14 lb. and 12 1/4 lb. last July Field & Stream magazine of New York. 4 out of the five prizes were won in B.C. and 3 of them were in Capilano—the second prize won in Okanagan Lake with a fish around 15 1/2 lbs...*

Paul Moody Smith too competed for prizes and writes in a July 22, 1949, letter to the *Field & Stream* fishing editor:

> *The following facts, in connection with the steelhead I am entering in your competition, may prove of interest. The fish was a male of the summer run [steelhead]. As is almost invariably the case with male fish some progress towards spawning colouration had been made, but this had not advanced to the point where the rainbow band was obviously in evidence...*
>
> *Due to river conditions, at the point where I caught the fish, I had a long and exhausting time landing it. In the end I was unfortunate in the point my*

The upper reaches of the Capilano, now drowned, were favorite waters for the dry-fly man.

gaff entered for the fish bled profusely and was still bleeding on the scales in Vancouver three hours later. I feel confident that the witnessed weight of 15 lbs 12 oz. was a minimum of 2 oz. less than the fresh out-of-water weight.

I was alone, as is my usual practice when steelhead fishing and in consequence have no eye witness that it was taken on a dry fly. I am, however, very well known in fishing circles in this part of the world and no one could be found to state that during the past 30 years he ever saw me fishing for steelhead or any other species of the trout family except with the fly. I have, in fact, no other kind of tackle. I am very well know to Mr. Straight, one of my witnesses. Mr. Straight is editor for fishing and hunting news on The Vancouver Sun. I am well known to the members of the firm of Harkley and Haywood, Sporting Goods, Cordova Street, Vancouver and could produce many other reputable witnesses to the fact that for many years I have never been seen fishing except with a fly.

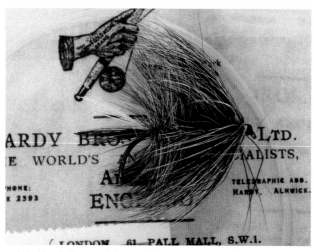

A Harkley & Haywood-dressed Whiskey and Soda dry fly from Paul Moody Smith's box (circa 1949).

Paul Dorien Smith, PM's son, wrote me years later and told me that his dad was a little miffed that his fish only placed sixth that year. In *The American Angler* (1954), A. J. McClane listed the largest 50 fish for a number of categories taken in the last ten years of *Field & Stream* contests. In the Western Rainbow Trout—Fly Casting category, P. M. Smith's fish ranked 39th. However, McClane listed month of capture, river and fly, and an examination of those 50 entries showed Smith's was the only one, thus the largest, taken on a dry fly. Quite an achievement.

That Capilano steelhead rose to the dry fly was a first for British Columbia and steelhead on a dry fly made the Cap a special place indeed. Catching steelhead on a dry fly on the Capilano was not an incidental thing. Practitioners of the sport attested to the use of dry flies for more than a quarter of a century.

Frank Darling made reference to fishing with a dry fly in a letter to my father's cousin—Jim Carlson—dated January 6, 1934:

I have caught them up to about 15 lbs.—run from 4 to 24 lbs. but larger ones not so liable to take the fly at least never heard of them. I hooked one once that might have been a big one but tangled me in a snag and I lost a new double tapered line cost $11 during war [First World War] I think or later...In summer I use floating flies and it's a [thrill] when one of 9 to 12 lbs. comes up and smacks at your fly. I am not as spry as I used to be so sometimes when they start down the river they are liable to beat me to it or leave me feeling pretty blown trying to keep up with them. I use a light rod and it's wonderful sport.

Paul Moody Smith in a letter to Mike Ball of *Field & Stream* dated April 15, 1950 noted that he "*took seven fish, including the one I entered in the contest and all these on the dry fly.*" He also lost an equal or greater number.

About floating flies Arthur Bryan Williams in *Fish and Game in British Columbia* (1935) writes:

There are two large grey hackles, the light-coloured one, which is almost white, and the darker grey. These are used for Steelheads, particularly on the Capilano. (p. 48)

That large Grey Hackle became known as Whiskey and Soda and along with the Bi-Visible they were British Columbia's first steelhead dry flies.

Although the history of this province's steelhead fly-fishing is short, few know that this province's first steelhead dry fly—the Whiskey and Soda—was developed in the 1920s for the Capilano summer-runs by the Provincial game warden, Austin Spencer. Spencer's Pool in the lower canyon was named after him. As for the odd name Whiskey and Soda, we have to look elsewhere for that history.

Totem fly-fisher, Bob Taylor knows. He got the story from one of the Capilano's first-generation fly-fishermen. Bob met Bill Cunliffe in the early 1950s and, during one of their many conversations, Bill explained that the Whiskey and Soda got its name from Black and White scotch whiskey, the favoured drink of many Capilano fly-fishermen. On the label of the dark-colored whiskey bottle were two Scotty dogs, one black and one white. According to Bill, the black Scotty represented the whiskey, the white represented the soda. The name Whiskey and Soda stems from the fact that it is dressed with only black and white hackle feathers:

Hook: 4, 6 or 8.

Tail: A black and white hackle tip.

Body: Black and white hackles tied in at the hook bend and wound thick and full.

Head: Black thread, varnished.

To make the fly ride high on its hackle tips, the Capilano fly-fishermen treated it with musclin or ceroline. It's important to remember the Whiskey and Soda was invented for dry-fly fishing and that dry-fly fishing—of a kind, never mind the steelhead fishing variety—is a recent innovation. It was introduced to British trout streams less than one and one-half centuries ago. The method didn't really develop a worldwide following until the turn of the

Tommy Mayo with a fine 21-pound Capilano steelhead, circa 1950.

COURTESY OF EARL ANDERSON

century. For that, the angling fraternity can thank England's F. M. Halford and his book *Dry-fly fishing in Theory and Practice,* published in 1889. That volume soon became the dry-fly fisherman's bible. Dry-fly fishing for anadromous fish is even more recent. It developed around the turn of the century and was popularized by Americans fishing for Canadian Atlantic salmon. Among the pioneers were E. R. Hewitt, Colonel Monell, and George La Branche. The Whiskey and Soda resembles the flies developed by these gentlemen. It was used, not skated over the surface causing a wake, but as the true, upstream dry fly.

Skating, as so many fly-fishermen nowadays call dry-fly fishing, has roots dating back at least three centuries. Until recently, it was never called "dry-fly" fishing. Indeed those who use the euphemism "dry fly" for the skated fly could be accused of insulting the originators and true disciples of the dry fly—Halford, La Branche, Hewitt, Monell and, closer to home, British Columbia's Frank Darling, Paul Moody Smith and Roderick Haig-Brown.

King White remembers meeting Frank Darling on the Upper Capilano in 1932. Darling was sitting on a log "resting" the Crown Creek Pool. He had just lost a fish, but had seen another surface in the lower part of the pool, and was getting ready to give it a try. In a letter to me, not too long before he died, King recalls his meeting with Darling and the fish Darling caught that day. King says:

I invited him to fish the pool while I rested after my long walk. He did and was soon working the pool casting a big grey Whiskey and Soda dry fly. Soon I got up and walked towards the river's edge just above Mr. Darling to watch more closely. I could see his fly sitting up high on the surface riding the waves down to the lower end of the reach. Just then a large fish shouldered through a wave just below the fly, and as it disappeared Mr. Darling's rod lifted to form an arc. The fish fought hard and remained in the pool for about ten minutes. By now I was sure he would land it on

the beach, but suddenly the fish tore away and on out of the pool downstream. There was a long steep rapid below, and the river finally rushed against a long cribbing on our side. If the fish stayed on and reached the cribbing it would be gone. I still had my wading staff-gaff over my shoulder, and down along the edge of the rapid I raced over large uneven boulders in my hip waders. Finally I stopped and on looking back up river I soon saw sunlight flashing on part of the flyline at least seventy-five yards below the figure of Mr. Darling. By now he had waded out to the edge of the pool all the while holding his nine foot Payne rod as high as he could. Suddenly I saw the flash of the fish's body behind a big low rock close to my shore and a little above me. In a few moments I made a lucky stroke and gaffed the seventeen pound summer henfish just behind the gill cover. The fly was till in the corner of her jaw, leader and line intact too, all the way to Mr. Darling who was standing on the shore way above me. Late that afternoon I was chauffeured from the river right to my front gate in Mr. Darling's big black sedan.

What of the river today? Go there most days and you will see tourist buses parked in the Cleveland Dam parking lot and groups walking over the dam looking at the impounded water and peering over the 300-foot spillway usually devoid of water. The Capilano River lives in name only. Gone is the clear, boulder-studded river. Gone, too, are the wild summer-runs. In the last nine years, a total of just over 100 summer-run steelhead were trapped in the hatchery holding tank, mostly hatchery marked fish. The river, its fish and its fly-fishers, though, have left us something quite precious: the steelhead dry-fly technique.

References

Lingren, Arthur James. *Fly Patterns of British Columbia.* Portland: Frank Amato Publications, 1996.

___. "Whiskey & Soda" Totem Flyfisher's *Totem Topics,* Issue 91 (1991): 3-7.

McClane, A. J. *The American Angler.* New York: Henry Holt and Company, 1954.

Smith, Henry Badeley. "Vancouver Water Works" Paper No. 35, of *The Proceedings of the Canadian Society of Civil Engineers,* Volume III, 1889.

Williams, A. Bryan. *Rod & Creel in British Columbia.* Vancouver: Progress Publishing Co., 1919.

___. *Fish and Game in British Columbia.* Vancouver: Sun Directories Ltd., 1935.

5

The Coquihalla River

A Tom Brayshaw painting of a steelhead.

THE NATIVE TRANSLATION OF COQUIHALLA IS "GREEDY OR hungry waters." Exactly in which context the Natives gave to the meaning is difficult to determine. Steelhead fly-fishers, however, may be able to derive some symbolic interpretation such as river with summer-run steelhead hungry or greedy for our flies. With its 1860s or earlier roots, British Columbia steelheading was born on this river.

The Coquihalla has a long fishing history with written records going back to the days of the fledgling crown colony of British Columbia, established in 1858. British Columbia and Vancouver

Island were separate colonies until they became one in 1866. Matthew MacFie spent five years in the colonies from 1859 and, upon his return to England, wrote his book, *Vancouver Island and British Columbia*, published in 1865. About the trout in the waters and a good catch, he writes:

> *Trout are found in the waters of both colonies, and often weigh from 4 lbs. to 6 lbs.... A superior kind of trout abound in the lower Fraser, weighing 7 lbs. or 8 lbs., and another of a smaller description in the tributaries of that river. Mr. Brown states that twenty*

mountain-trout were recently caught in a stream near Hope, whose aggregate weight was 146 lbs., and two of them weighed 11 lbs. each. (p. 167)

The method of capture was not given, but undoubtedly, MacFie is referring to the Coquihalla River, and the mountain-trout are the Coquihalla's summer-run steelhead. Although it is just a few short words, fly-fisher John Keast Lord, the naturalist attached to the Canada USA Boundary Commission, reported in his two-volume book *The Naturalist in British Columbia* that in September he:

> *was going trout-fishing in a beautiful stream, the Qua-que-alla, [sic] that comes thundering and dancing down the Cascade Mountains, cold and clear as crystal...* (Vol. 1, p. 59).

Lord, who spent four years from 1858 to 1862 in British Columbia, was the first naturalist to identify the steelhead trout in British Columbia waters. But he did not indicate in his book the date or place of capture. He did comment about the cutthroat, jack coho and Dolly Varden having a fondness for gaudy flies. On his Coquihalla trip he did not mention how far up the river he went nor the fish he caught, but in the 1860s the river was accessible above the canyon. A. C. Anderson, who was in charge of the Hudson Bay Company's Fort Alexandria near Quesnel on the Fraser River, searched for an easier route to the Company's Fort Langley that would bypass the Fraser Canyon. In 1846, he secured one by way of the Coquihalla River, that, until replaced by the Hope Princeton (Dewdney Trail) and Fraser Canyon roads built in the late 1850s and early 1860s by the Royal Engineers, was the route to the southeastern interior. Anderson's Coquihalla Trail was improved in 1876 and was used for cattle drives from Nicola to Hope.

In search of angling experience in British Columbia along the CPR line, H. W. Seton-Karr stopped and fly-fished the Coquihalla in September of 1890. About his fishing and the town of Hope, in *Bear-Hunting in the White Mountains or Alaska and British Columbia Revisited,* published in 1891, he says:

> *Hope is one of the most beautiful and picturesque villages I have seen on the Fraser, or indeed anywhere... It is surrounded by mountains not so rugged as to be repellent, but high enough to lend a grandeur to the scenery...For a consideration a small boy accompanied me for about a mile to the banks of the Coquihalla River, as a guide to a place where fly-fishing might be had. He bore a small can of salmon-roe and rod of his own, but I caught more trout than he with the artificial fly, about a dozen in all, none over half a pound. But the day was fine, the trail picturesque and flat, and the river easy to fish and very pretty, while there was in many places a broad expanse or stones and gravel between the stream and the trees on either bank, allowing one plenty of elbow-room to cast the line.* (pp. 133-134)

Seton-Karr fished the lower river and in September the summer-run steelhead would have been either in or above the Coquihalla canyon. The small size of the fish caught by Seton-Karr

indicates that they were probably cutthroat or, perhaps, steelhead smolts.

Anglers wouldn't make a point of journeying to Hope to fish the Coquihalla River if they had not heard favourable reports of good catches. The reports of the fishing did draw anglers to Hope and the Coquihalla became a destination for visiting anglers. Nonetheless, it took the angler and writer Dr. Thomas Wilson Lambert, the surgeon attached to the CPR's Western Division, who sampled much of the fishing along the line of the CPR, to provide the documentation of those large fish that attracted anglers. Lambert fished the lower three miles of Coquihalla many times in July of 1892, when the summer-run steelhead would be migrating through. He writes:

> *A very beautiful river called the Coquehalla [sic] joins the Fraser at this place [Hope], which I used to fish in 1892...But I found that the pools of this river contained very large fish, which were then to me quite*

Tommy Brayshaw with a Coquihalla steelhead.

Bill Cunliffe displaying his double-handed rod-casting technique.

unknown monsters, and I spent many long days on its banks in attempts to capture some.

I used to try each pool first with the [Devon] min-now and then with the fly, which was, of course, exactly the opposite of the right course. Several good fish of 5lb. or so were landed and many lost. On one occasion, as I was hauling in a small trout to remove it from the fly, I was startled by an immense fish which lept out of the water at it, close to my feet. It must have been a fish of anything from 10lb. to 15lb. or more. It jumped high in the air, drenching me with spray as it fell back into the water. I supposed it to be a large salmon, but as a bright red stripe was clearly seen along its side I know that it was a rainbow trout. Twice in this river small trout were seized as they were being drawn in, but each time the single gut was snapped by the fish. The higher parts of the river were never tried by me, though once or twice I saw large strings of trout brought in by cowboys. No doubt at this time of year the best fishing was in the upper waters. Probably the steel-head or sea-run comes up the Fraser as far as the Coquehalla. (pp. 67-68)

Lambert was right. The steelhead did come up as far as Hope and further. That large, red-striped fish that broke his line was undoubtedly a Coquihalla summer-run steelhead.

By the time A. Bryan Williams wrote *Rod & Creel in British Columbia,* published in 1919, the Coquihalla was well known as a steelhead stream. Williams mentions the fishing to be had in "the famous Steelhead Pool" about a ten- to fifteen-minute walk from the hotel. About the trout fly-fishing, he says:

During August and September the water gets to its lowest stage and about this time there is always a run of rainbows and cutthroat, some of them running to quite a good size, and nice fly-fishing may then be had...It is, however, for steelheads that the river is famous, and for these fish there are few streams its equal. (p. 120.)

Williams says that the steelhead run all winter with March and April the best months. It is highly probable that the large rainbows found in August and September mentioned by Williams and MacFie's mountain trout are the prized summer-run steelhead.

Commissioned for service in 1916, the Kettle Valley Railway, with Shakespearean station names along the track in the Coquihalla Subdivision, wound its way through the Coquihalla Valley. With daily passenger service, fishermen had a much quicker way to get to the river above the canyon. Andrew McCulloch, construction engineer and, later, the railway general superintendent, loved Shakespeare and named the stations after characters from the bard's works. Lear and Othello would become popular fly-fishing spots and remained so even after the railway was decommissioned in 1961. When the Coquihalla Highway was constructed in the 1980s, signs along a portion of the highway bearing the original Shakespearean names mark the old railway station stops.

The Coquihalla was a magnet and I a chunk of iron ore. I had heard so much about the Coquihalla River and with Beverley and son Charles in tow I headed for a look-see. We camped at Lear Bridge Pool and the next morning, a lovely summer September one, with a low clear river with a water temperature in the low fifties, I wandered along the old access road searching the glistening, bubbling waters for steelhead. In those days a logging bridge crossed at Othello and peering from the bridge into that deep pool I spotted a couple of summer-runs. Although this was a family outing, I just happened to have my fly gear in the camper. I eagerly put the equipment together and scurried down the steep river bank. I decided that the low, clear but reasonably warm water needed an upstream approach and a dry fly. I put on a Stacked Deerhair, a simple dry fly consisting of clumps of deer hair fixed from bend to hook eye on a number four Wilson dry-fly hook.

Starting well below the fish, I worked my way up river. Trigger happy I yanked a trout from the water when it rose and took the fly. A couple of moves and casts later the fly landed, rode the waves and disappeared. It is amazing how large fish can at times take a fly with so little surface disturbance and at other times the take looks and sounds like an explosion on the surface. I tightened and felt a solid weight. About 10:30 on my first morning fishing the river I slid my first Coquihalla summer-run steelhead onto the beach—a good fish of about eight pounds.

Brayshaw's Coquihalla Orange was one of the flies featured on Canada Post's fly-fishing flies stamp series.

In 1944, with retirement in mind when World War II ended, Tommy Brayshaw scouted the Coquihalla River while searching for a place in Hope to retire. The Brayshaws found what they wanted and bought a lot on the Fraser's right bank across from the Coquihalla's mouth. In March 1946, after building their house, they settled in. Brayshaw would haunt the Coquihalla's summer-runs through his golden years.

After catching his first summer-run steelhead on a Devon minnow on June 28th, 1946, Brayshaw took only his fly rod to the Rock Pool on July 9. He "*fished the stream down with a #4 L[ow] W[ater] hook and black & silver... saw a steelhead rise, cast over it & rose it at once. (Brayshaw Diaries)*" The steelhead made fine long runs and then while it sulked the hook came away. Later that evening, he rose two more but ended the day with no fish on the beach. On August 9, he went to Othello and fished the Station House Pool, rising one fish on his first pass through. He changed to a number six Teal & Red and in almost the same place he rose and hooked a dour, stubborn fighter eventually landing an 8 1/2 pound fish, his first fly-caught Coquihalla summer-run steelhead.

Over the next couple of decades Brayshaw became synonymous with the Coquihalla. It was during his Coquihalla retirement years that Brayshaw developed his many steelhead patterns, the most famous being the Coquihalla series: the Red, Orange (both

Light and Dark), and Silver. It was also during those years that he became famous for his paintings, fish carvings and bamboo rods. A number of years after he passed away, a book about Brayshaw was written by Stanley Read the long-time honourary secretary of the Harry Hawthorn Foundation, a group dedicated to "*the inculcation and propagation of the principles and ethics of fly-fishing.*" The title of Read's book *Tommy Brayshaw: The Ardent Angler-Artist* (1977) depicts a man engrossed in his sport and art. Read quoted Brayshaw when one of his (Brayshaw's) fishing friends passed away saying that he has "*crossed the River Styx to join the band of anglers in the Elysian Fields* (p. 41)." And now that Brayshaw has joined that friend on the River Styx he is referred to as the Legendary Tommy Brayshaw.

During the early years of Coquihalla steelheading not many cast flies to this great fish. Brayshaw in a September 1959 letter to Dr. Dwight A. Webster of Cornell University said that, "*the number of fly-fishermen whom I know, for steelhead, could almost be counted on the fingers of one hand.*" Filling out that one-hand list would be fly-fishers such as Roderick Haig-Brown, Denny Boulton, Lee Richardson, Ralph Wahl and Bill Cunliffe. Cunliffe stands tall next to Brayshaw as one the Coquihalla's most dedicated steelhead fly-fishers.

Bachelor Bill Cunliffe, an industrial arts teacher and a veteran Capilano fly-fisher, spent a good part of his summer break on the Coquihalla River. He rented a cabin near the Coquihalla Fishing Camp lodge on the Camp Pool located just above the Othello railway station. During the summer months wielding his two-handed rod, Cunliffe was a familiar sight along the river's pools above the canyon.

One visit to this river will provide living proof that this small river—the birthplace of British Columbia steelheading—has suffered at the hands of men. A transportation corridor from the day that Anderson found his trail to the interior in 1846, it was followed by the Kettle Valley Railway in 1916, and the many-laned Coquihalla freeway completed for Expo '86. Gas, oil, and telecommunication companies found the valley to be the most convenient route to the Lower Fraser Valley for their utilities. The railway line and gas and oil pipelines were built when there was little concern for the environment. In addition, forestry, since the railway was built, has taken a toll on fish habitat. In 1970s a gold mine was established on Ladner Creek, a tributary steelhead spawning stream, and, in 1982, tailings laced with cyanide spilled from the mine's tailing pond killing juvenile and adult steelhead and affecting many different year classes and adult returns for at least a decade after the event.

Fishermen, too, played a role in the demise of the runs. When Brayshaw arrived in 1946, the limit was three steelhead a day, 15 trout a day—steelhead smolts mostly—no annual limit and year-round fishing with any kind of gear. The anglers of the day mined the river and when Brayshaw left Hope in the early 1960s there

were few fish left. Through much of the 1960s, the river was closed to summer-run steelhead fishing. The river had long ago seen its glory days. The 1960s' closure helped bring the fish back and in the 1970s, under very restrictive angling regulations—catch and release, bait-ban below the canyon, fly-fishing-only above—the fly-fishers were back casting their flies on pools above the canyon. In the mid-1980s with excellent ocean survival the river saw abundant returns. The fly-fishing was superb and we thought the Coquihalla was back to its former glory days. Then the 1990s and the years of poor ocean survival hit. The Coquihalla has had only one year, 1996, where the minimum 300-fish spawning escapement was achieved. In 1996 almost 600 fish returned and there was a brief 6-week opening on the upper river through September and October. The only year that decade when flies floated over Coquihalla summer-runs.

Hopefully, good ocean survival as well as fisheries' work will result in better returns. However, present and future generations of fly-fishers will never experience those unspoiled days that anglers found in the first half of this century and before. There are just too many people wanting a piece of the outdoors. But when the runs become strong enough, Fisheries need to consider very restrictive regulations that will do the least harm to fragile stocks while at the same time permitting some angling. For example, the fly-fishing-only section could be opened to floating lines only, no weighted flies and none above size six. Perhaps it's time for upstream dry-fly only. Also, on small streams like the Coquihalla, close to large urban populations, it's time for a new ethic and a new kind of limit for

Some Brayshaw-dressed Coquihalla steelhead flies.

On June 28, 1946, Brayshaw took his first Coquihalla River steelhead. He carved this model and gave it to Ralph Wahl of Bellingham, Washington.

catch-and-release steelhead fishing. The limit would be set at one or two released steelhead and you are off the water. This sharing of water and resource is alien to most steelheaders' thinking, but it is the future. Some may argue that their rights to fish are being violated by restrictive regulations. We have no right to fish guaranteed in the Constitution, only the Native people have that right. Anglers are granted permission from the state to fish, providing the rules set out are obeyed. Restrictions on gear type and technique are not discriminatory. For example, anyone can learn to fly-fish and take part in a fly-fishing-only fishery.

The Thompson wasn't worth the long drive. September 24th was just too early and the river too high. What to do? The Coquihalla was two hours away and might be okay. The drive down the Thompson and Fraser canyons went quickly. I parked the truck at the top end of Trackside, a short distance above the Coquihalla/Hope interchange. The railway tracks used to pass along the right bank of the river, but now the old rail bed is used as an access road to Lear bridge. I walked up to Gold Pan, a popular steelhead holding spot, but drew a blank.

The Coquihalla Highway was in full construction and as part of the fish habitat mitigation, boulders had been strategically placed, providing lies for steelhead in the Trackside section of river. The water looked promising and a bold wade put me on the left bank. Evening was coming on quickly and with no more than an hour left to fish I cast my Black GP into the first piece of water bringing my fly through the slick caused by a placed boulder. The fish took well and about 15 minutes later I took the hook from a 28-inch female. During the fight, the fish took me down to the next spot. It looked good so I threw the Black GP into it and was into another fish almost instantly. Minutes later I took the hook from a 29 1/4-inch female. I mused, what a good night: two small pieces of water and two fish landed. I didn't expect any more steelhead but in the next

pool another fish took. It was after 6 p.m. and dark when I took the hook from a 29 1/2-inch male steelhead. Hat tricks don't come easy and I will remember that evening on the Coquihalla forever. It is the river where I took three beautiful summer-run steelhead from three pools in 45 minutes of fishing.

May the runs return and, once again, may fly-fishers cast flies to the Coquihalla's magnificent summer-run steelhead in the river that has lured anglers to her banks for nearly 150 years.

References

Begg, Alexander. *History of British Columbia.* Toronto: William Briggs, 1894.

Hill, Beth. *Sappers: The Royal Engineers in British Columbia.* Ganges; Horsdal & Schubert, 1987.

Lambert, T. W. *Fishing in British Columbia.* London: Horace Cox, 1907.

Lingren Arthur James. *Fly Patterns of British Columbia.* Portland: Frank Amato Publications, 1996.

Lord, John Keast. *The Naturalist in British Columbia.* London: Richard Bentley, 1866.

Read, Stanley E. *Tommy Brayshaw: The Ardent Angler-Artist.* Vancouver: University of British Columbia, 1977.

Sanford, Barrie. *Steel Rails and Iron Men.* Vancouver & Toronto: Whitecap Books, 1990.

Seton-Karr, H. W. *Bear-Hunting in the White Mountains or Alaska and British Columbia Revisited.* London: Chapman and Hall, 1891.

Williams, A. Bryan. *Rod & Creel in British Columbia.* Vancouver: Progress Publishing Co., 1919.

The Cowichan River

WE GLIDED THROUGH THE POOLS AND RUNS CASTING OUR lines, sometimes getting out to wade and fish, then we rounded a bend and there it was. The pool! Twenty years had lapsed since that January 1967 morning when my former brother-in-law took me fishing on the Cowichan. I remember driving along a winding road, walking along a railway track, dropping down a steep trail and wading a side channel to get to a small island caused by the high water. Etched in my mind was the picture of that spot where I caught an eight-pound steelhead that morning. My first from the Cowichan. I returned often to fish the Cowichan and wondered about that spot. Seeing that run brought back fond memories of days of wandering this river so steeped in fly-fishing lore.

Never has a British Columbian river received such attention and accolades in its early days. Even princes of the realm came to fish this jewel of Vancouver Island. Most of British Columbia's coastal rivers are not insect rich, in fact, most produce little food. Some salmon use the nutrient-poor streams only for spawning and the fry migrate to sea as soon as they pop through the gravel. However, trout and coho salmon rear in them, often taking one to three years to become smolts before they migrate to the sea and grow large. Unique to the Cowichan Valley and noted by Colonial Office explorers in the mid-1800s was the type of soil with minerals that when leached into the water generated nutrient-rich waters. Those nutrients fed the organisms that resulted in the river's prodigious insect life. Oliver Wells, in his 1860 *General Report on the Cowichan Valley,* writes:

> *High ranges of mountains believed to be of secondary formation, with Calcareous Freestone, or Carbonate of Lime, form almost impassable barriers towards the North and South, and the whole subsidence of land between these mountains is evidently a deposit brought down by the waters. The distinctive nature of the soils throughout the Cowichan Valley is Calcareous, seemingly formed by the decomposition of Limestone rock, for while the other principles occur in different degrees, the properties of Carbonate of Lime almost invariably predominates.* (pp. 1-2)

Wells goes on to describe a valley lush with trees, plants, game and a river and bay full of fish. It is the soil, however, with its limestone base that fed the chain of life, resulting in good trout populations. The first sportsmen were attracted to the river by the trout fly-fishing in the summer months.

Since time immemorial, in their cedar duguot canoes, the Cowichan First Nations people traveled up and down the river from

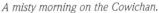

A misty morning on the Cowichan.

Cam Proctor, Charles Lingren and Mark Shannon on a Cowichan drift.

Cowichan Lake to Cowichan Bay hunting, fishing and gathering. The river was their highway and the early sportsmen wanting to fish the river hired Native guides. Lady Somerset (Mrs. Algernon Saint Maur) and her husband, after spending a few days trolling spoons on the lake, journeyed down the Cowichan with Native guides. About the Natives' canoemanship, scenery, the trip down river and the joys of the outdoors in her *Impressions of a Tenderfoot* (1890), she says:

> *Sometimes, as we got into heavy rapids, it seemed impossible that they would allow themselves to be guided, but as we glided through the water at about ten miles an hour, sometimes rushing past a large rock, at others within a few inches of a sweeper, as they call the trees which hang across the river just clear of the water, we saw how skillfully the Indians steered, and felt when each danger was passed...The banks of the river were lovely, green with maiden hair ferns and mosses, whilst high on both sides towered big trees.*

> *The day's work being over, we camped on a bank, and amused ourselves fishing for an hour or two before supper, and were able with the fly to catch a few nice trout, and after a good supper were willed to sleep by the murmur of running waters.*

> *Wonderful is the rest to body and mind in the kind of wild life, I marvel no more that weary disappointed men go into the woods to find oblivion*
> *'No tears,*

> *Dim the sweet look which Nature wears.'*
> *There is often solace in the sight of God's grand and glorious works, and care is dwarfed, for human plans appear insignificant, compared with the great designs of creation.* (pp. 95-96)

Mrs. St. Maur mentioned the Cowichan Hotel, built by Frank Green in 1887. That log structure was one of first fishing lodges built on Vancouver Island. In *Fishing Adventures in Canada and U.S.A.* (1950), G. D. Luard includes a month-long trip by his friend, called only Dick, to the Cowichan Lake and River in 1899. It is early September and about the sport Dick found on the trip down river, Luard writes:

> *The following day Dick fished the Cowichan river with flies and caught sixty-three trout, and the day after set out down the river accompanied by the fat and jolly Doc., in a small boat, 'with camping outfit and provisions for four days, and had great sport fly-fishing'—the best fish being 3 lb.* (p. 131)

It was trout catches like Dick's that drew King George V when he was Duke of York and later his son the Prince of Wales to fish the Cowichan.

Arthur Bryan Williams in *Rod & Creel in British Columbia* (1919) gives a glowing testimonial to the river, its trout and steelhead fly-fishing:

> *Of all the magnificent rivers of this province none have attained greater fame and justly so, than the*

A nice specimen of a Cowichan brown trout.

Cowichan. It has been fished by white men of all degree, including Royalty. It has been fished with the fly, minnow and baits of all descriptions: it has been fished by Indians with nets and weirs; it has been fished by every method, legal and illegal whereby fish can be caught, for the past thirty years, and yet to-day in spite of all, it is still a splendid river for a good fisherman.

You can fish the lower reaches from Cowichan Bay, four of five miles higher up from Duncans, or the head waters where it empties from the lake at Cowichan Lake. At all these places there is excellent accommodation.... At Duncans there is a cozy little Club, and if you can get an introduction, you will find a number of first-class fishermen amongst its members who will willingly afford you all the information you desire.

Trains run from Duncans to Cowichan Lake two or three times a week, on other days there is an auto stage. By taking the morning stage you can get off at

either of the two famous pools, the Falls pool is twelve miles from Duncans, the Rips pool four miles from the lake, having plenty of time to fish and return in the evening...

With regards to the fish to be caught. It is an excellent stream for steelheads in the winter and early spring months up to March 25th when the season closes on Vancouver Island for this species of fish. Some of the local anglers catch them entirely on the fly, generally using a fly very similar to a large Grouse and Claret. The Jock Scott and Silver Doctor are sometimes good...

After the first freshet in the spring the rainbow and cutthroats begin to run and afford sport to the fly-fishermen all summer (May and June being the best) except after a long drought, when the water gets too low...

There is always the chance of hooking a spring salmon on the fly during April, May and June and cohoes in the fall. The best salmon water is about 10 miles up stream from Duncans.

Some of the best flies are Cowichan Coachman, March Brown and Jock Scott for rainbows.

For steelheads a Grouse and Claret tied on a 6/0 hook. (pp. 67-68.)

An excellent trout stream, it attracted many fly-fishers but the trout's larger cousin the mighty steelhead offered special appeal to those seeking big fish in flowing waters. About this magnificent game fish, the sport of fly-fishing for them, the best fly-fishing technique and the Cowichan, J. R. Dymond, in *Game Fishes of British Columbia* (1932), writes:

There are few finer game fishes than the steelhead... The smaller sizes rise more readily to the fly than larger ones...However, thirteen and fourteen pound fish have been taken on the fly, and it is probable that when anglers think more of their sport and less of the number or weight of fish which they take, that more and more of the larger steelheads will be taken on the fly...In the Cowichan River, steelhead fishing is at its best in January, February and March. There, according to A. A. Easton, Fishery Inspector, they are taken on medium-sized salmon flies, the best being Parmachene Belle, Jock Scott, Silver Doctor, and Dusty Miller. The best method is said to be to fish above where one expects the fish to be, casting across and up stream and allowing the fly to sink well by the time it reaches where the fish is expected to be lying. Mr. Easton adds, 'Steelheads are game fighters to the end, and good tackle is essential. I recommend a double-handed, sixteen foot rod, at least three hundred feet of medium salmon line and heavy sea trout casts. When hooked, these fish generally go away with a tremendous rush for perhaps sixty or seventy feet, and at the end of it leap high out of the water, and should they succeed in getting into rough and broken water, as they usually attempt to do, you have all your work cut out to hold them.' (pp. 15-16)

The Cowichan was the stream on Vancouver Island to take winter steelhead on the fly. The cutthroat and rainbow are the native trout of this river, but in 1932 the Cowichan received its first and largest plant of European brown trout. Just over 300,000 eggs were hatched at the Lake Cowichan hatchery with 176,000 fry released to the Cowichan and 50,000 in the Little Qualicum. The balance were reared in ponds at the hatchery and released as one-year and two-year olds in 1933 and 1934. With good mayfly, stone-fly, caddisfly populations, as well as salmon fry and salmon eggs in season to eat, the habitat suited the brown trout. And they grew large indeed, some to steelhead size. Two of the largest landed are Ron Saysell's 14-pounder and Ian Sutherland's 14 1/2-pounder, both taken in the 1960s. Nowadays there is the odd fish that might attain weights of 10 pounds or larger, but a five-pound Cowichan brown is a very good fish.

The Cowichan's habitat suited the coho salmon exceptionally well. Sometime in the 1920s the prolific runs of returning coho salmon drew fly-fishers to Cowichan Bay. In a 6 January 1934 letter to Jim Carlson, about coho fly-fishing, Vancouver fly-fisher Frank Darling writes:

In Sept. & Oct. I go over to Van. Island to Cowichan Bay with Mr. Hunt and fly-fishing for Cohoe salmon in the saltchuck and it's about the best sport I know of. They certainly can smash at your fly and have lots of pep. We use a small launch to chase them up [if the fish] gets out too much of your line. I use 150 yards and sometimes it gets down to 15 yds or less with a good fish.

W. F. Pochin in his 1946 book, *Angling and Hunting in British Columbia*, writes about the sport's popularity:

During recent years Cowichan Bay has become so popular for its Cohoe fly-fishing that anglers wishing to fish for trophy or button winners must make reservations long in advance...But during September and October Cohoes that range upwards of twenty pounds are caught on flies, and those who have taken them

Joe Saysell (left) and Bob Taylor discussing which fly to use.

claim this type of fishing to be the very tops in angling.
(p. 62)

In the early days of the sport, fly-fishing for coho was uniquely British Columbian; it was practiced by early British visitors and evolved over a number of years from the cast to trolled fly. Moreover, with the introduction of the hairwings, or bucktails as they became known, the flies became larger and eventually became difficult to cast. The fly-fishers of the day found that the larger flies trolled were more productive, and the term bucktailing was born to describe a trolled fly made from a deer's tail. About fly-fishing for sea-run cutthroat and coho salmon fly-fishing, Darling says:

> *We use a long streamer fly made of bucktail. Trout and salmon both take it. I use polar bear, black and brown bear hair…It's a bit hard to cast, have to heave it like a spoon.*

Charlie Stroulger's family lived on the bay for most of the 20th century. As a teenager in the late 1920s and early '30s, he remembers the bay teeming with coho and the fly-fishing he and his brother enjoyed. After Charlie took up fly-tying, he became one of Vancouver Island's premier bucktail-fly dressers. Stroulger-dressed bucktails were a must if you wanted to increase your chances of success on the bay. Charlie's legacy to the sport is his Grey Ghost bucktail.

These testimonials spanning 60 years show a river rich with trout and steelhead and a bay teeming with coho. In any exceptional fishery, some fishermen stand out from the crowd. Henry Ashdown Green is foremost among the Cowichan's earliest fly-fishers. Green was a surveyor and engineer with a passion for fly-fishing and lived in Duncan when not away working. He was part of Walter Moberly's engineering team back in the 1870s when Moberly was exploring routes through the Rocky Mountains for the trans-continental railway. Introduced to the Cowichan around 1889, his Ashdown Green fly was *the* fly to use and it was one of the few Canadian flies that graced the back of Sportsman cigarette packages. With a red goose tail, claret body and throat and white swan wing it is almost identical to a fly that Bryan Williams called the Cowichan Coachman, differing only by the absence of the red goose tail.

Bryan Williams left his mark on the river's fly-fishing with Williams' Yellow-bodied sedge, Vancouver Island's first trout dry fly.

Long the domain of Victoria fly-fishers, many of the well-to-do from the province's capital built fishing and summer-holiday retreats on the Cowichan. Great uncle of Victoria politician David Anderson, Ken Gillespie was born and raised in Victoria. When Gillespie returned from overseas at the end World War I, after spending four years as a POW, he had had enough of city life. He moved to Cowichan Lake and became a trapper and fishing guide

Right: Charles Lingren fishing the Cabins Pool.
Left: With the wildflowers blooming,
spring is a nice time to be on the Cowichan.

Brown trout were first planted in the 1930s.

with a somewhat colourful reputation. About his uncle, Anderson writes:

> *There are many stories of his time there. I cannot vouch for the truth of any of them. Once, after he had refused to clear the snow from the road in front of his house the provincial police arrested him, so he spent Christmas in jail. All his fishing clients from Victoria made a point of driving up to visit him, bringing many bottles of scotch, so Christmas was an eventful and uproarious event...Ken had a launch on the lake, and would transport loggers and millworkers in the outlying camps of Lake Cowichan for an evening in the pub. He would join them, and then get them back to their camps by first light. One story has it that after a particularly enjoyable evening the group piled into his launch, which was started and Ken hunkered down in the stern to steer it up the lake. Only at daybreak did they discover that the launch had not been cast off, and they had spent the previous two hours at the Lake Cowichan dock.*
>
> *Ken also had a dugout canoe, which he would pole up the river. He was asked to take the Prince of Wales on the river when he visited in the late '30s. Ken refused point blank. Victoria society was horrified at this slight to the future King!*

Gillespie made his living guiding and trapping and the canoe was vital to those endeavors. He refused the future king because he was worried that he might wreck his canoe on a rock or shallow bar in the low water. Trips down the Cowichan with Gillespie consisted of four or five days of drifting, camping and fly-fishing. Before outboard motors became popular, Gillespie poled his long canoe up and down the river like the Natives had done for millennia.

Nearly 30 years ago I remember seeing a television program about the Cowichan, featuring Richard Ciccimarra, one of the river's most devoted fly-fishers of the day. Ciccimarra lived in Victoria but made frequent pilgrimages to the Cowichan. European-born, he probably realized the value of access to common-property far more than British Columbian-born anglers. In Europe most waters are private with its best waters reserved by the wealthy and, on those not open, anglers are charged daily-use fees. Ciccimarra treasured the Cowichan and delighted in casting his flies to the planted European brown trout.

Many fly-fishers from the Haig-Brown Flyfishing Association, formed in the early '70s, cast their lines on the water carrying on this Victoria tradition. Joining them are fly-fishers from Duncan's Cowichan fly-fishers and other up-Island clubs. They too love this river with a passion and are actively involved in protecting it against despoilers.

However, a river as superb as this one attracted many and some came to fish and ended staying. Gillespie was one and he guided for nearly 50 years. He befriended a young Ron Saysell after Ron, in 1935, started coming from Vancouver to fly-fish the Cowichan. In 1947 Saysell moved to the Island, bought Gillespie's property with a small cabin on the Willow Run and became a guide. One year later, Joe Saysell, the conscience and protector of the Cowichan, was born.

Joe was brought up with a fly rod in his hand. When he was eight years old he took his first steelhead from a pool not too far from his home. Ron taught his son well the lore of fly-fishing and Joe had his first boat when he was 12 years old. Father, son and clients would go hand in hand down the river. The river boats used by the guides were similar to those used by the Natives and Saysell's father's was 24 feet long. They were replaced by flat-bottom McKenzie River-type drift boats in the late 1970s or early 1980s.

During the summer months while he was growing up, Joe would swim parts of the river near his home, not just for fun. The young guide scouted trout holding spots and on one of these swims in the early 1960s, Joe noticed a huge brown trout. A friend of his father, ardent brown trout fly-fisherman Harry Robinson, was talking with Joe shortly after Saysell had found this large brown. Robinson wanted to try for this fish and Saysell recalls Robinson's dry fly drifting over the lie and then disappearing. The huge fish showed itself a couple of times during the brief battle then it sought refuge in its lie along the deep, tree-rooted bank, fouling the leader and breaking off. Robinson was not too disappointed. Like a true angler, he had his chance and the fish won, but he would remember that encounter to his dying day.

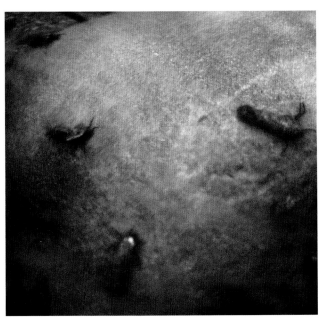

The Cowichan has ample caddisfly larvae and other insects on which the trout feed.

Like many young Vancouver Island men of his generation, Joe went to work in the woods as a tree faller. He bought property a short distance upstream of the family home, built his house where Gail and he raised their family. During steelhead and trout season, he guided on weekends and holidays. The years passed and as

logging practices changed from bad to worse, always an environmentalist, Saysell became more outspoken. In the 1980s, BC's forest practices received worldwide attention, especially the barren moonscape clear-cuts on Vancouver Island. With a long history of overharvesting, the industry now in decline blamed environmentalists because they fought for sustainable forest practices. The logging-based Lake Cowichan saw their way of life disappearing and blamed the environmentalists rather than face reality. But truth be told: the forest industry, aided and abetted by the Ministry of Forests with its non-sustainable practices, had destroyed the livelihood of so many relying on it. It was during that time that Joe had a serious accident in the bush and he never went back to work in the woods. His life now revolves around fly-fishing, hunting and protecting rivers, especially the Cowichan.

Noted by early fly-fishers were the huge trees in the valley. "*Many of them are six to eight feet in diameter, and rise to a great height, the bole clean of branches for a hundred feet or more and then thrusting out broad green arms to form a wonderful roof which almost excludes the sunlight, in places,*" reported N. de Bertrand Lugrin for *Rod and Gun in Canada* in 1923.

Those huge trees attracted the loggers. In the early days they did as they pleased. The valley was stripped to the river bank, logs were dragged across spawning streams and in November of each year they drove logs down the river with no regard for the freshly laid salmon eggs. Log jams too often blocked the river and, after the river scoured new channels, it left piles of logs as testimonials of that practice. The log drives stopped in 1908, not because they were doing harm to the fish resource but because the industry lost too many logs.

Through the following decades, the valley was clearcut and now you see the scars as the second growth and timber high on the mountains that was too hard to get at the first time through is cut.

The river and valley has long been a provider to many. To the loggers it provided a source of trees and a transportation corridor, to Lake Cowichan and Duncan it provided a source of potable water as well as a place to dump their sewage, to Crofton Pulp Mill it provided the water needed to produce paper, to the fishermen it provided a variety of sport nearly year-round in a beautiful setting, and to those who lived along its banks it provided a beautiful setting in which to live and raise a family. Each activity has an effect on the river and its fish, some more so than others.

In the 1980s many users of the Cowichan became concerned about the river. The second-growth timber was ripe for logging, riverbank developments threatened habitat, more people were moving into the area resulting in more outdoor users; all were having their affect which, when considered collectively, may destroy what was left of this jewel of a river. To examine the larger context of all those activities—starting back in the late 1980s and through the early 1990s—a Cowichan River Recreation Management Plan was developed.

Flowing from that plan's development, some private valley-bottom lands were bought and with public lands owned by the crown much of the undeveloped land above and below Skutz Falls became part of the Cowichan River Park, with provincial campgrounds at Stolz and Skutz Falls.

With liberal quotas, sport fishermen too had a detrimental effect on fish stocks. But progressive regulations, such as catch-and-release, bait-ban, fly-fishing-only, no-fishing during trout spawning in the upper river as well as many others, have helped trout stocks.

The target of Gulf of Georgia commercial and sport fishermen, the coho salmon that returned in the thousands to the Cowichan suffered badly. It has been years, but they are coming back and, perhaps, Charlie Stroulger might again see the scrappy coho chasing his Grey Ghost bucktail and hear the line screaming from his reel.

Poor ocean survival through many years in the 1990s has affected steelhead stocks all along the east coast of Vancouver Island. Few Cowichan steelhead fly-fishers have felt the pull of that grand game fish during the past decade. Most search the waters for the Cowichan's fabled trout.

The Cowichan has a few road access points, and much of the waters are abutted by private lands. Because of that, many anglers drift the river. A good part of the river is accessible to the angler willing to use his or her legs and hike the riverbank trails. The most popular section for fly-fishers is the section above Skutz Falls to Stanley Creek. However, once you reach the Spring Hole the trail leads back to Lake Cowichan Road. The pools above the Spring Hole to Stanley creek have abutting private property and most who

want to fish this section do a day drift from the Road Pool to Skutz Falls.

The Haig-Brown fly-fishing Association publishes a map of the river from Lake Cowichan to Cowichan Bay. The map shows roads, trails and names most pools. A river is a dynamic living thing and this river has changed over the years, blowing out pools that had existed for decades and scouring new ones. Many years ago the local rod and gun club posted signs naming some of the pools along the trail and some signs still exist.

Pool names are intriguing but, to a newcomer, unless you are accompanied by someone knowledgeable or the pool names are posted along the river bank it is a search-and-find proposition. The river flows from run to run and even after more than 30 years on this river I can't name more than a few runs where I have caught fish. I just wander along fishing likely spots. About five years ago Saysell and I drifted from his place to Skutz. Along the way, as we approached a good-looking pool, I could see trout surfacing taking salmon fry. This was one of his favourite spots, although to the practiced eye it was a logical one to fish and any fly-fisher with basic knowledge wouldn't pass it by, especially with trout showing. As we left Saysell said, "Please keep the spot to yourself."

The next year my son and a couple of his University of Victoria friends wanted to spend a day with me on the Cowichan. We did the drift from the Road Pool to Skutz and part way down we stopped for lunch a couple of runs above the spot I had good sport

Bucktails dressed by Charlie Stroulger when he was in his early 80s.

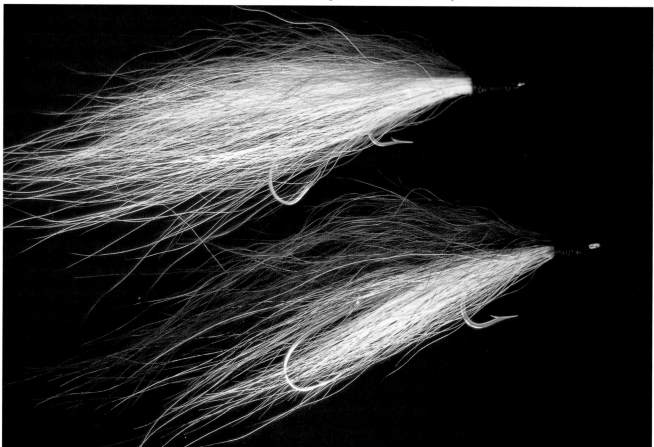

Jack and Charlie Stroulger. Charlie took the 22 1/2-pound coho from Cowichan Bay on his Grey Ghost Bucktail in 1950.

COURTESY OF CHARLIE STROULGER

with Saysell the year before. Cam Proctor told me that he fished the Cowichan whenever breaks from studying allowed and that he had caught his first steelhead from the Cowichan a couple of weeks earlier. We talked about the trout fishing and he mentioned the name of his favourite pool. It didn't mean much to me. I don't remember names too well, just good fishing spots. I asked him where that run was and he pointed downstream to the run that I had fished with Joe last year. Robinson's Fly Shop in Victoria had directed Cam to that spot when he first came to UVic, and he claimed all the University's Cowichan fly-fishers think it is one of the best spots for trout on the river. "Please keep it to yourself," brought a smile to my face. The whole bloody town of Victoria knew about the Black Hole.

But names are important to local fishing lore, and the Cowichan has more than its share of lore. For example, Hancock's is named after local fly-fisher Art Hancock, Green's is named after the Green family who have lived on that property since the 1880s, Saysell's is in front of Joe's house, Cook's is named after Norm Cook, a local fly-fisher, Collis' after Don Collis a former member of the Haig-Brown fly-fishing Association who, in the 1980s, bought the property fronting the pool, Rip's Run was mentioned by Williams in his 1919 book and is still a popular fishing pool, Wrixon's after Maurice Wrixon another Haig-Browner who favoured this water, and Robinson's after Harry Robinson. Other pools take names of landmarks such as tributary streams or waterfalls. All tell a story revealing part of the river's history and can connect past and future generations of fly-fishers.

My spring steelheading trip to Vancouver Island had been a bust. I had fished low, cold and clear Nanaimo, Gold and Nimpkish rivers and drew blanks. I hooked and lost a fish of about 10 pounds in the Campbell, my only steelhead in five days of fly-fishing. Before I caught the ferry back to Vancouver, I thought I would scoot down to the Cowichan. Often when the rivers up Island are low and clear, the Cowichan is in good shape because of the lake's balancing effect. It was 10:30 when I hiked through the bush to the river. The sun was shining on this early April morning, the river running clear with good flow, and the water temperature was 47 F. Under almost ideal spring conditions—I would have preferred an overcast day—I swam my number four Silver Lady through the pool and had only fished 15 minutes when a steelhead took the fly. Pleased, I slid an eight-pound male onto the beach; the Cowichan had saved the day and the trip.

Seduced by its magical charm, the Cowichan has lured me to her banks for over three decades. With second-growth evergreens towering above, I have enjoyed many a day wandering the trails above Skutz Falls casting my flies into the waters in search of browns, rainbows and steelhead. May the river and its fish be preserved so it can seduce many more generations of fly-fishers.

References

Dymond, J. R. *The Trout and Other Game Fishes of British Columbia.* Ottawa: Department of Fisheries, 1932.

Lugrin, N. de Bertrand. "Fishing and Filming on the Cowichan." *Rod and Gun in Canada,* XXV, 1. (1923), 12-14.

Luard, G. D. *Fishing Adventures in Canada and U.S.A.* London: Faber and Faber, 1950.

MacFie. *Vancouver Island and British Columbia.* London: Longman, Green, Longman, Roberts & Green, 1865 (Facsimile Edition 1972).

Obee, Bruce. "The Cowichan." *Beautiful British Columbia.* (circa 1990), 5-14

Paterson. T. W. "Fourth Generation Moves to McKinstry." *Cowichan Valley Citizen.* February 14, 1999, p. 19.

Pochin, W. F. *Angling and Hunting in British Columbia.* Vancouver: Sun Directories, 1946.

Saint Maur, Mrs. Algernon. *Impression of a Tenderfoot.* London: John Murray, 1890.

Wells, Oliver. *General Report on the Cowichan Valley.* Victoria: Colonial Office, 1860.

Williams, A. Bryan. *Rod & Creel in British Columbia.* Vancouver: Progress Publishing Co., 1919.

___. *Fish and Game in British Columbia.* Vancouver: Sun Directories, 1935.

CHAPTER 7

The Bella Coola and Dean Rivers

BRITISH COLUMBIA HAS A RUGGED COASTLINE, MAKING IT difficult to access remote areas. Even today, once you leave the Lower Mainland and Sunshine Coast, road access to the coast is limited. There are some logging roads, but only two Provincial Highways branch off Highway 97 at Williams Lake and Prince George, providing access to the coast at Bella Coola, Kitimat and Prince Rupert.

The Bella Coola River flows into the head of North Bentinck Arm and the Dean River, the next major river drainage to the north, flows into Dean Channel a few miles south of the Dean Channel's head. In 1946, W. F. Pochin's book *Angling & Hunting Guide in British Columbia* was published and, about the northern part of the province, he says that it is "*practically untouched by the sportsmen.*" Under his Atnarko River heading Pochin provides the first reference to fly-fishing Dean steelhead and its good rainbow trout fishing:

> *Atnarko River—Length 40 miles. Rainbow and Dolly Varden, from 1 1/4 to 10 lbs. Also, Steelhead. Season, early July to late fall. Steelhead can be taken with fly at Tanya Lake (4 days pack) in August. Excellent Rainbow fishing in nearby Dean River. (p.121)*

Tommy A. Walker, operator of Tweedsmuir Lodge on the Bella Coola River, took expeditions into Tanya Lake and the Upper Dean in those early days. Tanya Lake is on the headwaters of the Takia River, a major tributary of the Dean.

A few years later in his short book *100 Steelhead Streams* (Revised 1956 edition), Lee Straight gave glowing reports for both the Bella Coola and Dean rivers. He writes:

> *Bella Coola—One of the finest rivers in B.C., not only for steelheads but for coho salmon in fall, spring salmon during the summer freshet when water is murky, resident rainbow trout in its upper reaches, cutthroat trout in the lower reaches, Dolly Varden trout and Rocky Mountain whitefish throughout it length—all readily caught at the time of writing this. Steelheads are taken as far up as the Atnarko, a major tributary 50 miles from the sea. A road skirts the river, never more than a mile from it, right up to the Atnarko. It contains a heavy winter run of fish, giving*

A fresh-from-the-sea Dean River summer-run steelhead.

good sport as early as November and as late as April.

As rivers go, the Bella Coola has a very high per-centage of easily fished water and its gentle rapids are navigable by small boat from Stuie, 40 miles up-stream, to its mouth. Contains much good fly water and is a clear stream from fall to early summer. Accessible by boat to Bella Coola village and, when the road to Anahim Lake and Williams Lake is improved, by car in two days from Vancouver. A future steelhead Mecca.

Dean—Enters Dean Channel opposite the village of Kimsquit. A virgin, lightly fished river that is said to be as productive as the fabulous Bella Coola River. Accessible by boat to Kimsquit then by trail and possi-bly by river boat up the Dean River. Steelheads are caught here almost year round, up to, according to reports, a series of impassable falls about 40 miles from the sea.

The upper reaches are accessible by pack horse trip from Anahim or Nimpo Lakes, on the road west from Williams Lake. September is said to be the best month for steelheads in the lower reaches, as well as for trout above the falls. The writer has heard of a "Long Lake" [Tanya Lake], likely bearing some Indian name on the map, which affords lake fly-fishing for steelhead, a rare thing in B.C. (pp. 24-25)

It is noteworthy that the fishing on these two rivers so close together ended up so differently. The Bella Coola runs opaque once the freshet gets established in the spring and continues to run coloured until the frosts of fall seal glacial runoff. Because of that, the best fly-fishing opportunities for cutthroat, salmon, and steel-head occur during the months when the river is clear and cold. Even though a few fly-fishermen made regular journeys to fish the Bella Coola ever since Tweedsmuir Lodge started catering to fish-ers, the river was and still is favoured more by bait and lure fishers. The steelhead Mecca that Straight predicted in the mid-1950s lived a short life. The runs became decimated through Native and sport overharvest, habitat destruction and poor ocean survival. For the past five years the Bella Coola has been closed to all steelhead angling, but through those severe measures the run is recovering. It has some good salmon and cutthroat fishing. My fondest memo-ry of that river and its fish is a day I spent drifting and fly-fishing with Bob Taylor.

My diary for April 27, 1987 reminded me that Bob and I drift-ed from Walker Island to Indian Reserve takeout while Van Egan and Lee Straight did the Sallompt to Walker Island drift. In a gale-force wind Bob and I struggled to cast and, for the most part, the fishing was slow. With one pool left to fish, I left Bob to work the top end and I disappeared below the bend to fish the lower end. Shortly after I started fishing, salmon fry moved into the pool and the cutts and Dollys went crazy chasing and pouncing on them. In the next couple of hours, fishing a floating line and silver-bodied flies near the surface, I beached 25 fish to about 2 pounds and lost an equal or greater amount. Straight was picking us up at 6 p.m. and at 5:30 I pulled myself away and wandered up river to find

Taylor. When I asked if he had had as good action as I, he looked at me blankly and said that he grew tired of fighting the wind and opted for a snooze. He missed most of the action.

The Dean River's reputation is that of a fly-tosser's haven. Most of the early fishers chucked other gear, but from the earliest days of discovery some faithful to their sport fly-fished. Over the past four decades, fly-fishing became the way to catch the Dean's trout and steelhead. It is now a fly-fisher's haven and a river that produces ever-lasting fly-fishing memories.

I have journeyed to the Dean every season since my first in 1983 and can tell many stories about the river, its fish and the fly-fishers. However, some of the most exciting adventures are those experienced by first-timers to the Dean.

I had seen his colourful fish paintings and then met Loucas Raptis at the British Columbia Federation of Fly Fishers convention in Kamloops in May, 2000. When one of the fellows in my Totem Flyfisher's Dean River group canceled, I called Loucas in Victoria and asked if he would be interested in replacing our dropout. As soon as I made the offer I detected excitement in his voice, but he had to clear things with his wife and work. The next day he called me saying "yes, he could go" and through the next month or so we exchanged e-mails. Loucas arrived on the Dean with everything brand-new—rod, reel, line, waders, wading boots, vest and rain jacket. He spent a fortune on new equipment. Although he was an avid and accomplished trout fly-fisher, he had never caught a steel-head on the fly. The steelhead runs on his home rivers on Vancouver Island had diminished to such an extent that Loucas felt guilty casting a line to them. Evident through his artwork and

Martin Tolley made his first trip to the Dean in '69, circa 1970.

The Bella Coola is best fished in the spring when the salmon fry are emerging.

talking with him, his passion for the sport and the fish runs deep indeed.

The Dean is a good steelhead producer but catching steelhead requires effort, albeit pleasant, it is still work. The first day all the group except Loucas managed to land a steelhead, but he had learned some of the basics and some of the waters to fish.

Enthusiasm is a grand asset and on the afternoon of the next day Loucas wandered off by himself. When he returned from the Victoria Run, Peter Broomhall asked, "Did you catch a fish and do you have a story for us?" Not one to gloat or brag, Loucas said as modestly as he could but with great pride, "Yes, I caught a 31-inch female on a Black GP from the Victoria Run." There are many things to learn and experience when fly-fishing for steelhead and Loucas learned quickly. I remember the day he came back from the Cottonwood Run mumbling something about violent fish. Steelhead can take a fly softly, sometimes the fly just stops and at first you think it's snagged bottom until it moves. Then there are some fish that see the fly coming, charge and grab it on the run, often with disastrous results. Loucas had just experienced his first violent attack. Visibly shaken by the experience, he didn't get that fish.

A steelhead river constantly changes and we had some rain that brought up the river, colouring it. A large bulky fly is often necessary in coloured water and Loucas had few so he put something together, a mongrel of a fly owing its origins to my Marabou Black GP and a Black Bunny Leech. Called the Dean River Cuss, a name derived from Peter Broomhall's "good natured cuss" expression repeated throughout Pete's storytelling. The new pattern worked well indeed for Loucas and Rob. Rob Williams took the largest of the trip, a 38 1/2-inch fish from the Camp Run on one of Loucas' Cusses.

The days passed and Loucas connected with other fish. But some days not much moved through the river and you can work all day for a strike or two. Some days you draw blanks and Loucas experienced some blank days. Due to leave the next day, Loucas managed to hook five steelhead on Friday and landed a 34-inch male, his largest ever steelhead on the fly and the largest on any gear type. When we tallied the scores for the trip Loucas had hooked 18 steelhead, unfortunately he managed to land only four. But engraved in Loucas' mind are many rewarding memories from the famous Dean River and its magnificent summer-run steelhead.

The Dean River originates up in the Chilcotin Plateau and meanders through the interior high-altitude forests and grass lands picking up nutrients from the soils and eventually cascading its way through the eastern part of the Coast Mountain Range to the sea. Anyone flying over the Coast Mountain Range even in the middle of summer can't help but notice the sea of white. The cap of the range is almost all glacial and as the Dean passes through the Coast Mountain Range many of the tributaries add glacial tint to the river. The degree of the tint has profound effects on selection of fly-fishing technique.

Above the natural anadromous fish barrier some miles above Salmon House Falls, the Dean River watershed is primarily the

*Lana Manuel guides for Lower Dean River Lodge;
their blue boats are a familiar sight on the lower river.*

domain of the rainbow trout. Because of the make-up of soil found in the Chilcotin Plateau, the water is richer in dissolved minerals than coastal steelhead streams. The nutrient-rich water produces larger quantities of insects, resulting in a stream with good trout populations. That section of the Upper Dean River is accessed through Anahim Lake and provides excellent fly-fishing for trout. However, another characteristic of the Chilcotin Plateau is its climate: long extremely cold winter with relatively short but hot summers. Although the streams are rich in insect life, because of the short trout growing season, trout, although plentiful, take a number of years to become large. Most anglers journey from far and wide to the Lower Dean, natal birthplace of the chinook, coho, chum, and pink salmon and the anadromous cutthroat and steelhead trout, to sample the Dean's world-class summer-run steelhead fly-fishing.

For years the Natives said that the Dean River had a large population of steelhead, and later this was confirmed by commercial gillnetters fishing Burke and Dean channels with catches of summer-run steelhead in their nets. The lower Dean River started to draw interest from sport fishers in the 1950s. The first rod-caught steelhead were taken from Tanya Lake during pack horse trips into the Rainbow Mountains by Bella Coola guide Tommy Walker in the mid-1940s. Walker also recalls observing Natives catching steelhead in baskets. However, it was the runs as they came through the Lower Dean above the 5-Km canyon which would bring worldwide fame to the Dean.

Since time immemorial, the Kimsquit people poled their canoes to pools above the Dean's canyon and caught steelhead using traditional Native fishing techniques. It wasn't until Al Elsey came to the Bella Coola valley, settled there and purchased guide Tommy Walker's house, started Talchako Lodge and through conversations with natives on the logging crew found that steelhead could be netted in pools above the canyon, that the sport potential of the Lower Dean was realized. In September 1954, Esley took Bob Hendron into the Dean where they hiked above the canyon and caught a 16-pound steelhead.

The group returned to the pool above the canyon during the next few days and hooked numerous coho and nine steelhead. Convinced he had discovered a gold mine, Elsey didn't tell a soul and returned with clients in the late summer of 1955, '56 and '57. Elsey introduced Dick Blewett and Bob Stewart to the Dean in 1957. Afterwards Blewett and Stewart realizing the potential of the Lower Dean, decided to go into the steelhead-guiding business. However, because the native trail over the canyon was the only access to the Dean it wasn't until a third person arrived on the scene, a flier named Dick Poet, that the steelhead guiding operation above the canyon became a feasible venture. They explored the river and found a spot near Stewart's present Lower Dean River Lodge camp where a plane could land with guests for the camp.

Because of all the energy that Blewett put into learning about run timing, extent of the fishes' migration through the system,

The Dean River Cuss produced the largest steelhead of the trip.

developing the first guiding operation and designing the river boats that are used on the river today, he is credited with developing the Dean River steelhead fishery. For more than 10 years Blewett guided on the Dean and during some of those years was assisted by Bob Stewart's son Rob and Daryll Hodson. Rob Stewart would eventually buy out Blewett's share of the Lower Dean River Lodge. In 2000 Stewart sold the Lower Dean River Lodge to an American company. Rob remains involved with Billy Blewett, Dick's son, looking after the day-to-day management of the operation.

Daryll Hodson arrived in Bella Coola in 1963 and Bob Stewart hired him as a guide for the Bella Coola spring fishery and the summer-fall Nimpo Lake fishery. In ensuing years Daryll guided on the Dean and by 1968 had learned enough and ventured out on his own establishing his camp about two miles below Stewart's on the North bank of the river. He ran a popular fly-fishing operation until his tragic helicopter death in 1991. He was only 49 years old. However, his wife Nancy, daughter of crop duster and founder of Wilderness Airlines, Dick Poet, along with son Danny and daughter Jill with her husband Bobby Hull, continue to operate Hodson's Guiding Service.

Access to the Dean in those early years was by the Native trail over the canyon and in the early 1960s by float plane. Because of the Dean's remote location and difficult access, it didn't attract large numbers of anglers. Blewett had to pack a lot of the equipment for his guiding operation over the Indian trail, including boats and motors. However, logging started in earnest in 1961 below the canyon and in the winter of 1963 and spring of 1964, Mayo Logging extended the road above the canyon reaching the vicinity of Blewett's camp. The large-scale logging operation with the construction of the airstrip at tidewater and the logging road had two effects on the Dean River and its steelhead. Access was opened up which made it easier for Blewett to get supplies and equipment to his camp, but it also provided access for non-guided anglers. Increased angling pressure combined with generous catch limits— 40 steelhead per year and a limit of three fish per day with a two-day possession limit—the influx of non-conservation-minded loggers, and commercial interception by the gill-net fleet, the steelhead runs suffered and continued to decline even after 1976 when logging operations ceased.

In the mid-'60s, after Blewett established his camp, he soon had a steady clientele. Although the percentage of the early fishermen who fly-fished was small, the numbers increased until eventually now 100 percent of Stewart's and Hodson's clients are fly-fishers. And when word of their catches became known in the steelhead fly-fishing community, more and more fly-fishers ventured to the Dean. Dr. Joe Sladen was one of Blewett's early fly-fishing customers. Sladen recalls fishing the Jamb Hole with his father in that first-ever 1966 trip and says that "they caught about eight steelhead during the short stay at that pool." Joe fished the Dean River for many years as a guest of Blewett and later Rob Stewart. After the Totem Flyfishers was formed in 1967, Sladen became a member and the large size of the summer-run steelhead that he entered in the competition for the Totem's steelhead trophy brought the Dean to the attention of many in that group. Sladen took the trophy in 1969, 1972, and 1974 all with steelhead from the Dean that were over 20 pounds.

A beautiful setting for a couple of fly-fishers to cast their lines.

Good catches of large summer-run steelhead are difficult to keep secret and the Dean was now known. Anglers were making their way to her banks. In 1966, Peter McVey made his first trip, hiking above the canyon and sleeping on the banks of the Jamb Hole. McVey is a masterful steelhead and trout fly-fisher, bamboo-rod builder, and great storyteller. Peter got to know Rob Stewart and when Stewart opened his upper camp, located at 18-mile, Stewart hired Pete to look after the camp guests. McVey, a chef by profession and addicted fly-fisherman, thought he was in heaven. After the guests left in the morning to search the upper waters and Pete completed his chores, he had free time to fly-fish the waters around camp before he had to come in and prepare dinner. And fly-fish those waters he has. For thirty seasons he has worked for Stewart's lodge and each season he has spent five or six weeks fly-fishing for Dean River steelhead. Peter believes he has probably fly-fished for Dean River steelhead more than any other fisherman.

In his early Dean River steelheading years, McVey with his British roots, favoured the Zulu fly, an old-time Scottish trout and salmon pattern. But he soon became enamoured with taking fish on surface patterns and in the early 1970s, the black-bodied, red-tailed Zulu was transformed in what is now known as the McVey Ugly. This fly is unique in that it is the first Pacific Northwest steelhead fly with moose-hair wings that angle down the shank and protrude horizontally from the body. This design adds to the fly's contact with the water surface and when brought across on a down-and-across swing, the fly stays on the surface producing a wake. Some summer-run steelhead love to attack a waked fly.

Since the early 1970s when not on the Dean, Pete can be found at his own Corbett Lake Country Inn, near Merritt. An energetic individual, he is always full of ideas. Before Corbett, he attempted to develop a camp at Minnie and Stoney lakes. After diverting a stream into Stoney Lake in the hopes that the running water would help keep part of this lake ice-free during the winter, he stocked it with trout. The trout did grow large on Minnie and Stoney, but the plan didn't work and McVey gave up the idea of the camp at Minnie and Stoney and eventually settled permanently at Corbett Lake Country Inn. Over many years Peter has turned Corbett Lake into a fine fishing lake where his guests can enjoy fine dining prepared by Peter as well as being entertained by one of British Columbia's finest fly-fishing storytellers.

During the cold winter months, McVey spends much of his time crafting bamboo rods, a skill he learned from one of the master English bamboo-rod builders, Bob Southwell. Peter has honed that skill over more than 30 years of rod building. One of my most cherished angling possessions is the McVey-built fly rod given to me by my co-workers when I retired in January 2000.

Peter's enthusiasm for fly-fishing for trout and steelhead continues to give him rewarding experiences. Back in the 1960s the steelhead fly-fishing fraternity was small and they did share information with like-minded fly-fishers.

In 1969 one of British Columbia's leading steelhead fly-fishing advocates and founding Totem Flyfishers' president, Martin Tolley, made his first trip. Martin was writing for *Northwest Sportsman* magazine in those days. His 1960s and 70s articles "Steelhead on

Two masters of the art and craft of fly-fishing: Harry Lemire (left) admiring a bamboo rod made by Peter McVey (right).

the Fly? First, Break Your Bait Rod," "Steelhead on the Fly, There isn't any Other Way," "Float Line Fishing for Steelhead" and "Steelhead a Take of Pure Artistry" certainly influenced this then-starting-out steelhead-fisher. Peter McVey's good friend, Harry Lemire, famed Washingtonian steelhead fly-fisher, wasn't far behind Tolley with his first trip in 1971. In the early 1970s, Lee Straight and Bob Taylor made their inaugural trip.

During most of the last half century, Robert Taylor of Vancouver—expert steelhead fly-fisher, fly-designer and tyer, book collector, rod maker, and all-round fly tackle craftsman—has journeyed through most of British Columbia and Washington State pursuing the mighty sea-run trouts that frequent most coast and some interior rivers. Taylor loves and fishes many rivers but prefers those of large size with big fish. The Dean is his favourite.

A masterful fly-tyer, he created Taylor's Golden Spey, unique in that it is the first Spey pattern that incorporates the flat feather wing of the General Practitioner while still maintaining the other features of classic Spey patterns such as the thin body, double rib, heron hackle and a barred duck flank throat. Characteristic of Taylor's fly-tying craftsmanship are his small, neat heads.

Taylor has long been a supporter of the conservation movement and, before it was in vogue, a catch-and-release fisher. Through his continual fly-fishing and conservation activities, he has been instrumental in influencing the regulations on the Dean River.

A man of great knowledge and with a willingness to share it with like-minded fly-fishers, he remains as committed as ever to preserving and protecting the interest of ordinary anglers to enjoy British Columbia's freshwater fisheries.

After his early trips to the Dean, Taylor insisted that he share his Dean experiences with his fellow Totem Flyfishers and the Totems started their expeditions to the river in 1976.

Renowned British Columbian river-hopper Jerry Wintle and chum Dave Winters wet their lines on the Dean in 1973. Jerry and his wife Jean have been a summer fixture on the river ever since.

In 1957 Felix Lederer moved to the Dean River and did various jobs for Fisheries or the logging companies. The logging road opened up the river above the canyon and in the early 1970s some American bought a truck and hired Felix to run anglers up the river. The anglers were dropped off and drifted back down fishing along the way. Felix soon tired of working for others and went into business as a packer on the Dean which he did until his death in the fall of 1984. Felix used to charge the Totems $50 return for four people.

After Felix passed on, Tony Hill became the packer, while at the same time he constructed his Nakia Lodge below the canyon not far from the airstrip. Tony also met an untimely death in 1991, the same year Hodson was killed. Hill had delivered a couple of Forest Service employees up the rain-swollen river to do some silviculture

Bob Taylor, the Dean of the
Totem Flyfishers' Dean River fly-fishers, has been
instrumental in influencing the regulations on the Dean River.

work and didn't return in the evening to pick them up. They found bits and pieces of his boat above and below the canyon. Apparently he became tangled in his anchor rope and was drowned. That year, 1991, was not a good year for the guides.

The Hills were not the first lodge built on the large gravel spit at the river mouth. Bella Coola residents Graham Hall and Tom Carmichael were hired by Charlie Morse the owner of Rimarko Ranch to build a camp on the Dean in the mid-1960s. On his first day at the Dean, Graham Hall hooked three steelhead, keeping one for supper. After the camp was finished, they stayed for a few more days and drifted the Dean in rubber rafts, experiencing some fine fishing. Ever since those early fly-catches became known the word spread and particularly so through the mid-1980s when all Pacific Northwest rivers experienced phenomenal runs of steelhead, the Dean became "the destination" river. Many anglers came to sample its famous summer-runs.

I retired in 2000 from a long career in regional government and I intended to fly-fish a lot before I started writing this book. Rather than just one week on the Dean I spent 25 days. Over my 18 Dean seasons I have had some good fishing and some not so good fishing. This trip I remember for many reasons. Foremost is witnessing Loucas Raptis's introduction into the world of steelhead fly-fishing, Rob Williams' ardent desire with his dawn-to-dusk efforts on the river, and of course trips with Peter Broomhall are always memorable.

After my time in the Totem Flyfisher's camp on August 2, I took the helicopter up river 15 or so miles and did a solitary 10-day, drift-and-camp trip starting from the Eagle Run. I loved parts of that upper river, but few fish had moved up river and settled into the pools. Etched in my mind are the five full days I went without a touch from a steelhead and I fished some fine pieces of water. I didn't start finding fish again until I reached Shannon's Run about a mile below the Sakumtha's confluence with the Dean. Like Loucas' last day my last full day fishing also provided me with some memories and my last fish of the trip proved to be a classic.

In the morning I fished the Grizzly Run and soon saw a fish move in behind my Woolly Bear Bomber. Then the fish disappeared into the depths of the pool. I couldn't get it back so I carried on down the run, thinking about coming back later to the pool head for another try. As I swung my waking Woolly Bear through the glassy glide near the tailout it suddenly disappeared. Some steelhead make a huge commotion when they take a waked fly and some sip it down like a trout does a dry fly. A few minutes later I took the fly from a 34-inch male. Content, I left the pool and fished the opposite side. I watched a steelhead come to the fly and in my haste I pulled the fly from its mouth, that was followed by a good-sized cutthroat and again I watched mesmerized as a large steelhead bolted out of the depths to the surface, taking my Woolly Bear on the run with such force that my line overran the reel and jammed, breaking the leader. A violent fish, shaking I returned to camp.

It is difficult leaving a beautiful wild place like the Dean and often nostalgia sets in as a trip ends. It was with that feeling that I

Darkness had enveloped the river when I slid my prize into shallow water. To get an idea of size I hastily laid my rod along the fish marking the spot close to a guide. Too dark for pictures, I slipped the fish back into the river and walked back to camp. The fish was inches longer than the morning's 34-incher but not wanting to exaggerate I told Gil that it was 36 inches plus. It proved to be closer to 38 inches and, although I have had a number of Dean fish that size and larger, this was the trip's largest and a classic grand finale to this Dean River adventure.

What of the future? The Forest Service still has its eye on timber in the watershed and practices silviculture operations in the Dean regularly. There is an active logging license issued for the Dean and the valley continues to be threatened by forestry activity. However, the Dean River Advisory Committee has recommended the Dean for a Protected Area study zone with the long-term goal of acquiring Protected Area Status. This land-use designation, which is the highest protection that could be given, short of park's status, would be the savior, protecting the Dean not only from logging but also other detrimental uses such as mining and hydro-electric development. However, lurking on the ocean are other threats to the Dean's fish stocks and Protected Area Status will have little value if those other threats are not neutralized.

During a steelhead's migration along the coast and up Burke, Dean and Fisher channels it falls prey to the nets of commercial fishermen. Throughout the Pacific Northwest, commercial interception of non-targeted stocks is a serious problem for weak stocks migrating with stronger. In fact, many Pacific Northwest stocks of coho, chinook, and steelhead are facing extinction because of the century-long mixed-stock fishery strategy. Furthermore, enhancement activities such as the chum and pinks on the Bella Coola system work to the detriment of the steelhead and other less numerous stocks. Better long-term strategies, with goals such as area licensing of boats, terminal fisheries and sport status for steelhead, coho and chinook, are an absolute necessity. A sport-caught fish generates 10 to 20 times the value to the economy of the province over a commercially-caught fish.

The Dean is one of the Province's crown jewels. May the Dean River, its valley and its fish be protected so that future generations of anglers can make the pilgrimage to this beautiful wild place and experience those wild violent takes from steelhead in the lower river or trout sipping dries in the upper river.

What a way to spend the summer—working as a river guardian on the Dean River!

left camp to fish that last evening. I decided to work a piece of water that looked good and fished it hard. Only one steelhead came to inspect the Woolly Bear, but it didn't take or come back.

Evening was turning into night as I walked along the bank towards my camp when I spotted Gil Sage from the Totem's camp fishing the top part of the Cottonwood Run. Gil was fishing a sink tip and I asked if it was okay if I walked down and fished the bottom part of the run. With the lateness of the evening he couldn't possibly fish the whole run and he said, "Sure." I started at the sunken stumps, knowing that Gil couldn't fish them properly without getting hung up with his sink-tip, and that left him a large piece of water. I would have no difficulty with my floating line and waked fly. The evening was shortened by the clouds that had moved in and it was with only about 15 or so minutes left to fish that I cast my line. I figured I should be able to cover the water down to the cottonwood root wad. I heard the noise and then saw the boil of a good fish breaking water and taking my size 10 Woolly Bear.

References

Lingren, Art. *Steelhead River Journal: Dean River*. Portland: Frank Amato Publications, 2000.

Pochin, W. F. *Angling and Hunting in British Columbia*. Vancouver: Sun Directories Ltd. 1946.

Straight, Lee. *100 Steelhead Streams*. Vancouver: The Sun Publishing Co., Revised Edition 1956.

8

The Harrison River

A fly-fisher casts his flies into the rainbow hoping for a big one.

FLOWING OUT OF HARRISON LAKE, TEN-MILE-LONG HARRISON River joins the Fraser River about a half mile below the Canadian Pacific Railway bridge at Kilby Park. Explored by the Hudson Bay Company as a fur trade route to the Interior, the river was named after Benjamin Harrison, a company official. The river did become the gateway to the Interior when gold was discovered east of Quesnel in 1859. It remained the route to the Cariboo gold fields until the construction of the Cariboo wagon road through the Fraser Canyon was completed in 1863.

The river is the gateway for salmon migrating into the Harrison Lake and Lillooet River systems. It is home to all species of Pacific salmonids. These copious runs of salmon sustained the Salishan First Nation people since the last ice age. The abundant runs of salmon proved useful to the Hudson Bay Company who operated a salmon saltery at the mouth of the river from 1848 to 1858.

The Harrison is a relatively low-gradient stream with the odd section of fast-flowing water. A large portion of the river bed provides ideal spawning gravel for pinks, chums and chinooks in the main river with runs of steelhead, coho and sockeye migrating into

tributaries to spawn. Besides the salmon, the river provides ideal habitat for cutthroat trout. During late summer and fall, the spawning salmon provide a diet of salmon eggs for the cutthroat. Later, after the salmon have died, the decaying bodies provide the cutthroat with another source of food through the winter months. And in the spring when the salmon fry emerge from the gravel the cutthroat gorge on them. For a change of pace the river provides insects and a multitude of three-spined stickleback for the cutthroat to eat through the summer and fall. It was the cutthroat that attracted the first fly-fishers and it was the cutthroat fly-fishing for which the Harrison became famous.

The Harrison became a tourist destination after the first hotel was built at Harrison Hot Springs in 1886. The visitors came to bathe in the natural hot springs and to fly-fish in the river and lake that teemed with cutthroat.

Dr. Thomas Lambert, in *Fishing in British Columbia* (1907), writes about the Harrison and its fishing:

> *The Harrison River affords excellent fishing as early as April. The fish run from 1lb. to 2lb., and take the fly*

freely. The river flows out of Harrison Lake to the Fraser at Harrison Station. It must be fished from a boat. Bags of thirty and forty fish are by no means uncommon...The Hot Springs Hotel affords good accommodation. (p. 66)

The cutthroat fly-fishing in the lake attracted the more affluent fly-fishers who could afford the luxury of hiring a launch to take them to the best spots. About the Harrison Lake fly-fishing, Bryan Williams in *Rod & Creel in British Columbia* (1919) says that "*some excellent fly-fishing can be had more or less all summer, but the best times are April and May and then again in the fall* (p. 111)."

Through the first half of the 20th century, Harrison Lake and Harrison River increasingly became the playground of Lower Mainland fly-fishers. Some, like the example following, recorded their catches in diaries:

Brougham & I Harrison Lake 20 miles at Carey's, caught 40 fish weighing 48 lb. All on fly using Siwash and Silver & Teal. All large fish.

That testimonial for March 8, 1925 came from George Reifel's diary and is typical of the sport found on the lake. Wilfred Francis Brougham, Reifel's fishing partner on many trips, developed a number of fly-fishing patterns. Most notable is Brougham's Coho, a fly I have used with good success, taking coho, cutthroat and chums on the Harrison, Tlell, and other British Columbia rivers.

There was no doubt that the fly-fishing for cutthroat was superb during the first half of the century. W. F. Pochin, in *Angling and Hunting in British Columbia* (1946), gives a glowing report:

Commissioner Sandys-Wunch of the Royal Canadian Mounted Police is one of Canada's outstanding authorities on salmon and trout. He has fished the length and breadth of the Dominion and is credited with creating many patterns of flies that have proven successful in taking both trout and salmon. Above everything else he is a fly-fisherman.

On a recent visit to Vancouver the Commissioner said, that in his opinion, two of the finest rivers in Canada are the Harrison and Nicomekl. Both are located on the lower mainland of B.C. and are easily accessible.

The Harrison is big water. It is clear, and in some places quite fast. It flows out of the southern end of Harrison Lake and empties into the Fraser ten miles to the south. Harrison River offers the finest native cutthroat trout fishing in southern British Columbia and is reached over an excellent highway just sixty-five miles from Vancouver.

The Harrison cutthroat, while not one of the largest of game fishes, is one of the sportiest. Three pounders have been taken, but he rarely attains that weight. However, a good day's catch will include fish up to and over two pounds. Best of all he rises freely to flies...

He first puts in an appearance in late December in the lower reaches of the river. At times great catches are made just a few yards above and below the Highway bridge. A migrant from the sea, via the Fraser River, he is full fleshed and resembles a bar of shimmering silver. Fishing in the River remains good until about mid-April, when the water rises, covering the bars and making wading impossible.

The Harrison cutthroat is ever in search of salmon

Fly-fishing the Harrison system started in the 1880s.

The Harrison cutthroat are a fine game fish.

fry, upon which he feeds, and the best flies are silver bodied. Cumming's Fancy has always been a favourite, with a tied down minnow and Silver Doctor running a close second. Popular sizes are sixes and eights...

At times the trout feed so close to shore that the angler must stand well back on the gravel, often taking fish not much more than a leader length out. Then again they may be feeding in pockets fifty or sixty feet out...The rise of the fish to the fly can be seen practically every time and greased lines are recommended.

The season opens at Harrison Lake on February 1 [year-round fishing permitted now], and over its entire 46 miles are numerous shallow beaches where Cutthroats feed. Fishing is similar to that in the River, in that the same flies are used, with the exception of late April when there is a hatch of black ants upon which the trout gorge themselves. Anglers have found the trout harder to take than when feeding on fry, but in late years dry fly-fishermen, using small black bi-visibles attached to three X gut have made incredible catches. (pp. 41-42)

I would be hard pressed to find a better tribute to a fishery than those words of Pochin. When there is an increasing and uncontrolled demand on any common property resource, however, history shows that it suffers. In the last half of the 20th century with more and more pressure on the river's fish stocks, the Harrison

cutthroat populations plummeted. It has taken considerable work by the Provincial fishery staff to rebuild cutthroat stocks. The Harrison wild-fish stocks have been augmented with hatchery fish, but they will never reach historical abundance. The 20-fish-a-day limit of long ago has eroded to the release of all wild fish. Two hatchery cutthroat can be killed with only one greater than 20 inches. Not many fly-fishermen kill hatchery cutthroat, especially the large ones. It takes about six years to grow a 20-inch cutthroat in Lower Mainland streams and if a wild or hatchery cutt can live that long it deserves a better fate than a frying pan.

The cutthroat fly-fishing remains as popular today as it has ever was. Silver-bodied flies representative of salmon fry or stickleback such as Murray's Rolled Muddler, the Muddler Minnow and variations of Mallard and Silver, and Teal, Silver & Blue are the preferred poisons. Harold Lohr, a Vancouver-based fly-fisher, dresses an amazing-looking epoxy fry pattern that produces well. One thing that can be critically important with fry imitations: the fly should be about the same size as the salmon fry the cutthroat are targeting. We can never reproduce the wiggle that salmon fry exhibit as they move through the river, but we can at least replicate with fur, feather and tinsel the size, shape and colour. I remember one evening fly-fishing across from Kilby Park where cutthroat chased fry between my legs. The fish that night were extremely selective and difficult to take. But that is part of the fun. We would get terribly bored if we caught fish on every cast. Every now and then, the fish seem to go crazy taking whatever is thrown at them, adding even more intrigue to the sport. You just can't predict when that might happen.

In early March, 1992, Bob Taylor and I had returned from an enjoyable but not too productive trip, fish-wise, to the Queen Charlottes Islands. One would think that we had enough of fishing for a while, but the weather was pleasant and I was restless. I suggested a trip to the Harrison. Just why the Harrison I don't know. Sometimes fate—or perhaps a sixth sense—guides these matters. I seem to get more than my share of unusual, unexpected, but rewarding, fishing experiences. Often I am at the right place at the right time.

I picked Bob up on the Friday night and we drove to Kilby Park on the Lower Harrison and stayed the night. After breakfast and getting the boat and gear ready, we headed up river. In those days, I didn't do much trout fishing. I was not expecting much more than an enjoyable day afield with a fishing chum. We started fishing the water below the Pilings and above Vincent's Spit.

During the morning I worked hard fighting the wind and big water with my number-5 outfit, but the two of us did manage to connect with 1/2 dozen cutts, with my 19-incher the largest. We left the morning's fishing for lunch, content with our results. We couldn't guess what the afternoon might bring, but to counter the problems with the elements, I switched to a more stout, number-seven line and a 11'-3" rod. A wise decision.

What an afternoon of fishing it turned out to be! Everywhere we went we found fish "showing" and by days-end we had connected with around four dozen nice cutthroats up to 19 inches long. Some connections were brief, but many fish showed their mettle with good fights before they threw the hook or were beached.

As most Harrison River trouters know, this river does not offer its treasures easily. But on this day the river gave us a good sampling of those treasures, and the unexpected trout fishing that Bob and I experienced on this exceptional, shirt-sleeve, spring day is an everlasting memory of the river and its fish.

The Harrison's slow-moving, crystal-clear waters produce another excellent fly-fishery and that is for its coho salmon. In the mid 1800s, it was commonly believed that Pacific salmon would not take the fly. Indeed, it was also rumoured that England's Foreign Secretary in the 1840s, Lord Aberdeen (on the advice of his brother-in-law, Captain John Gordon, who actually fished for Pacific Coast salmon), suggested giving Washington and Oregon to the Americans in order to avoid war. The territory was evidently not considered worth fighting for simply because the Pacific salmon would not take the fly. That story—a favourite along the Pacific Coast—circulated for many years. Clearly, Captain Gordon was not impressed with the country he saw or with the methods used for catching Pacific salmon.

It is no secret that Pacific salmon can be hard to catch on the fly once they enter fresh water. The problem has been documented for many years. Consider this passage from John Keast Lord's *A Naturalist in British Columbia*, published one and one-third centuries ago:

> I tried every lure I could think of, to tempt these lordly salmon. The most killing salmon-flies of Scotch,

There are places on the Harrison where you can get away from the two million-plus people in the lower Fraser's watershed.

> *Irish, and English ties, thrown in the most approved fashion, were trailed close to their noses; such flies as would have coaxed any old experienced salmon in the civilized world of waters to forget his caution.* (Vol. I, p. 45)

Passages such as this are common in the early writings about salmon angling in British Columbia. Perhaps that's why many British sport fishermen who came to this province tried to prove that salmon could be taken on the fly. If those early anglers had only ventured to the Harrison River, doubtless they would have fared much, much better.

The Deputy Commissioner of Fisheries for the Province, John Pease Babcock, in his 1910 book, *The Game Fishes of British Columbia*, refuted the claim by many that salmon do not take the fly. About that and the Harrison River fly-fishing for salmon, he says:

> *It is often stated that the Pacific salmon do not take a fly, but having caught both Spring and Coho salmon in the Province with a fly, the writer feels justified in denying this statement...*
>
> *On the Mainland, the Harrison River, above the city of Vancouver, is the most accessible and productive waters for those who desire to take salmon with a fly. Very few Spring salmon there are taken by that method, but one may take a good many Coho in October and even as late as November.*

Bob Taylor's Harrison River coho was one of the chunkiest I have ever seen.

One November evening in 1986, Bob Taylor and I were late getting to the river, with little daylight left we dropped anchor just below the bridge pier. Shortly after, Taylor, throwing an Umpqua fly on a sink-tip line, connected with a big coho. The fish put up a good scrap and with no net I had to take the boat to shore so Taylor could beach the fish. It remains one of the chunkiest coho I have seen from this or any other river.

The Harrison coho, as well as its other salmon and trout, have suffered from man's presence. The Harrison/Lillooet is a huge watershed with many salmon-producing streams and much work has been done by fisheries people to bring back salmon and trout stocks. Natural reproduction is augmented by fish from many enhancement projects such as the Chehalis River hatchery, Weaver Creek spawning channel and other upriver facilities. Whenever you have large runs of hatchery fish with generous kill quotas close to a large urban population you produce fisheries of the lowest level. The Harrison does provide some good fly-fishing for sockeye, pink, coho and chums with the odd chinook thrown in. During some of the salmon fishing, when the people are there only for meat, snagging is common. You wonder what happened to the concept of fair play that Bryan Williams envisioned when he became Provincial Game warden so long ago.

The river will continue to be an important urban fly-fishery. In the last half of the 20th century many fly-fishers have cast flies to the Harrison's game fish. But none was more devoted to the river and its fish than Earl Anderson and Jack Vincent.

Fly-fishing expert, professional fly-tyer and instructor, fly-casting teacher, sporting goods salesman, and rod and reel repairman, Earl Anderson spent most of his long life involved with many aspects of the sport. Through such activity, Anderson became acquainted with and influenced hundreds—perhaps thousands—of fly-fishers.

Earl was a self-taught fly-caster and one of the achievements he was most proud of was his first-place finish in the 1950 Vancouver Sportsman Show dry-fly casting competition. In 1951, he started professionally teaching fly-fishing, casting and fly-tying. Thirty-one years later, School District 39 presented him with a plaque commemorating his service and thanking him for his devotion to teaching. Over those many years, Earl introduced about 1,200 students to the sport.

Born in 1911 on the Prairies, Earl came to British Columbia with his family after World War I, where they settled in Vancouver. One of six boys, Earl started to fish in 1927 at age 16.

In their steady search for cutthroat, steelhead and salmon, the fishing Andersons—Earl, Arne, Frank and Willard—frequented many lower mainland streams. Earl reminisced at length about the

Capilano, Allouette, Nicomekl, Serpentine, Stave, Silver, Coquihalla and Harrison rivers and the glorious fishing of the olden days. His favourite stream for cutthroat fly-fishing was the Harrison River.

Earl spent much of his work-life in retail sporting goods sales and spent the last 15, up to retirement in 1975, at Woodwards downtown department store.

It was during his Woodwards' years that I first became acquainted with Earl. In the mid 1960s, as newly-weds we lived in the Kitsilano district and Woodwards was a convenient place for my wife, Beverley, and I to do our shopping. Friday night often found us there, Bev in the grocery department or ladies' clothing, and I in sporting goods, looking at fishing equipment and talking to Earl. I purchased my first Silex casting reel from Earl in 1968, for the terrible sum of $40. It took some effort convincing Bev that an expensive reel like that was a necessary tool for steelhead.

Although I didn't yet fly-fish in those early years I was already a Haig-Brown enthusiast and reading his books convinced me that one of my goals in life was to become a fly-fisherman. I bought my first fly rod from Anderson in the late 1960s and, shortly after that purchase, learned to cast in one of his and Reg Campbell's fly-casting classes at Vancouver Technical School. Earl also introduced me to fly-tying.

Earl Anderson introduced hundreds to fly-fishing.

COURTESY EARL ANDERSON

A boat is a good way of getting around the Harrison if it works. Dennis Lingren had a little problem with his motor this day.

As the years pass, each angler develops skills and a philosophy about our sport. Haig-Brown and many of the other writers whose books line the wall of my library, have influenced me considerably. I am happy that I became acquainted with Earl in my early years. He provided sound advice and helped feed the desires of not only this budding angler and fly-tyer but many hundreds more. Earl Anderson passed away on February 26, 1995. He was 84 years old.

Jack Clifford Vincent, like Earl, spent most of his adult life working in the fishing business as a professional fly tyer and salesman. Jack worked in Woodwards Oakridge sporting goods department for many years. In the early 1980s, he left Woodwards to work in a shop on Kingsway called The Fishing Hole, which unfortunately had a short life. When it folded, he went back to work at Woodwards until his death at age 62 in 1984.

In the last half of the 20th century, few were better fly-fishing ambassadors or more devoted to the Harrison than Vincent. Even though he left us early, he spent many decades fishing his favourite river for his beloved cutthroat. On his days off work he could be found wandering the river in search of its cutthroat and coho. About a 1/4 mile above the highway bridge on the river's right bank is a long spit separating the main Harrison from a huge bay into which much of the braided Chehalis River flows. Jack liked the spot so much and was seen fishing there so frequently that it became known as Vincent's Spit and it remains a popular fly-fishing place to this day.

As a long-time member of the Totem Flyfishers and their President in 1975, Jack introduced many of the club members to the Harrison.

Great anglers have inquiring minds and Jack was a great fisherman always trying to improve local patterns to make them more effective. Salmon fry imitations have always presented challenges to the fly dresser and Vincent thought that tying the wing down would make a more representative salmon fry imitation. Some of his thoughts he shared with Rod Haig-Brown and in a 7 March 1956 letter to Jack this is what Haig-Brown had to say:

> *I think your tied-down fly is a very good one indeed. Generally, I don't like a tied-down wing, but you have an excellent point when you say an ordinary wing may not work properly with the current. Hardy's makes what they call a "fly-minnow", very like yours, though larger. I have had one for years and have occasionally taken fish with it. But yours has one very important advantage—a flat sided body instead of a round body;*

> *it seems to me your fly will have a much better action when drifted or at slow speeds, for this reason, I enclose one of my own favourite fry imitations, a streamer variation of the Silver Lady, which does work on searun cutthroats. The wing can be tied down on this, too, and I sometimes use dyed blue swan and teal in the wing (better, I think, on streams where spring and dog salmon fry predominate). But I am curious now about the effect of thicker bodies, like yours, and of flies with more "substance" in the water…Good luck to you on the Harrison—that really is a stream to try the ingenuity of the fly-fisherman and to break the heart if it's breakable.*

Vincent's experiments with tied-down fry imitations have been copied by other fly tyers. The debate among fly-fishers continues about whether trout are attracted to the moving fibres on wings not tied down versus the more exact shape and size depicted on tied-down versions.

When Vincent passed away, some Totems were told that he wished his ashes strewn on the crystal-clear water at Vincent's Spit. Not on just any fishing day, but on a day when the cutts are rising and slashing after salmon fry or sticklebacks.

A fine cutthroat taken on a stickleback imitation.

COURTESY UBC SPECIAL COLLECTIONS

Studies of Harrison Lake cutthroat by Tommy Brayshaw.

It was already early November and I hadn't made a trip to the Harrison. My month-long trip to the Skeena and shorter trips to the Thompson had satiated my fly-fishing urges. I was hard at work writing this book and had a good excuse. But the lure of a favourite river was too strong and on November 3, 2000 I drove into Kilby Park late in the afternoon.

Fishing the Harrison in the fall can be quite a pleasant experience, but at times the weather can make it an impossible place to fish. My two trips this fall fell into the latter category. Weather fronts funnel through the valley causing great winds. If the storm is coming inland from the coast, the wind howls across Harrison Bay and up the river churning the bay and river into a stormy sea making fishing next to impossible. Sometimes when an Arctic front moves down, the wind funnels down the lake and valley in such force that it makes the highway bridge sing. The front was moving inland on November 3 and a frightful night I spent camped at Kilby with the wind shaking the camper and howling through the campsite's huge cottonwoods.

This was the Loons Fly-Fishing Club's Harrison outing and Ron Schiefke and I were joining them for a day of coho fishing. Schiefke pulled in with his boat at 6 a.m. and during breakfast we decided that discretion is the better part of valour and we would not boat in such dangerous conditions. We reasoned that we might be protected somewhat from the wind by the dike along the left bank of the

river. The rain accompanied the wind. Not just a shower, but sheets of rain were being whipped along by the wind.

I was eager to try my new multi-tip Air Flo fly line and chose the slime line tip. My stickleback imitation, a size six, was my poison. When we walked to the clearing along the dike there were about four or five other fishermen lining the banks. One fellow reported that no one had connected with a fish and they had been there since daylight fishing mostly spoons, although they packed along their fly rods just in case the fish were plentiful and close to shore. Ron went up to his favourite piling. I fished below him and then walked upriver with one of the spoon fishermen. As we walked and talked we spotted a few coho showing not too far off the edge of the log booms. Certainly out of range of fly-tossers, but then a fish or two showed closer to shore. I waded a little deeper to my waist. Fortunately the wind was at my back and helped the forward cast sail out over the water. The fly landed past the rise and as I was stripping the fly through the water just below the surface, the fish took. The Harrison is slow moving below the highway bridge along the left bank and it was like fighting a fish in still water. Just before 8 a.m. I pulled a small hatchery coho only 21 inches long onto the sandy beach. Ron had his chance but the coho he hooked threw the hook. The weather didn't abate as the morning passed and by lunch time it had driven all from the river. I went home content, my coho and the cutthroat I caught a little later, from one of British Columbia's most popular fly-fishing rivers, had made my day.

References

Babcock, John Pease. *The Game Fishes of British Columbia.* Victoria: Bureau of Provincial Information, second edition, 1910.

Grantham, Ron, (Ed). *Totem Topics 25th Anniversary Issue.* Vancouver: Totem Flyfishers, 1993.

Lambert, T. W. *Fishing in British Columbia.* London: Horace Cox, 1907.

Lingren, Arthur James. *Fly Patterns of Roderick Haig-Brown.* Portland: Frank Amato Publications, 1993.

___. "Earl Anderson." BCFFF's *Fly Lines.* Issue 54 (1993): 7-8.

___. "The Unexpected." *British Columbia Sport Fishing.* 11, 6 (1993): 35-36.

Lord, John Keast. *The Naturalist in British Columbia.* London: Richard Bentley, 1866.

Pochin, W. F. *Angling and Hunting in British Columbia.* Vancouver: Sun Directories Limited, 1946.

Seton-Karr, H. W. *Bear-Hunting in the White Mountains of Alaska and British Columbia Revisited.* London: Chapman and Hall, 1891.

Williams, A. Bryan. *Rod & Creel in British Columbia.* Vancouver: Progress Publishing Co., 1919.

___. *Fish and Game in British Columbia,* Vancouver: Sun Directories, 1935.

The Bill Nation Kamloops Area Lakes

A catch from Lac Le Jeune (Fish Lake), circa 1900.

IN THE CRADLE OF BRITISH COLUMBIA'S STILLWATER FLY-fishery, Bill Nation is synomymous with the halycon days of fishing for large rainbow trout in the lakes around Kamloops. During the 1920s and 1930s, Nation fished and helped make Lac Le Jeune, Pinantan, Hyas, Knouff and Paul Lake famous.

Kamloops, an early trading post, grew slowly, becoming the hub of the Interior in 1885 after the Canadian Pacific Railway (CPR) reached the town. It was during the early railway years that fly-fishers started to explore the lakes in the area.

Starting in the 1880s and with the good catches though the 1890s, Fish Lake became the local fly-fishing hot spot. In 1928, Fish Lake would be renamed Lac Le Jeune, to recognize Father Le Jeune's missionary work with the Native people. Le Jeune with its prodigious population of rainbow trout drew fly-fishers to its shore and many provided glowing testimonials on the fishing they experienced.

Dr. T. W. Lambert devotes over half a chapter to Fish Lake (Lac Le Jeune) in his valuable treatise, *Fishing in British Columbia* (1907). He writes:

About twenty-three miles from Kamloops is a lake known as Fish Lake, in which the fishing is so extra-ordinary as to border on the regions of romance, though locally it is considered a matter of course. For lake fishing, in point of numbers, it is impossible that this piece of water could be beaten; it is like a battue in shooting, the number to be caught is only limited by the skill and endurance of the angler; indeed, little skill is needed, for anyone to catch fish there, though a good fisherman will catch the most. (pp. 48-49)

Lambert also provides a few words about the Natives' fishery at the lake and of an 1897 catch by an American friend and himself of 1500 trout in three days. The "*true bait for Fish Lake is the fly*" and about the fly-fishing, fly patterns and fly sizes, he says:

Flies were abundant, and the fish were ravenous for both real and artificial; they almost seemed to fight for our flies as soon as they touched the water. Even when almost every feather had been torn off they would take the bare hook. We fished with three flies, and often had three fish on at one time...Almost any ordinary Scotch loch flies are suitable for this water, a brown wing being perhaps the best, with a red body; the Zulu is a killing fly, as also a minute Jock Scott, size being the chief matter of importance. The fly must not be too large. (p. 51)

Lambert gives an example of a group of fly-fishers using too large a fly and catching only 30 fish in a long day's fishing. Those fly-fishers claimed the lake to be fished out, but Lambert, using smaller flies, caught 300 the following day.

In the mid 1880s, Dave Lusk, one of Le Jeune's early sport fishers, built a log cabin on the lake. He was the first person to make Lac Le Jeune a fishing retreat. Over the next 100 years many more would be drawn to the lake's shores to build summer and permanent homes. Later, in 1905, he and partner Robert Cowan built the first Fish Lake Hotel, a primitive but successful hotel, one of the first fishing-lodge type hotels in the Interior. Lusk retired in 1906 and Cowan built a new and larger hotel called the Rainbow Lodge that became a popular retreat for CPR management people and other wealthy patrons. The current Lac Le Jeune resort is located on the same property that Lusk and Cowan built their first lodge almost 100 years ago.

After a harrowing nighttime journey to get to "Rainbow Cottage" one of the hotel visitors, F. G. Aflalo wrote about Lac Le Jeune, which he called Trout Lake, its fly-fishing, the rainbow's fighting ability, and fly patterns in *Sunset Playgrounds* (1909):

For ordinary tastes Trout Lake should be good enough. I gladly threw back anything under a pound, and as I may add, as a further tribute to the fishing, that my action in throwing a trout-fly is unlike Basonquet's on a slow wicket. Yet at the very first cast I hooked two, one of close on two pounds, the other half a pound less. These lake rainbows jump like tarpon six or eight times, and they fight like demons...Many flies do well on the shallows, and among them a red-bodied Montreal, a green-bodied cow-dung, a March brown, a Zulu, a Parmachene belle, and a silver doctor, all tied on No. 5 or 6 hook. (p. 203)

In *Rod & Creel in British Columbia* (1919), A. Bryan Williams describes Fish Lake as "*the Mecca for fly-fishermen* (p. 114)." It was, and still remains, a popular fly-fishing lake to this day. Its fame, however, was to be shaded by some lakes north of Kamloops: Paul, Pinantan, Hyas and Knouff as well as Peterhope southeast of Kamloops. These lakes all had one thing in common. Early settlers discovered that trout quickly grew to enormous size when put into

Hisaichi Kamizawa casting into a crystal-clear, calm, mirrored Walloper Lake.

A couple of Nation Special flies, circa 1930.

barren lakes containing large populations of aquatic insects. Stocked in 1909 with 5,000 Kamloops trout fry of Scotch Creek origin, Paul Lake was the first of the barren lakes to produce very large trout—with specimens weighing between 4 and 14 pounds—four years later. Pinantan Lake, stocked the same year as Paul, is a smaller, more shallow lake and the fish there also grew to enormous size. About Paul's and Pinantan's trout, Williams says that Paul's fish are "not so plentiful as in Fish Lake but they run much larger in size" and that Pinantan "has some enormous trout in it, fish up to twelve and fourteen pounds have been taken..." (*Rod & Creel In British Columbia*, p. 116). Because of the rapid fish growth and resulting good fishing in Paul and Pinantan, Knouff was planted in 1917, Hyas in 1923 and Peterhope in the 1935. They would become renowned in the world of stillwater fly-fishing—and partly so because of one man.

Bill Nation became the undisputed master of British Columbia's Interior trout fly-fishing. Rod Haig-Brown relied on Nation for information about Interior fly-fishing for his classic, *The Western Angler*, published by The Derrydale Press in 1939.

In the later 1947 trade edition of *The Western Angler*, Haig-Brown paid tribute to Nation saying that:

> he brought to Kamloops trout fishing the most original mind it has yet known. In a very real way he made the Kamloops trout his own special fish and his active mind seemed never to rest from thinking about them...He was a really good fly-fisherman himself and as fine a guide as man could want—excellent

> company on the water and tireless in searching for fish even on the worst days...
>
> Other men may solve more Kamloops trout problems than Bill did, make more ingenious imitations and develop more perfect ways of fishing them. But for me and for many others Bill will always be the true pioneer of the fishing, the man whose life was closer to those particular fish than any other man's has been or is likely to be. (pp. 114-117)

Arthur William Nation, a quiet, small, bespectacled man, was born in Bristol, England on June 29, 1881. He emmigrated to Canada and ended up in British Columbia, fishing the Kamloops area in the early 1920s. At first he guided around the Little River area, but in 1927 he moved his headquarters to Paul Lake and continued to operate out of Paul until his death in November 1940.

His unique letterhead states that he is an Anglers' Guide:
- *Specializing in fly-fishing and in trout fishing tackle of the finest quality*
- Offering *Fishing, among others: Paul, Knouff, Le Jeune, Hyas, Long, Dee, Jewel, Pillar, Hi Hume, Big Bar, Canim, Mahood, Murtle, and the two Beaver Lakes: The Thompson, Adams and Little Rivers, with a guarantee of at least 100 trout a week—Taupo and Rotorua districts in New Zealand.*
- And *Originator of the Nation's Special and Silver tip trout flies and the new series of nymphs of the dragon flies and sedges.*
- With *Special flies for large rainbow and steelhead trout, including six original patterns tied personally, $2.00 a dozen.*
- Offering *Hardy and Allcock tackle.*
- With *Headquarters at Echo Lodge, Paul Lake, Kamloops, BC.*

Nation, a man of the times, was a masterful fly-fisher and guide who came to the Interior when waters yielded large fish and many of them. Even with railroad and primitive road access, getting to the Kamloops area lakes and streams was a chore, and costly, so there were few fishers. In 1927 Nation headquartered at Echo Lodge on Paul Lake. The lodge, built by J. Arthur Scott in 1922, offered Nation's well-to-do clients appropriate accommodations in the heart of Kamloops fly-fishing country. His clients could enjoy the sport Paul Lake offered, but he could also take guests on day or longer trips to other exceptional waters, many that he advertised on his letterhead.

The lake fishing drew many to the area because in those waters the trout grew large. By the time Nation moved his headquarters to Paul Lake, the fish were not as large as they once were. Nonetheless, every season fly-fishers consistently took trout in the three- to five-pound range. Mature specimens were averaging 8 to 10 pounds.

Nation developed a number of flies for rainbow trout with some being the first imitations of insects in those still waters he fished and some are the first-ever imitations of certain species of insects.

Bill Nation's gravestone in the Kamloops cemetery.

Bill Nation with the first trout of 1939 on a stonefly nymph of his own tying.

On his Nation's Black, British Columbia's first Chironomid imitation, consisting of a few strands of deer hair and black floss, he took fish up to 8 pounds. His Grey and Green Nymphs were the first-ever attempts at imitating a dragonfly nymph. Bulky creations, difficult to cast, and made fun of by some fishermen, Nation says that "The Special and the grey and green dragon nymphs account for the bulk of the larger rainbows. The largest on fly in recent years weighed 17 lbs., and took a #4 grey nymph." Nation's Blue was an imitation of coupled damselfly adults, Nation's Red was an imitation of coupled dragonflies, Nation's Green Sedge and Nation's Silver Tipped-sedge were both imitations of the green sedge nymph, common to many Kamloops-area lakes. Nation's Fancy, Silver Tip and Special were more general wet-fly patterns.

That he was an innovative fly designer, there is no dispute. However, today's fly-fisherman would classify many of his patterns as fancy flies and not many have survived the passage of time. But it was Nation's skills as an observer of the natural world and as a

Row boats very similar to those Pete McVey has at Corbett Lake were the standard during Nation's day.

fly-fisherman, adopting and improvising techniques to stillwater fly-fishing, that made his flies effective fish-catchers.

Many anglers developed a special attachment to Nation's Special. Bruce Hutchinson in *The Fraser* (1950) says:

> His [Nation's] *memorial is the Nation Special, the unique fly that he constructed out of his unequaled knowledge of insect life and the appetite of the Kamloops trout. No fisherman can afford to be without Bill's masterpiece.* (p. 325)

On examining Echo Lodge's Honour Book, Haig-Brown noticed that of the 119 large trout between 3 1/2 to 7 1/2 pounds, a Nation's Special deceived 46. The Jock Scott, with nine fish, was next closest.

Wilderness, solitude, large fish and plenty of them are some of the attractions that past and present-day fly-fishers covet. It is true that Nation experienced all those things, but not all were serene days back in the 1920s and '30s. Canada did not have the Medicare system that we take for granted today. Throat cancer robbed Nation of a long life. He claims the cancer was a result of inhaling contaminated air when using a spraygun to paint the rowboats, probably with lead-based paints. He died rich in fishing friends but poor in material goods and the owners of Echo Lodge had to sell his fishing equipment to pay for his burial service. Located in the Kamloops Cemetery, his grave is marked with a memorial gravestone paid for by his fishing friends. It states:

Erected in the memory of Bill Nation of Paul Lake, Kamloops, by his many fishermen friends and admirers. Died Nov. 27, 1940.

The 1930s may have been the best of days for Kamloops area fly-fishing. Nation was instrumental in bringing fame to the area. In *Fish and Game in British Columbia* A. Bryan Williams says:

Paul Lake

Very fine fly-fishing can be had from the time the season opens until the water becomes too warm, usually in July and again in September. Dry fly-fishing usually commences in June, the best fly to use being the Green-Bodied Sedge and occasionally the Black Gnat. The fish run from one to three pounds, with an occasional one up to five pounds. (p. 120)

Pinantan Lake

Size of fish, 1 to 6 lbs. Kamloops trout. The fishing in this lake is best as soon as the season opens. With hot weather the water gets too warm until cool nights come in September. There is often a good hatch of Black Gnats. (p. 122)

Knouff Lake

This is one of the most beautiful of the interior lakes and also one of the best for fishing...for fly-fishing, it is best to wait until the first week of June, when the Sedges begin to hatch. This lake is known for enormous numbers of Grey-Bodied Sedges. When they are in the water you need to be a dry fly-fisherman or your chances of hooking a fish on the wet fly are not good, except just at the start of the rise.

The weights of the fish in this lake vary considerably from year to year. Some years they average about 3 pounds, another year they will go 6 or 7. You never can tell what sized fish you will hook; but the best fish I know of was a magnificent specimen of 17 1/4 pounds, caught on a dry fly (Sedge). Numbers of 8, 9 and 10-pound fish have been taken.

For dry fly-fishing, use the Grey-bodied Sedge and Bi-visibles. After the sedges are gone, the small blue Dragon Flies come in numbers. A nymph is very killing then. (p. 107)

Hyas Long Lake

This lake is about the same size as Knouff Lake and the fishing is very similar, except that the Sedges there are of the green-bodied kind, and the trout average somewhat larger. The best fish caught on a dry fly that I know of weighed 15 1/4 lbs. (p. 99)

Fish Lake

The fish do not run to very large size, going from 1 to 2 pounds, with an occasional larger one...For dry fly-fishing, use the Green-Bodied Sedge and occasionally the Black Gnat or Bi-visible. (p. 93)

Noteworthy is the decline in the size of trout in Paul and Pinantan. Those huge fish weighing into the mid-teens just after initial plantings lasted a few short years. Through natural spawning in tributary creeks, and or by too large of stockings, the lakes became overpopulated, the fish gobbled up the food supply, until an equilibrium developed between fish and food production. In the late 1930s, Peterhope also showed rapid growth with Heber Smith's 16-pound trout in 1945 one of the largest fly-caught. Heber's fish won third prize in the *Field & Stream* Western Trout Fly Casting Category that year. Notable also is the size of Lac Le Jeune fish. Le Jeune was never a barren lake and there existed a balance between fish size and food production and, in 1935, 50 years after the first sport fishers arrived, the fish still averaged in the one- to two-pound range.

Anglers such Dr. Lambert, Bill Nation, Tommy Brayshaw, Colonel Carey, Arthur Bryan Williams and others of that era who fly-fished one or more of the Nation Lakes, birthed many of the stillwater fly-fishing techniques, which spread throughout the province. The first fly-fishers used eastern North American and British fly patterns but through the 1920s and 1930s and onward, local patterns, many fancy, were produced. Nation dressed the first Chironomid pupa and dragonfly nymphs and Colonel Carey developed his famous Carey Special. In the early 1920s, Bryan Williams collected traveling sedge specimens from Knouff Lake and had Harkley and Haywood in Vancouver dress the Grey-Bodied Sedge and Green-Bodied Sedge, B.C.'s first local stillwater dry flies. It was on the Grey-Bodied Sedge that Earl L. Hodson took his 17 1/4-pound Knouff Lake trout, the largest dry-fly-caught rainbow from these lakes. Nation was on the lake the day that Hodson caught his large fish and his client took one of 16 pounds, also on the Grey-Bodied Sedge. The sedge hatches on Knouff made that water the

Paul Lake looking towards the provincial campsite.

Jack Shaw playing an acrobatic Kamloops trout.

premier dry-fly lake in North America and perhaps the world.

The Nation lakes and those that fished those waters during Nation's era laid the foundations from which a large following of fly-fishers sprouted. Some, such as Jim Kilburn, Jack Shaw and Brian Chan, became the masters of the sport.

During the 1960s and early 1970s, Kilburn, a founding member of the Totem Flyfishers, B.C.'s oldest fly-fishing club, wrote many articles on the Interior lakes' fly-fishing, fly patterns and aquatic insects. He was at the forefront of the group dedicated to improving fly-fishing by dressing patterns more representative of trout food. He influenced many fly-tyers and fly-fishers.

Next to Bill Nation, Jack Shaw stands tall as a master of the sport and no work about fly-fishing the lakes around Kamloops would be complete without something about this legendary fly-fisher. When Jack went fishing it seems that trout, realizing their fate and Shaw's skills as a fly-fisher and fly dresser, lined up waiting their turn to be caught on Shaw-dressed fly patterns. When less-skilled fishers experience good catches, they can be attributed more to luck, however, consistent good catches don't just happen. Skill, knowledge, experience, and observation, with a little luck thrown in, are traits possessed by the great fly-fishers.

Montreal-born Shaw moved to Burnaby at age nine in 1925 and, like most youngsters with a yen for the outdoors and fishing, started his angling career with bait and hand-line fishing Burnaby's south-slope creeks and the sea around Burrard Inlet, False Creek, and English Bay. Those early day catches consisted of small 8- to 10-inch rainbow trout, bullheads, rock cod and flounder.

In 1940, Shaw moved to Kamloops and Jack started his lake fishing career. In those early Kamloops years, Shaw relied on his bait-fishing background and used gang troll and worm, but soon, he realized the errors of his ways and his fly-fishing career was born.

Shaw was irritated by the existing trout patterns with names that didn't identify what insect they represented. In the early 1950s, Shaw developed his own patterns and named them after the creatures they represented. Later, when he became allergic to dust from his automobile body-shop vocation, his love of fishing proved the provider when he took a fly-fishing representative and fly-tyer position in a local sporting-goods store. The store owner persuaded Jack to tie some of his flies and offer them for sale, but the Shaw-invented wingless patterns didn't sell. Being an observer of nature, Shaw, an innovative fly tyer, developed patterns to represent the insects on which fish fed. He raised the insects in an aquarium and from macro photographs dressed his imitations. However, they didn't look like the normal winged-fly patterns of the day, and fishermen are extremely conservative and not quick to change unless convinced otherwise. Jack was determined to persuade them otherwise.

Jack's concern about wingless, more-representative flies and the resolve to persuade fishermen to use his style of pattern has been well illustrated in previous writings. However, as a fly-fishing/tying teacher, Shaw did convince many of them otherwise and, although some of those winged standards are still popular, all lake fishermen fly inventory include non-winged Shaw-type patterns.

Jack Shaw's book, *Fly Fish the Trout Lakes,* came out in 1976,

Brian Chan is now synonymous with Kamloops Lake fly-fishing.

it detailed the equipment and techniques for fishing the Kamloops area. However, Shaw showed, by careful trimming of hackle or wing, how to convert many of the standard-of-the-day patterns into more life-like imitations of the insects on which fish fed. Reprinted many times it has become a standard reference for anglers fishing the Interior.

Jack's second book, *Tying Flies For Trophy Trout* was published in 1992. In it he utilizes his vast reservoir of skill and knowledge—obtained from nearly 70 years of fishing, 50 years of fly-fishing, 40 years of fly tying, and many years as a fly-fishing/fly-tying teacher and sales representative—to give present and future generations of anglers sound advice to catch those prized trophy Kamloops rainbow trout. Jack passed away on February 2, 2000. Through his writing and his teaching he contributed greatly to the lore of Interior fly-fishing.

Inspired by masters like Jack Shaw, Heber Smith, Barney Rushton and others and through an inquisitive scientific mind, Brian Chan honed his skills as a stillwater fly-fisher over three decades and is now synonymous with Kamloops' lake fly-fishing. Chan, a fishery biologist by profession working for provincial fisheries, transferred to Kamloops in the early 1970s. Over the years since he moved to what he claims is trout-fishing paradise, he has become the undisputed master of stillwater, fly-fishing techniques, with a specific interest in Chironomid fishing, his fly-fishing love.

Chan makes fishing Chironomids sound easy and claims that it is once you understand the life cycle of the Chironomid. Chan's book, *Flyfishing Strategies for Stillwaters,* published in 1991 provides some insight into that subject. In his book, Chan details the entomology of most trout foods available in British Columbia's stillwater fisheries, plus much more on how to catch stillwater trout. He recommends two Chironomid fishing techniques. The floating line with varying lengths of leader from 12 to 24 feet depending on the depth of water to be fished. The pupae should be fished close to the bottom with a dead-slow retrieve or wind drift. However, in the deeper water, often a full-sinking line is effective when it is permitted to sink to the vertical and slowly retrieved.

In 1999, *Morris & Chan on Fly Fishing Trout Lakes* co-authored by Brian Chan and Skip Morris was released. Brian also teaches fly-fishing and entomology through fishing schools and stars in his videos *Flyfishing Strategies for Stillwaters*, Vol. I and II.

With its myriad lakes, in addition to those lakes highlighted in this chapter, the Kamloops area lures many fly-fishers to its productive waters. About the Bill Nation lakes, Chan sums up their current status and writes:

Paul Lake

The current fishery is made up of about 60% wild recruitment and 40% annual stocking. We are releasing yearling Pennask strain rainbows and Blackwater strains. The Blackwaters are definitely feeding on the shiners, to what extent they will impact the shiner population is not known. Suffice to say this strain of rainbows are getting well conditioned when on the forage fish. Expect rainbows to 2 kg with an average

size of 0.75 kg. Still excellent Chironomid and callibaetis mayfly hatches. Shrimp, dragonflies and damselfies still prominent.

Best flies: Pheasant Tail mayfly nymphs, bead head Hares Ear, Adams, Chironomid pupae in a variety of colours, shrimp patterns, damselfly nymphs and lillebulidae and darner dragonfly nymphs. Also shiner patterns.

Pinantan Lake

Similar stocks as Paul Lake, Light Pennask and Blackwater stockings with about 25% of fishery composed of wild fish. Good population of shiners. Overall, an abundant population of trout with max. size of 1 kg and average of 0.5 kg.

Shiner patterns effective as well as more attractor style patterns, leeches, Woolly Buggers, some Chironomids and dragonflies but invertebrate populations not as prolific as Paul Lake.

Hyas Lake

Currently a good fishery with annual stockings of Pennask strain of rainbow trout. Pure culture and abundant populations of shrimp and Chironomids. Still has traveler caddis hatch. Fish to 2.5 kg with average of 0.75 kg.

Closed to fishing in the winter months. Best fly patterns, bloodworms, Chironomid pupae of various colours, Hyalella shrimp, caddis larval and pupal patterns, leeches, damselfly nymphs, and water boatman in the fall.

This pure culture lake continues to support a quality fishery. It is stocked with Pennask rainbow trout on an annual basis. Water quality remains good and invertebrate life is abundant. Shrimp, Chironomid, caddis and leeches are the trouts' staple food items. Traveler sedge hatch still present. Fish to 2 kg. with an average of 0.75 kg.

Knouff Lake

Stocked on an annual basis with all female rainbow trout stocks. Limited natural recruitment. Caddis hatches still occurring and definite following of anglers who enjoy this famous hatch. Good Chironomid and callibaetis emergences. Water quality still good, clear water, white marl shoals. Fish to 3 kg. Regulations: 2 fish/day and single hook restriction. Very popular fishery particularly with fly anglers.

Patterns to consider: mayfly nymphs, Adams, Chironomid pupae, particular small green patterns, caddis pupa, Mikaluk sedges, damselfly nymphs, Hyalella shrimp and dragonfly nymphs.

Lac Le Jeune

Still an excellent fishery although fish are quite spooky when on the shoals. Water quality still good. Callibaetis and Chironomid hatches still prominent as well as good caddis hatches. Also, small damselfly emergences. Good populations of Hyalella shrimp.

Very popular fishery with large provincial park and

many permanent homes on both south and north shores of lake, Lac Le Jeune resort still operating. Fish to 1.75 kg with average of 0.75 kg.

Best patterns, callibaetis mayfly nymph imitations (Skip Nymphs, bead-head Hare's Ear, Pheasant Tail), dun imitations (parachute Adams, Chopaka May), Chironomid pupae of various colours, and shrimp patterns.

Peterhope Lake

Still an excellent fishery, stocked with Pennask yearlings each spring. Limited natural recruitment. Quality regulations: 2 fish limit, single barbless hook, bait ban and winter closure. Forest Service recreation site plus newly redeveloped lodge. Fish to 4 kg. with average of 0.75 kg. Recent conversion of irrigation licenses to conservation will maintain stable water

Dave Locke and Beau enjoying a BCFFF outing on Paul Lake.

The author's uncle Andrew Lingren and Grandfather Lingren with an August 21, 1939 catch from Pinantan Lake.

levels in the lake ensuring shoal areas remain productive and habitable by fish. Excellent Chironomid, some mayfly and caddis emergences. Fish often feeding on Hyalella shrimp and small Chironomid pupae. Nocturnal fishing with leeches and dragonflies can be productive.

"Kami, let's go to Kamloops and try fly-fishing," I said. Earlier that year in April, Hisaichi Kamizawa (Kami), Gary Baker and I celebrated Peter Blain's 50th birthday on the Cowichan River. High and dirty it flowed, and we didn't fish long but I managed a 22-inch brown in that water. Impressed by that fly-caught catch, Kami wanted to try fly-fishing.

Two months later we drove north over the Coquihalla Highway and that night stayed at Lac Le Jeune campsite. I brought along a spare fly-fishing outfit for Kami. It was his first attempt fly-fishing and I didn't expect him to have any fly gear. But he had purchased a new Hardy graphite rod, Hardy reel, and floating line, spending about $1000 on his outfit. My friend loves his fishing and good equipment, but he said, "Don't mention to Akiko what I paid for this."

The next morning we fished the shoal across the lake from the campsite. Kami couldn't fly-cast so I rowed, trailing our lines behind the boat. In one of my books Kami had spotted a picture of a trout that I had caught with a Black Carey dangling from its mouth. He insisted on using this leech-type pattern and not long after we started he was playing a trout of about two pounds. He hooked two more, landing one trout over a pound and losing the other before the wind blew us from the lake. I could tell that Kami was quite pleased with his catch. He had the same look in his eyes that I noticed way back in 1972 when, as a new Canadian, he took

his first steelhead from the Gold River. He confided in me then his pride of accomplishment when he said, "I am so happy I could kiss that fish."

It pleased me that I could introduce my friend to fly-fishing and that his first catch came from Lac Le Jeune, one of the Bill Nation lakes in the cradle of British Columbia's Interior stillwater fly-fishing.

References

Aflalo, F. G., *Sunset Playgrounds*, London: Witherby & Co., 1909.

Chan, Brian. *Flyfishing Strategies for Stillwaters*. Kamloops: Privately printed, 1991.

Haig-Brown, Roderick, *The Western Angler*, New York: The Derrydale Press, 1939.

____. *The Western Angler*, New York: William Morrow, 1947.

Lambert, T. W., *Fishing in British Columbia*, London: Horace Cox, 1907.

Raymond, Steve, *Kamloops*, New York: Winchester Press, 1971.

Williams, Arthur Bryan, *Rod & Creel in British Columbia*, Vancouver: Progress Publishing, 1919.

____. *Fish and Game in British Columbia*, Vancouver: Sun Directories, 1935.

CHAPTER
10

The Skagit River

A colourful rosy-sided Skagit River rainbow.

FLOWING OUT OF THE CASCADE MOUNTAINS AND crossing Highway 3, about 30 km east of Hope, this river and its rainbow trout have attracted fly-fishers to its banks for well over 100 years. In 1887, Sir Clive Phillipps-Wolley, seeking adventure with rod and gun, journeyed from his Victoria home and departed the train at the station across the Fraser at Hope. At Fort Hope he hired guides and packers to take him east through the Hope Mountains over the Dewdney Trail constructed from Hope to Princeton in 1861. He was directed to a spot by the 14-mile house owner and a cast with two Norwegian trout flies he had some good sport. In *A Sportsman's Eden* (1888), he writes:

> *Our halting-place the first night was at the 'fourteen-mile' house, a rough log cabin...The first cast in one of the pale blue pools showed me that there were fish there worth having and willing to be had. As the flies went out over the first pale blue pool, its surface was troubled, and as they lit, two great trout came half-way out of the water for them...(p. 54)*

He lost both fish by a "smash," but undaunted he put on another cast and, with an alder fly, he was at it again:

> *In a moment I was into a big fellow, and ye gods! how he fought! How savagely he headed for an unpromising looking stake, whose broken end rose from the other side of the pool! But the gut held, and at last I piloted him safely through the sunken logs and boughs which fringed the edge of the pool, and knocked him on the head, first of two dozen, whose rosy sides glistened that evening on the pebbles behind me. (p. 55)*

With a bag of two dozen glistening, rosy-sided trout, he returned to his lodgings having experienced good sport. Later on the return trip, in September, he stopped to fish the same waters. From his bank he saw trout rising on the far bank. Rather than wade, he rode his horse across the river almost losing it in quicksand and soaking himself in the crossing. Wet to his neck, he dismounted his horse and waded in casting his flies. Wondering what kind of brilliantly coloured fish he caught and about where he caught them, he writes:

> I have learned since, however, that all the big trout of the Skagit (of which the stream I was fishing is a tributary) are of this brilliant hue. In spite of his colour, he was a true trout, and hung at my saddle-bow, I should think, a good four pounds, the best fish I ever caught in [North] America. (p. 149)

Sir Clive was probably not the first to wet a line in these waters. He mentions in his book that the 14-mile house had maybe a dozen visitors a year and it was the proprietor who told him about the trout fishing. The stream he fished was part of the Sumallo system and was probably around where Sunshine Valley is today.

The Natives living in the Lower Skagit used the Skagit Valley as a route to the Interior and, in 1858, Captain Walter De Lacy of the US Army built the Whatcom Trail, which traversed the Upper Skagit from Silvertip Mountain, joining up with the Dewdney Trail. The Skagit River trail from Sumallo Grove follows the route of the original Whatcom Trail, still the only access to that section of the river below the Hope Princeton Highway.

Gold fever enveloped the Skagit with the first discovery in 1859. One later strike found on Shawatum Mountain in 1910, and the salting of the area with gold nuggets by two Nevada miners, resulted in a claim-staking rush. By 1911 there were more than 1200 claims and three surveyed town sites with two hotels built in the valley. The mining boom didn't last once the truth about the salting became known, but through that early mining activity, access into the Skagit was improved.

In *Rod & Creel in British Columbia* (1919), about the river, how to get there, its fishing and flies to use, A. Bryan Williams writes:

> The Skagit River rises in the Cascade Mountains in British Columbia, but after running for about thirty miles, crosses the boundary line into the United States. The last twenty miles of the river in this province is one of the best streams in southern British Columbia for the fly-fisherman, and anybody wanting a ten-days or a fortnight's fishing trip cannot do better than pay this stream a visit any time after the first week of July.
>
> To get there you go to Hope and engage a man with pack horses to take you in, unless you feel like doing thirty miles with a pack on your back. There is no accommodation after you leave Hope and you have to camp out.
>
> From Hope the trail follows up Nicolum Creek to the divide at Lake House, a distance of fourteen miles. Small fish can be caught here. You then strike Sumallow [sic] Creek, which is a tributary of the Skagit, and follow it down for nine miles to where it joins the main river. You can now begin to catch fish, but they are not very big and you had better keep on going down stream until you get within four or five miles of the boundary line. Here you will catch fish on the fly

> of all sizes up to three or four pounds in weight, more than you know what to do with, unless you smoke them. If you care to try spinning for a change, you will get some good big dolly vardens.
>
> There is seldom much choice of a fly but you had better take some March Browns, Royal Coachman, Black Gnat, Teal and Red and a Jock Scott or two. (pp. 124-125.)

In 1946, Tommy Brayshaw moved to Hope and made his first trip with his wife and son into the Upper Skagit through the Sumallo. In his diary for September 11, 1946, he writes:

> Becky, Chris & I left Hope 6:15 a.m. & drove about a mile beyond camp at 23 up Hope-Princeton Rd. at 8 a.m. Walked about a mile and found a trail down to the Skagit.
>
> Quite a small stream & very clear—caught one about 9 inches & returned it. Slipped on rocks & fell, got badly shaken so quit. Came back to car to about 21 mile & had lunch—very bright & hot, dug up a few rhododendrons then found a road leading to junction of Sumallo & Skagit. Saw trout rising but could not raise them on wet fly so changed to dry, got one on a ginger hackle & dun wing size 12 of 1 lb. 10 oz., then crossed & stalked rises, got another of 3/4 lb. on badger hackle size 12 after which they refused the fly so

Gil Sage helped save the Skagit from flooding.

changed to a size 14, March Brown & got two more of 1 lb. 11 oz. and 11 ozs.—quit at 3:30 when sun left river—a very satisfactory hour & a half 2-2:30. An awful road for 5 or 6 miles.

In 1948, Roderick Haig-Brown visited Brayshaw to fish the Coquihalla but rain put that river out and on September 24th they fished the Skagit. About the fishing, the flies used and the bugs the fish were eating, Brayshaw writes:

A beautiful day. Rod & I started at 11 for the Skagit owing to the road having been built since last year, along the left bank of the Sumallo we missed Bill Robinson's place & the turnoff to the junction of the Sumallo & Skagit. Inquired at the camp & had to turn back for 1 1/2 miles and dug up some rhododendrons on the way. Reached the river about 1 p.m. just at junction of Sumallo and Skagit and went downstream.

Roddy fished dry—about size 12 mostly Mackenzie River patterns of hackle and hair wings. He got 3 of 1 lb. 1/4 lb. and 1/4 lb. in one pool besides losing two good ones. I lost one on wet fly through the dropper snagging. Not much rise up to 2:30 then at a pool about 3/4 mile lower we saw a few rising. Rod took the bottom & I the top. He hooked a big one which snagged & broke him in the overhanging bushes on the far side, it was the biggest one we hooked all day. I got 3 on a King Rio Grande, a sort of Coachman, of 12 oz., 1 lb. 2 oz. and 1 lb. 10 oz. all in about twenty minutes and without moving more than a few yards.

When the sun got off the water about 4 the hatch and the rise was over & though we fished back to the Sumallo we didn't move another fish.

Cleaning the fish at home later we found them very full of caddis, nymphs and fully developed flies in that order, the caddis being farthest down & the flies little beyond the gullet so presumably that showed that in the morning they changed from caddis to nymph and later to flies.

How true Brayshaw's observations were. The Skagit has a good population of trout but when the fish aren't rising and you look at the shallow, crystal-clear pools you wonder if there are any fish. The river is bug rich with good mayfly, stonefly, caddisfly and midge populations. The trout are there feeding on bottom-living insects but become surface oriented when the hatch is on.

After spending a couple of days on the Coquihalla, and with only one 22-inch-long steelhead for my efforts, I thought the Skagit might be worth a try.

I walked down the trail and, as I arrived at the river, large mayflies started popping to the surface. The bubbly water, flowing without a sign of life a minute or two earlier, was now bothered with rising trout. I thumbed through my dry-fly box looking for a

Peter Caverhill worked behind the scenes, but his contributions towards saving this river are significant.

fly about the same size as the duns floating down the currents. A size-eight Grey Wulff looked right and I cast it onto the stream with fish rising everywhere. I didn't do too well during the 1/2 hour of feeding madness before the river went dead. I managed to hook three on the Grey Wulff and one other on a Dark Olive Wulff, landing two. I mumbled something about selective fish and continued fishing into the evening without another strike.

That evening nearly 20 years ago was the first time I experienced a Green Drake hatch. Like other times when I have witnessed a prolific insect hatch and the resulting trout feeding frenzy I went to bed that evening with visions of fish slurping down Green Drakes on dancing waters.

Hope remained the primary departure point to the Skagit until 1946 when the Silver-Skagit road was constructed into the valley. Today that road is the main access into the Lower Skagit and Ross Lake. This road leaves the trans-Canada Highway a few miles southwest of Hope, parallels Silver Creek past Silver Lake and over into the Skagit drainage. The Skagit's Canadian basin, which was to be flooded when the Ross Dam was raised, was to be logged and this road was built for that purpose.

On an earlier trip Brayshaw and his son Chris went to the Skagit along the new Silver-Skagit road to the Whitworth Ranch area. The Whitworth's moved into the valley in 1903, built a large six-bedroom house, but left when the ranch failed in 1910. The house remained until it burned to the ground in 1950. A place called Whitworth Meadows about 6 kilometers north of the International boundary marks the spot of the ranch. Brayshaw noted in his diary that, "The river is taking an awful beating from tourists and the men at Camp 5 and Skagit days are numbered."

The Skagit required an effort to get to before and the new road provided easy access. The limit on trout in 1946 was 15 a day or 25 pounds, plus 1 fish and three days' possession. That was reduced to 12 trout a day or 25 pounds plus 1 fish, and two days' possession in 1951. Very generous limits indeed. The increasing popularity of the Skagit proved to be a double-edged sword. While fish populations dwindled, some users fell in love with the place.

Those people introduced others to this wilderness paradise. Years later some of these people would rally and charge to the Skagit River's rescue when this precious valley was threatened.

The Ross Dam, owned by Seattle City Light, was to be raised in stages to 1735 feet above sea level, flooding the lower valley an additional nine miles to almost the 26-mile bridge near Silvertip campsite. The original dam constructed to elevation 1,380 feet was completed in 1940. Because the raising of the dam would flood Canadian lands, in 1941 Seattle City Light applied to the International Joint Commission (IJC) for permission to build the extension. The Commission, at a single two-hour meeting held in Seattle on September 12, 1941, was represented by 43 US government agencies. Only 12 Canadian agencies were notified of the meeting. Excluded from the invitation list, the only opposition came from J. G. Cunningham of the B.C. Game Commission. This is what he had to say about the flooding:

> I am not familiar with the subject discussed here today... our Commission was not on the list of those advised. I am here merely to present a brief on behalf of the sportsmen of the Skagit River. It is one of the best fly-fishing streams in the whole of British Columbia... the more of that stream you flood, the less fishing we are going to have. (A Citizen's Guide to the Skagit Valley, p. 54.)

It was war time. Canada was in the thick of the war effort and, at the time of the IJC meeting, flooding a British Columbia valley for power seemed trivial. The US tried to use the war scare to get the dam raising pushed through and more pressure was applied after Pearl Harbour had brought the Americans into the scuffle on December 7, 1941. On January 27, 1942, the IJC issued an Order of Approval on the condition that Seattle City Light and British Columbia come to a binding agreement on compensation. World War II ended with no signed agreement, but by 1949 Seattle City Light raised the dam to its current level of 1,615 feet in two stages.

They continued to put pressure on British Columbia to come to a compensation agreement, but W. A. C. Bennett stalled signing for years. On January 10, 1967 BC Resources Minister Ray Williston signed the terms of an agreement, which stated that for an annual rent of less than $35,000 and taxes of $10,000 a year, Seattle City Light gained the right to flood the lower Skagit and save itself millions per year by not having to buy power from an alternative source.

Seattle City Light did not proceed with construction immediately. Two years after Williston signed the agreement, Liberal MLA Dave Brousson raised the High Ross Dam issue in the legislature with an erupting storm. In November 1969, 12 B.C. outdoor and environmental groups formed the Run Out Skagit Spoilers (ROSS) Committee to coordinate the process in B.C. The North Cascades Conservation Council did likewise in the USA.

In the "Foreword" of A Citizen's Guide to the Skagit Valley (1981) by Tom Perry, John Fraser writes:

> The fight to save the Canadian Skagit River has been difficult, frustrating, and time consuming. Much

Ron Schiefke releasing a 12-incher.

has been accomplished. Since 1942, when the International Joint Commission gave its order allowing the flooding by Seattle City Light, to the present time, a remarkable change in the attitude of the public and of the government has taken place. In those far-off days, not only did no one care, no one really knew what was happening. It seems incredible today that responsible politicians of all parties could throw away, by neglect and indifference, a beautiful valley and river. Today, no political party supports the proposed flooding. (p. iii)

Dr. Tom Perry tells the whole story up to 1981 in his book *A Citizen's Guide to the Skagit Valley.* Perry and Ken Farquharson, the long-time secretary of ROSS, were awarded the Totem Flyfishers' Roderick Haig-Brown Award in 1982 for their efforts to save the Skagit.

Notable in their efforts to save the river but not named in Tom Perry's "Acknowledgments" were two fly-fishers, Gilbert Sage and Peter Caverhill. Pete and Gil rallied the anglers and formed the

A lovely day on the river.

Skagit Anglers Committee, while Pete edited the Skagit Anglers Committee newsletter. Both worked with the fledgling British Columbia Federation of Flyfishers, so that anglers' voices would be heard when the IJC reviewed the 1942 flooding decision. On April 28, 1982, the IJC handed down its decision. It did not rescind the 1942 flooding order, but stated that:

...in light of the views of Canada and British Columbia, the Skagit Valley should not be flooded beyond its current level provided that appropriate compensation in the form of money, energy or any other means is made to Seattle. (BCFFF *Flylines*, Issue 10, January 1983)

Almost one year later, in March 1983, British Columbia and Seattle City Light signed an eighty-year agreement. It was a lengthy battle taking many years and reaching the highest political offices in the land, but the efforts of a few saved it for many.

The publicity surrounding the fight to save the river increased the pressure on the river and with wide-open fishing the trout populations plummeted. Knowing the stocks were in decline, the Fish and Wildlife Branch surveyed the river and learned that in 1982 and 1983 there were approximately 2400 trout of eight inches or greater, only about a sixth of what the habitat was capable of producing. It has taken considerable effort to improve fish populations and size. In 1987 restrictive regulations were implemented and the Skagit became a single-point barbless, no-bait, with two-fish limit, 12-inch minimum size fishery. But even then that was not enough and in the early 1990s the river became a catch-and-release fishery, the reservoir had quotas reduced and larger minimum size limits implemented. These regulation changes, above anything, were the savior of the fish. Through the 1990s and on, the trout population—as well as the size of trout—has increased.

In 1973 the provincial government declared the Skagit Valley to be a Provincial Recreational Area. That status provided some protection, but it didn't eliminate industrial activity such as logging and mining. However, in 1997, the Valley received official BC Park status, giving the watershed park protection. The Skagit Anglers surfaced again during the park-planning process. Early park proposals included such things as increased river-bank access with trails for horseback riding, and hiking along both banks and the removing of logjams to improve the river for canoeing. The Skagit Anglers Committee proposed that the Valley's wilderness attributes should be foremost in the park's development. As a result, the logjams were left in place providing refuge for trout and access was made more difficult rather than easier. Between the 26-mile bridge and Ross Lake there were forty access points, some of which were old roads where anglers could drive right to the river. Rather than enhance those access points, most were closed. Now there are eight access points where forty existed and at those eight there is roadside parking and anglers must hike trails to the river. The river and valley maintains much of its wilderness setting. Unfortunately, with fly-fishing's booming popularity, we're loving the river to death. Now and on some weekends during the summer fly-fishing season, it is hard to find an open pool.

But the trout are there, often taking nymphal imitations of stone, caddis and mayflies, and at other times thrilling fly-fishers by

This beauty rose to a Tom Thumb.

rising to a well-presented Tom Thumb, Green- or Yellow-bodied Humpy, Adams, Elk Hair Caddis, Royal Wulff, No-hackle Green Drake, Yellow Stonefly, Simple Sedge, Madame X and many other dry flies, providing they approximate the size and, perhaps, colouration of the natural.

Today was the Loons Fly Fishing Club's Skagit River outing and Alan Steeves, who grew up and fished the river since boyhood, organized and deployed the group along the river so we wouldn't be bumping into one another. An old-time Hope family, the Steeves' have fished the Sumallo and Upper Skagit for decades and know it well. I opted for the one-hour hike down river to get away from the Sumallo Grove parking lot anglers.

I like to explore and enjoyed the day wandering around fishing wet and dry flies on a floating line. The river was high because of the late runoff from the heavy winter snow pack. With no flies coming off, I swam a size-6 Black GP through the rapids into a likely spot. The fish of about 16 or 17 inches was the largest of the day and the only fish to take until after lunch. During the afternoon, seven more fish took my flies, some to dries but most took a Black Caterpillar. This Haig-Brown pattern sat un-noticed in my box until it caught my eye, reminding me of other trout conquests I have had with it. I threw it into the water and brought it over a deep blue slot. The fish liked it and after a couple of quick fish I chucked it into the slot a little closer to the logjam. The fish felt strong, but

once it felt the hook, it sought safety, scurrying into the logjam, snagging my leader and breaking off. That was my only Black Caterpillar and although I fished the rest of the afternoon, no hatch developed and the trout that showed some interest only pecked at my flies.

At 5:30 p.m. I wandered into Sumallo Grove parking lot after an enjoyable day fishing with the Loons and being piloted by Alan Steeves to the Skagit waters that Brayshaw and Haig-Brown fished over half a century before.

References

Domer, Jerry. "The Skagit River." *Osprey News*, 33, 7 (2000): 1, 6, 7.

Hill, Beth. *Sappers: The Royal Engineers in British Columbia.* Ganges; Horsdal & Schubert, 1987.

Perry, Thomas L. *A Citizen's Guide to the Skagit Valley.* Vancouver: Run Out Skagit Spoilers Committee, 1981.

Phillips-Wolley, Sir Clive. *A Sportsman's Eden.* London: Richard Bentley and Son, 1888.

Sage, Gilbert. "Skagit River Report." BCFFF *Flylines*, 17 (May 1984): 7-9.

Williams, A. Bryan. *Rod & Creel in British Columbia.* Vancouver: Progress Publishing Co., 1919.

11

The Stamp River

Joe Wilkinson and "Dad" Chisholm, two veteran Stamp River fly-fishers.

VAN EGAN

EACH TIME I SIT DOWN AT MY DESK I LOOK AT A 1907 Hardy "Perfection" 10-foot 6-inch split bamboo, steel-centered fly rod sitting on my window sill. Not far away, in a glass-topped, black-velvet-lined display case, is a Hardy aluminum Atlantic salmon fly box with the initials N.M. on the front. The fly box, filled with steelhead patterns, has a few flies displayed around the initials on top of the box. Both fly rod and fly box belonged to General Noel Money.

Campbell River's great sport for large tyees drew General Noel Money to British Columbia in 1913. On his way there he took a liking to Qualicum Bay and in 1914 he made Qualicum Beach his home. Shortly after Money settled in Qualicum Beach, war broke out and he returned to England, serving with distinction. After the armistice was declared, he came home and opened the Qualicum Inn, which for the next half a century was a haven for Vancouver Island fishermen.

Since boyhood Money recorded his sport with rod and gun in what he referred to as his Game Book. Consisting of three volumes, the books are now part of the University of British Columbia's Special Collections Division. An examination of the Game Book shows blank years during the war. The entries resumed in August of 1920 with notes about his cutthroating on Nile Creek, using a Professor, Grouse & Purple and Yellow Sally flies. Fishing it for the first time, on September 15, 1920, a rainy day, Money fished a rising and colouring Stamp River. In his Game Book for that day, he recorded the details of the day's catch:

Sept. 15th, 1920 10 1/2 lbs., 9 3/4 lbs., 7 3/4 lbs., 4 lbs., 7 1/2 lbs., 6 1/2 lbs. 6 total. Stamp River. Caught them on a 10 ft. 6 inch trout rod & a Dusty Miller. A grand morning's sport, in heavy water.

For the next 20 years, the Stamp and General Money were inseparable. In 1922 Money built a cabin on the left bank overlooking what he called the Home Pool or Long Run. There he

*Roderick Haig-Brown introduced the greased-line technique to
General Money and the Stamp River in 1939.*

entertained the lords and ladies of the British aristocracy, Canadian
Governor Generals who came to fish with him, as well as
Hollywood notables such as Spencer Tracy, Phil Harris and Warner
Baxter. Over the years, Money named favourite fishing spots and
pools such as the Black Rock, Junction Pool, One Log, Two Log,
White Stone, Big Pool, Upper Ash Pool and First Below. Some
names such as the White Stone (Haig-Brown called this the white
kidney stone), One Log and Two Log are part of the Long Run or
Home Pool, known now as Money's Run or Pool and the White
Stone is still a place where summer-run steelhead lie.

He devised a number of flies for that river. For years after it was
developed, the General Money fly was "the fly" to use on British
Columbia steelhead streams. The General fished the Stamp for the
last time on October 17, 1940, and in his game book he recorded
that he "got one fish in one-log." He was 78 years old when he
passed away on May 26, the following year.

Rod Haig-Brown became friends with Money when the
General was well on in years. Fred Auger in his 1974 article on
"General Money" published in *Northwest Sportsman* included
Haig-Brown's recollections about the General. For that article, Haig-
Brown writes:

> He [Money] *fished just about every day he could, rain
> or shine, and worked the rivers and stream mouths
> north and south of Qualicum thoroughly and enjoy-
> ably, though his real enthusiasm was for summer steel-
> head of the Stamp. He understood this river and
> fished it almost as though it were his own private
> salmon stream in Scotland. There was in fact, very
> little competition in those days.*
>
> *It was General Money who first persuaded me
> that winter steelhead could be taken on a fly as a reg-
> ular thing and not just a fluke. He was deeply con-
> cerned about the life histories of salmon and steel-
> head as well as about catching them and he loved new
> methods. I recall one day when the Stamp was
> extremely low, that I showed him Wood's greased line
> technique and almost immediately he took a fish with
> it. The General promptly sent for suitable rods and
> low-water flies. When the new tackle arrived from
> England I remember sitting with him and Mrs. Money*

> *on the porch at Qualicum, watching the sun set over
> Hornby Island and planning the next day's fishing on
> the Stamp.*
>
> *The last time I saw General Money was when I
> was passing through Qualicum on leave from the
> Army, during the war. It was a December day, cold and
> wet, and he was sitting comfortably in front of an air-
> tight heater in a room upstairs with long johns and
> other clothing draped around him. He had been wad-
> ing the Little Qualicum that day and had managed to
> fall in. He was... still spare and active, still as enthusi-
> astic as ever about all aspects of fishing and totally
> indomitable.*

New to steelhead fly-fishing, it was during the summer of
1939, four years after Jock Scott documented Arthur Wood's technique in *Greased Line Fishing,* that Haig-Brown introduced Money
to the greased line technique on the Stamp River. Even though
Money was late in years when Haig-Brown met him, he had an
ever-lasting influence on the young writer. So much so that Haig-
Brown dedicated his classic work, *The Western Angler* (1939):

> *To General Noel Money of Qualicum Beach, finest of
> western anglers, and to his own Stamp River, loveliest
> and most generous of western streams.* (p. vii)

The General was highly regarded in British Columbia and, for
years, his big McLaughlin Buick bore License plate number one.
However, on February 16,1937, *The Daily Province* reported:

> *General Noel Money of Qualicum, leading Vancouver
> Island sportsman, has lost the coveted "number 1"*

General Noel Money, 1920.

A selection of General Money-dressed flies displayed around the initials N.M.

motor license plate of British Columbia. For many years General Money's car has carried the distinctive plate.

When anglers saw the car with the No. 1 plate parked along the Island Highway roadside, it was a sure giveaway that there were cutthroat, steelhead or salmon running in a nearby creek or river. Though named after Edward Stamp, who built the first-for-export saw mill in British Columbia on Alberni Inlet in the 1860s, the Stamp River will be forever known as General Money's river when it comes to steelhead fly-fishing.

Arthur Bryan Williams was one of the first to report about the fishing in the Stamp. In *Rod & Creel in British Columbia* (1919), he says that the "*best place to fish it from is the lodge on the lake.*" (p. 74). About the Ash River, a major tributary of the Stamp, Williams says that "*it is a splendid river if you want to get some real big trout, anywhere from three pounds to ten pounds, on the fly.*" (p. 73).

In the very early years, when anglers fished streams in the summer and fall months, more often than not, they referred to the summer-run steelhead they caught as rainbows or big trout. It was

thought that steelhead were a winter and spring fish and that British Columbia streams grew large resident trout. General Money referred to the Stamp fish as rainbows, not steelhead.

In his 1935 book, *Fish and Game in British Columbia,* Bryan Williams gives a glowing report for the Ash:

> *Excellent fishing during July, August and September...Steelhead are taken for about six miles up Ash River. These fish run up to 10 lbs...Good auto road to within 3 miles of river, from which point good trails connect with river and lakes.* (p. 71)

Williams also reported that the nine-mile-long Stamp River offered fly-fishing for cutthroat, steelhead and coho from 3 to 10 pounds and that the best fishing was in the early spring and again in the fall after the first heavy rain. From these reports it appears that the majority of the steelhead were returning to the Ash River. The life history and habits of summer-run steelhead confused early fishery scientists. That summer-runs needed to get through a section of water during optimum water conditions and that when they returned on their spawning run some summer-runs would spend the better part of a year in fresh water before spawning was not well understood.

About the steelhead's life history and habits, J. R. Dymond in his 1932 *The Trout and Other Game Fishes of British Columbia* writes:

The steelhead's visits to fresh water are not con-fined to its spawning migrations. In many localities it moves into streams at more or less regular intervals. Thus, at Port Alberni, on Vancouver Island, according to Mr. Waterhouse, steelheads usually run into the river at the end of June or beginning of July, when the snows in the mountains begin to melt. There is also a run in September when the autumn rains begin, and often another in November. In many places steelheads accompany salmon on their spawning migrations. At Stamp Falls, on Vancouver Island, during the late summer of 1926, it was necessary to catch the sockeyes below the falls, carry them up, and place them in the river above. By August 4th, about nine thousand sockeyes and six hundred steelheads had been thus placed above the falls. (p. 14)

The Stamp Falls fish ladder now permits fish to pass to waters above the falls at any time. Prior to the ladder's construction, the salmon and steelhead would congregate in the Falls Pool and when water conditions were ripe for passing the falls, the fish would make their move. Usually on coastal streams with a barrier like a falls, the first runs of summer steelhead would get through during the spring freshet, then other runs would go up the falls on certain rain events through the summer. But if a dry summer, fish would hold below the falls waiting for the first rains of fall and on the right water level, height and temperature would go through in a rush.

In the mid-1950s before the decline, Lee Straight in his little book *100 Steelhead Streams* gave one of the last glowing reports for the Ash and Stamp rivers. About the Ash River, he writes:

An excellent steelhead river, favored by fly-fisher-men...A clear river, it is nonetheless affected by fluc-tuating water levels. It can be a prolific producer in

August and September during the evenings, after the river has risen with rain freshet, then is dropping. (p. 19)

As most steelheaders are aware, steelhead fishing is probably at its best after a rain has stirred up the water and the river is receding and clearing. Stale fish become takers again and often new fish move into the water, and freshly arrived fish are grand takers. About the Stamp, Straight writes:

Excellent summer and winter steelhead runs, particularly the former. Renowned all over the continent for its summer fly and spinning sport for steelheads, and fall coho fishing. Best from July to September. (p. 23)

It was not many years later when it was hard to find a wild steelhead in the Stamp or the Ash. Van Egan of Campbell River saw the last of the glory days.

Intrigued by Haig-Brown's brief writings about the Stamp River, Wisconsin-born Egan made his first trip to the Stamp in 1954 and second trip in 1955. He remembers those trips well. First, while wandering the banks of the Stamp he came across a steelheader who would alter his life for his remaining days. Not just any steelheader but one of great fishing skill and beauty. One month after meeting Maxine Southerland, with Rod Haig-Brown acting as best man, Van and Maxine were married. They settled in the Campbell River area eventually buying a home a few doors up from Rod Haig-Brown where they live to this day.

However, it was on the Stamp and Ash that Egan came across the long double-handed rods then favoured by Vancouver Island steelhead fly-fishermen and, in particular, by the late General

The Long Run or Money's Pool.

A 1934 greeting from General Money to Ted Pengelley.

Money. The terrain surrounding the waters of the Stamp and Ash suited Spey casting with a double-handed rod. Money favoured Hardy rods and in a testimonial letter published in Hardy's Anglers Guide, in 1925, Money writes:

> Vancouver Island, 3/7/22. The 12 ft. 6 in. "Wye" rod you sent me last year suits me exactly for big trout. One day last week I got three good fish on it (all on fly, of 9 1/2 lbs., 6 1/2 lbs. The best rod I have ever had. Signed Brig. Gen. N. Money.

In 1929, the government Tourist Bureau's seven-minute-long *Seeking Steelhead* film was released. In this silent film General Money, tight against the bank or trees, can be seen Spey casting his double-handed "Wye" rod on the Long Run and catching steelhead after steelhead. About the double-handed rod and his introduction to Stamp River users, Egan writes:

> I first saw the Spey rod in action on the Ash River (Vancouver Island). I was fishing the lower end of a large pool, locally known as Log Jam, about three-quarters of a mile above the confluence of the Ash and Stamp. Log Jam was a large pool for such a medium sized river, deep against the jammed banks on the far side. My 55- to 60-foot casts with a single-handed rod

> fell short of this logical holding water. While casting near the tailout, my peripheral vision caught a slight disturbance in the slick of a glide at the far side of the head of the pool. I paid it no attention until it occurred two or three more times. Then looking up I saw the tall, slender fisherman. He was standing not more than ankle deep and sending out a long line that puts his fly almost against the far bank, a good 100 feet off the reel.

> I left the river then, taking a seat on the bank to watch as this master of the two-handed rod continued to cover the deep run against the jam of logs. Shortly he joined me. Intrigued by the performance, I was full of questions. He told me his name was Havilah Harford and the rod was a 13 and a half-foot Hardy Wye. "It was the choice of General Noel Money," he said, who had tried out a variety of two-handed rods on the Stamp, selecting this one for its capacity to deliver a long cast on wide pools where there was not room for an extended backcast...

> That winter I bought my first Spey rod, a 13 and a half-foot Hardy Wye, and fitted it with a four-inch Hardy Uniqua reel and a 40-yard salmon line with 100

The summer-runs penetrate above Stamp Falls. Below is the domain of the winter-run steelhead.

*Van Egan found this skilled steelheader wandering
the banks of the Stamp—and married Maxine.*

brought more and more people to the valley and, as the population increased, the commercial and sport fishers took too many fish. The watersheds were scalped to make pulp and the Stamp was dammed in the mid-1930s to supply water to the mill. By the 1970s the accumulated effect of all those activities combined with too many people killing too many fish, few fish were returning to this great watershed.

Watershed stewardship did not and still does not receive much attention and, in those days, hatcheries were the quick fix. At a huge cost to the other taxpayers of the province, Robertson Creek hatchery was built and it has produced large runs of coho and steelhead. The fish were back and the killers flocked to the banks of the Stamp in droves to get their "free fish." Lately, politicians favour a user pay and with a returning hatchery steelhead or coho costing taxpayers many dollars, perhaps it's time to start recouping the costs of operating a hatchery from those that use the product and charge a fee for a fish killed. A returning adult hatchery steelhead costs taxpayers a hell of a lot of money to produce.

Very little of the Stamp/Somass watershed enjoys Park protection. Perhaps not on such a grand a scale, but the sins of the past do haunt the future. The Ash and Stamp watersheds have partially

*Charles Lingren casts his fly
on waters that General Money fly-fished.*

yards of backing. I could barely stand the anticipation of a return to the Stamp River in June 1955, and hopefully showing my outfit to Harford. Finally arriving at Money's Pool, I met the Chisholms of Port Alberni, father in his 80s and his doctor son, both practitioners of the two-handed rod. Both were helpful in explaining the lies in Money's Pool, and I recall the exuberant cries of "Dad" Chisholm as his rod bowed with a fresh, bright steelhead skyrocketing across the mouth of Bear Creek. Later, when I asked about Hav Harford, I was grieved to learn he had died the previous winter. They had the upmost respect for Harford, agreeing that he was the best fly-fisherman on the Stamp since General Money.

General Money bought his 13-foot 6-inch Hardy Wye rod in 1925. He loved it and wrote Hardy telling them that he had used their rods for years, but that their latest the 13-foot 6-inch Wye was "the best of all." He also told them that he caught 5 fish on July 30 on his new rod, the best fish went 8 1/2 pounds. Hardy included Money's letter in their 1927 *Hardy's Anglers' Guide* testimonials for the "Wye" series of rods.

The Stamp and Somass watershed is one of the largest on Vancouver Island and in its pristine state produced large runs of salmon and steelhead. However, Port Alberni's economy was driven by commercial fishing and the pulp mill. Those activities

A catch of summer-runs from the Stamp, circa 1935.

recovered from the initial logging, but second growth is ripe and is being logged.

Ocean survival affected the coho and steelhead stocks returning to the Stamp system through the 1990s, but in the past couple of years the returns of steelhead and coho have increased and many Vancouver Island fly-fishers enjoy fishing this river. On any given day members of the Mid-Island Castaway Fly Fishers of Qualicum Beach and Parksville, wearing caps sporting General Money's blackbodied and red-winged fly, can be found casting flies on Money's Pool or on pools in the lower Ash. They and other fly-fishers from Vancouver Island fly-fishing clubs carry on the time-honoured sport of steelhead fly-fishing on the river that General Money spent so much time on when he was regarded as the premier fly-fisherman of Vancouver Island. Perhaps, it's time that we placed more importance on the historical significance of a river. If any water deserves fly-fishing-only status on Vancouver Island, it is the Stamp River above Stamp Falls and the Ash River that General Noel Money made famous.

Hugh Falkus, famed British Atlantic salmon and sea-trout fly-fishing author, had come to try for British Columbia summer-run steelhead. Before our September 20, 1987 evening meeting with Falkus, Bob Taylor and I wandered along the bank of Money's Run. The pool below the confluence with the Ash was ideal fly water.

It was a beautiful, warm Indian summer day and the river flowed crystal clear at 60 F. Nice to be out but the warm water and bright day were trying fishing conditions. Part of the river by the right bank was shaded by tall evergreens perched on the steep embankment and I thought by wading deep I might be able to reach the shaded portion of the river. I had strung up my favourite two-fisted, 12-foot Bruce & Walker rod with a floating line and because the water was so warm I knew a steelhead might rise to a large fly but after its look-see would most likely refuse it. I tied on

my smallest low-water pattern, a number-10 sparsely dressed, lowwater-style fly I simply call Black. Like the General had done years before, with little room to backcast I worked the pool Spey-casting a long line into the shaded portion of the river. On my first pass through I had a rise and hooked into a good summer-run. After a lively battle I slid the hook from a typical Stamp River summer-run steelhead 28 inches long.

It pleases me no end when I catch fish from hallowed waters. On this day I took that summer-run steelhead using the floating (greased) line, a sparsely dressed fly and Spey-casting a doublehanded rod using that British Atlantic salmon technique introduced to British Columbia nearly 50 years earlier by Rod Haig-Brown and General Money. I can't get much more connected to my fly-fishing roots than that.

References

Auger, F. S. "General Money" *Northwest Sportsman,* April May issue (1974): 5, 6, 8.

Dymond, J. R. *The Trout and Other Game Fishes of British Columbia.* Ottawa: Department of Fisheries, 1932.

Egan, Van Gorman. "The General's River, Another Look" *British Columbia Sport Fishing,* Vol. 12, 1 (1993): 32-36.

___. "A Legacy of the River Spey" *British Columbia Sport Fishing,* Vol. 16, 1 (1997): 26-29.

Straight, Lee. *100 Steelhead Streams.* Vancouver: The Sun Publishing Company, 1956 revised edition.

Sorenson, Roy. "Steelheading on the Stamp River" BCFFF *Fly Lines,* Issue 46 (1991): 9-10.

Williams, A. Bryan. *Rod and Creel in British Columbia.* Vancouver: Progress Publishing Company, 1919.

___. *Fish and Game in British Columbia.* Vancouver: Sun Directories Ltd., 1935.

CHAPTER 12

The Skeena and Its Famous Tributaries

The First Nation's people have been fishing the Skeena and its tributaries since time immemorial.

MONSTERS! IT'S NOT THE GHOST AND GOBLIN MONSTERS of Halloween to which I refer, but those magnificent wild summer-run steelhead lurking in waters of the Skeena, Kitsumkalum, Zymoetz, Kispiox, Bulkley, Morice, Sustut, Suskwa and Babine rivers. Those monster fish that get the fly-fisher's blood a-boiling.

In the foyer of Region 6 provincial fisheries branch offices in Smithers are two male summer-run steelhead. Both are near 44 inches long, both have girths of 26 inches or greater and both are 40-pounders. One was in its 9th year, returning for its second spawning. The other was, amazingly, in its 13th year, returning on its fourth spawning run. Unfortunately, on August 1, 1998, both fell victim to the Tyee Gillnet Test Fishery conducted in the lower reaches of the Skeena. Monsters, yes, but good ones deserving a better fate.

That the Skeena system is well known for its large chinook and steelhead there is no doubt. The record B.C. sport-caught chinook of 92 pounds taken in 1959—as well as many of the Province's largest steelhead, and world records at that—have come from its waters.

For well over a century, fishermen have searched the Skeena's waters for sport. Early adventurers exploring Canadian Pacific Railway (CPR) routes through the Northern valleys journeyed into the wilderness and tried their hand at fishing. While on a CPR northern route expedition, Rev. Daniel. M. Gordon is one of the first to mention fly-fishing the Skeena's tributaries. His 1880 book *Mountain and Prairie: A Journey from Victoria to Winnipeg Via the Peace River Pass* is an account of his travels. J. Turner-Turner also made the journey up the Skeena, through Babine Lake then into the Fraser watershed and recorded his adventures in *Three Year's Hunting and Trapping in America and the Great North-West* (1888). It took most of September for Turner-Turner's party to pole their way from the settlement at Metlakatla on the ocean up the

Skeena to the Forks at Old Hazelton. Turner-Turner intended to winter at Kispiox, but the Natives, fearing he was a land surveyor and there to take their land, wouldn't allow it. He returned to the Forks and built a cabin on the point of land bordered by the Skeena and Bulkley rivers, his home until he continued his journey the following June.

During the September journey up the Skeena, he noticed the salmon's abundance and tried spoon, Devon minnow and fly but could not entice them to take. He didn't catch any salmon, he did catch a fish he referred to as a sea-trout. He did not mention the size of the trout, they could have been cutthroat or even small summer-run steelhead. It's unfortunate that he didn't winter at the Kispiox. Perhaps Turner-Turner might have caught some of the large Kispiox summer-run steelhead. What adventures those early trips into the wilderness must have been!

In *Rod & Creel in British Columbia* (1919), A. Bryan Williams provides hints of the Skeena's great steelhead and trout fishing:

> *The line of the Grand Trunk Pacific follows the Skeena River for some hundred and fifty miles, and here and there along the line there are splendid streams for fishing. The majority of these streams have been hardly fished, as there is no accommodation in their vicinity, but they nearly all have lots of steelheads in them in winter and early spring; they are all affected by freshets as soon as the snow begins to melt and are unfishable most of May and June and some of them in July also. Those that run out of lakes such as the Kitsumkalum and Lakelse are nearly always clear and afford fishing for a longer period...*
>
> *The trout fishing along this line is the best there is in this Province...The Skeena itself is a big, swift river, principally noted for its great commercial salmon fishing...There are, however, numerous streams running into it, which afford magnificent steelhead, rainbow and Dolly Varden fishing, amongst which may be specially mentioned the Copper River, a few miles below Kitselas, and the Lakelse a mile or so below the Little Canyon. At present the only way to fish any of these streams is by camping out...Throughout the greater part of the country along this line, July, August and early September are the best months for fly-fishing. Among the flies commonly used may be mentioned the March Brown, Coachman, Royal Coachman, Cowichan Coachman, Black Gnat, Grouse & Claret, Parmachene Belle and Red and Brown Hackles and Professor.* (p. 137-138)

When Williams wrote these statements about the good trout fishing, steelhead were considered to be winter and spring fish. On those rivers that had summer-run steelhead, the fish were often referred to as rainbow trout. Also, the railway ran though parts of the Fraser watershed and some of its streams had good rainbow trout fly-fishing. Williams makes no distinction between a rainbow trout caught in the upper Skeena tributaries and those caught in the Nechako or Stellaco rivers. Williams must have only visited the Kitsumkalem River during the cold months for him to make the

statement that that river ran clear most of the time. This river runs opaque with glacial silt once the freshet begins and remains so until the frosts of fall.

Local fishermen were few, and those fishermen venturing into the north country in search of sport with rod and reel through the first half of the 20th Century found good sport. But distance and difficulty accessing the rivers were prime obstacles. World War I, the Great Depression and World War II kept all but the wealthy away as well.

Until it was eclipsed in 1944 by Len Hester's 26-pound summer-run from the Capilano, a 23 1/2 pound steelhead taken in the early 1920s from an unnamed Skeena tributary held the record for years as B.C.'s largest steelhead. After the First World War, Bryan Williams was dismissed as the Provincial Game Warden "due

The author christened his McVey-built bamboo rod with this 35-inch Bulkley River male, it too rose in cold water.

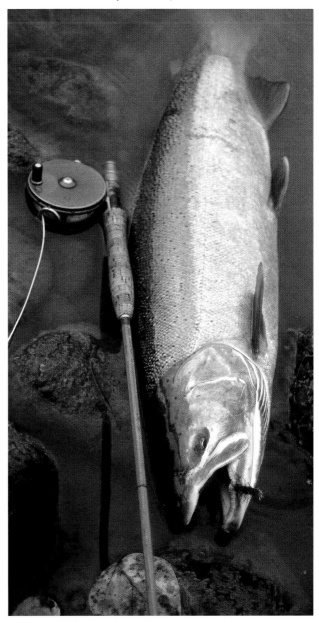

to the rigid economy." Before and after his government service, Williams spent a number of years hunting, trapping and guiding hunters and fishermen in the Skeena watershed. In *Game Trails in British Columbia* (1925), he took an experienced fisher on a first-time steelheading trip that ended with the capture of that 23 1/2-pound fish. He says:

> Before the yarn is continued it might be as well to explain that these steelheads are enormous sea trout which run anywhere from 5 to 25 lb. in weight. An average fish would go about 9 lb.; a 15-lb. fish is considered a very big one, and though it has been my good fortune to land several hundred of them, not more than three or four of my fish would go 17 lb. Therefore to kill one of 12 lb. was pretty lucky for a first attempt...
>
> When he began to fish it was at once noticeable that he was doing far better work than at any time previously; probably the fish he had already caught had inspired him with confidence. Anyway, he was not only reaching the "lie" of the fish, but was soon fast in one, and, though it did not break water immediately as they usually do, there was no room for doubt about it being a heavy one; moreover, its actions were such that it was also evident that it was a game fish and that he had a battle royal on his hands.
>
> How long he played that fish I cannot tell you. Such a thing as looking at my watch was out of the question. I was too intent on the struggle, far too busy hoping it was well hooked and that he would land it, far too busy racing first up stream and then down as the fish took him from one stretch of water to another. Once there were a few sickening moments when, after a mad rush up stream, it came down again like a streak of lightning, and a slack line made it appear that the fish had got off. Then, later on, when the fish had gone on and on down stream until we were nearly half a mile below where it had been hooked and we had reached the limit we could go without a boat, we had another agony of suspense. For a time that fish just hung on the edge of some rapids, and it took every ounce of strength the rod and tackle would stand to hold it from getting in to them. Nothing could have saved a smash had it done so. Even after that, when the fish gradually worked upstream a little, it was more nerve wracking than ever, as it then broke water several times and allowed us to see what a prize it would be...But game as that splendid fish was its endurance could not last for ever; shorter and shorter were its runs, until at last it was brought well in, and then, after making a half-roll over when about to make another effort, the gaff went home. and out on to the bank it came at last. The weight was an ounce or two over 19 lb.
>
> You might think that such good luck was enough for any one man, but there was even more to come. Later on he landed a steelhead that weighed 23 1/2

> lb., which is, as far as my knowledge goes, a record for a rod-caught fish. This fish, however, was not in such perfect condition nor did it put up an Homeric struggle, as, after making one fairly long run, it sulked most of the time. (pp. 328-330)

Those fish Williams' client landed were caught spinning, the method of choice for most people fishing rivers in the province. Fly-fishing for steelhead, trout and salmon was practiced by some.

In *Rod & Creel in British Columbia*, Williams was very positive about Skeena fishing opportunities, but in his follow up 1935 book, *Fish and Game in British Columbia*, of all the now-famous Skeena and her tributaries, he recommends only two pools on the Bulkley. One at the junction of the Telkwa and Bulkley rivers called the Bulkley Pool he says is worth fly-fishing:

This beauty rose from the depths in 40 F. water to take a Woolly Bear Bomber.

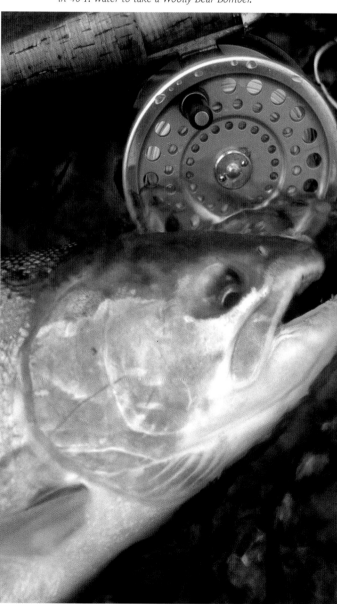

Kaili Clay with mother Kathy and Katari Clay walking upriver.

Spring and Cohoe salmon and steelhead are caught here, and some days limit bags are obtained. Steelhead run up to 10 lbs., and salmon up to 20 lbs. Experts have success with fly...(p. 76)

Admittedly, fly-fishers were few in those days. After World War II sportsmen started venturing into the North country in search of sport and in the early 1950s steelhead catches from the Skeena and Kispiox would bring world-wide attention to the area. In the October 1953 issue of *Northwest Sportsman* magazine, there is a picture of a man holding a large steelhead. The caption: "*World Record Steelhead is this 30-lb. 8-oz. fish caught September 6th, 1953, by Jeff Wilson of Hazelton, B.C. at the mouth of the Kispiox River where it meets the Skeena....*" World-record fever brought many anglers to the banks of the Kispiox, but many came to fish other tributaries as well. The first record I have come across naming local and American steelhead fly-fishers and referring to a large steelhead from the Skeena system taken on the fly appeared on page 6 and 7 in the January, 1955 issue of *Northwest Sportsman*. In the article titled "Steelhead Grow Big," publisher Jim Railton writes:

On our way north we met at Burns Lake a couple of keen steelheaders, Jeff Woodall and Cliff Cuningham, who fish these steelies with a fly. In fact this Woodall chap ties all his own patterns and his pet river is the Morice...Two days before I reached Hazelton, Jeff Wilson of Hazelton had caught a 30 1/2 pounder...

Naturally the publicity about such trophy fish by outdoor writers, press services of the transportation companies, attracted the attention of anglers interested to catch such fish. A party of anglers from Bakersfield, California visits this north-central area of B.C. every year. One of the party, Dr. Carl Moore, on his return home passing through Vancouver, called to

say one of their party took a steelhead on the fly that weighed 28 pounds.

By the early 1950s, fly-fishing for steelhead had its disciples. They were not many, but they persevered searching the more easily accessible rivers and runs with the fly. Some were rewarded. fly-fishing, now the method of choice by the majority of anglers on most Skeena tributaries, developed slowly.

John Fennelly, an American fly-fisher, was one of, if not, the first to document the fly-fishing sport he found on Skeena tributaries. Making his first trip in 1951, Fennelly learned from a fishing friend who received the information from expert dry-fly fisherman Mr. Kilpatrick of Burns Lake, that good steelhead fishing can be found on the Morice and Bulkley rivers. About the area and its fly-fishing in "Steelheading the Morice" article in *Northwest Sportsman* July 1956, issue, Fennelly says:

Except for a few small villages along the line of the Canadian National Railway [formerly the Grand Trunk Pacific] *the whole watershed is still a wild and rugged country. Planes and roads are now making much of the area accessible to hunters and fishermen, but as recently as World War II most of it was virgin wilderness visited only by trappers and Indians.*

During four separate visits to this country between 1951 and 1955 I pursued the elusive steelhead trout with a fly rod throughout a large part of the Skeena watershed...

My first steelhead were taken on the upper Morice about five miles below the outlet of the lake in August, 1953. I was fishing alone in a large pool while my guide Barry Grainger sat on the bank with his 30.06 rifle across his knees as protection from grizzlies...

Wading well out into the stream, I was casting a

dry fly into the edge of the current which swept in a semi-circle around the quiet water of the pool before emptying out into a long rapid below. The fly was a No. 12 Royal Wulff on a 2x nine foot leader. My rod was a 4 1/2 ounce nine foot Leonard and my reel was a small one, with only sixty yards of backing behind the fly line.

On my casts across the large pool my dry fly would float beautifully around the arc of the semi-circle and be pulled under briefly by the drag of the line at the foot of the pool. Just as the fly started to drag across the current on one of these casts, I had a heavy strike and found myself fast to what I thought was a large rainbow. Despite his acrobatics I managed to work him back into the quieter water of the pool and soon had him on the beach. Because my de-liar registered just over 5 pounds, I decided to keep him as the largest rainbow I had landed on the river.

Later in the article, after he spent a few days fishing the Bulkley

Karl Mausser with his 33-pound world record from the Kispiox River.

COURTESY KARL MAUSSER

at Houston during his 1954 trip, Fennelly tells the story of a large fish lost which he hooked dapping in the lower Bulkley:

I then moved downstream and fished three days at various spots on the lower Bulkley. Strangely enough, the only reaction I had from a steelhead came with a dry fly. I was fishing one morning in a huge pool just below a falls in the Bulkley at the Indian village of Old Hazelton. The whole pool was boiling with fish, mostly salmon, as they worked their way slowly up the fish ladder at the side of the falls.

After trying various wet flies without success for more than two hours. I shifted to a large dry squirrel tail fly on a No. 8 hook, made by Pat Barnes of West Yellowstone and known as a "Sofa Pillow." It had proved excellent in attracting steelhead on the Upper Morice. I was standing on a large boulder at the edge of the pool, and started idly dapping the "Sofa Pillow" on the water about 10 feet below me. Almost at once the fly was sucked quietly under the surface and I struck, thinking I had hooked a small fish.

Two seconds later, an enormous steelhead came straight up out of the water just below me. He was so close I could see every mark on his glistening body. With dark green on his massive back and upper sides he was pure silver underneath, and no sign of rainbow coloration anywhere....Even allowing for fevered imagination of an excited fisherman, the fish must have weighed 20 pounds.

After two tremendous leaps the big fish started on a run straight across the pool which was at least two hundred yards wide at this point. I applied as much pressure as I dared and suddenly felt the line go slack. I reeled in, and the tell-tale curl at the end of leader showed clearly the pull-out of the fly from the faulty knot.

Dry-fly fishing for steelhead had been practiced for at least a couple of decades on the Capilano River, but this passage was the first written that mentioned dry-fly use on the Skeena system. In the part where Fennelly tells of the capture of his first Morice steelhead, he mentions that the steelhead took the dry fly as it started to drag. Some Skeena steelhead, Morice ones in particular, will take the naturally drifted dry fly, but far more are taken on a fly brought across the surface in tension causing a wake. Fennelly was the first to record the response of Skeena-system steelhead to a dragged fly. Probably unintentionally, he introduced the ever-so-popular waked-fly technique to the Skeena. Fennelly and friends introduced the Sofa Pillow to the Morice and it remains a favourite for that river.

Fennelly fished the Kispiox for the first time in 1955. About that river and the anglers searching for that elusive record steelhead, he says:

Unfortunately, the water was high and fairly muddy from heavy rains and crawling with spin fishermen from all parts of North America. Most of them has been attracted to the river by a story reporting two world record steelhead from the Kispiox in the fall of

RAY MAKOWICHUK

Helge Byman was the steelhead fly-fishing ambassador on the Morice.

1954, 36 and 33 pounds. In all, six of the ten largest steelhead recorded in 1954 had come from the Kispiox…I landed just one steelhead of fifteen pounds and lost two others…Although we did not see the fish, we were told that the Indians had netted a 41 pounder near their village at the mouth of the river.

Field & Stream statistics for 1955 show an even more amazing record for the Kispiox. The six largest steelhead landed anywhere in 1955 on spinning tackle were taken from the Kispiox. These ran from 33 to 26 pounds. The three largest steelhead taken on flies also came from the Kispiox and ran from 29 to 26 pounds. Incidentally, my unreported 15 pounder was the same as the tenth largest fish taken on flies.

Much of Fennelly's early Skeena system fly-fishing adventures, as well as later exploits, are recorded in his classic, *Steelhead Paradise* (1963).

The publicity emanating from the Kispiox, mostly generated by the *Field & Stream* contests, and especially so after Ken McLeod took a 29-pound 2-ounce, world-record steelhead on the fly in 1955. McLeod's fish was later eclipsed by Karl Mausser's 33-pound steelhead in 1962. Those large fish made that river the destination of many fly-fishers. It remains so to this day.

Those early fly-fishers provided the roots from which a lasting summer-run steelhead fly-fishing tradition has developed on many of the famous Skeena rivers. Fly-fishing is now the method of choice for most fishermen wandering the banks of the Morice, Bulkley,

Kispiox, Babine, Sustut, Copper, and the Skeena. Some fly-fishers became the sport's ambassadors and deserve special recognition.

The Morice his river, Helge Byman was one such angler. Byman's family moved to Houston in 1926 when Helge was 15 years old. He went through the usual growing pains that many steelheaders experience. But according to reports from those who knew him well, he switched to fly-fishing some time between the late 1940s and early 1950s. He never looked back. During the early years steelhead fly-fishers struggled to fish deep and Byman's flies, dressed on large heavy hooks, are testimonials to that philosophy. Fennelly too was told that if you fished the Bulkley down near Houston you must fish deep. Some still suscribe to that theory.

In the late 1960s, Byman adopted and used almost exclusively the floating line with either a wet fly or a dry fly. The Billy Goat and Thompson runs on the Morice and the Propeller Run and Helge's Hole on the Bulkley were his favourite dry-fly waters. The Sofa Pillow, introduced to the Morice by John Fennelly and his fly-fishing companions in the 1950s, and the Black Bi-visible, recommended by A. Bryan Williams in *Fish and Game in British Columbia* (1935), "as being very important" for British Columbia dry-fly fishing, were Helge's favourite dry flies. Both remain Ray Makowichuk's favourites for dry-fly and waked-fly work on the Morice and upper Bulkley rivers.

On the Morice, Byman was fly-fishing's ambassador and fly-fishers venturing into Houston would stop by his Shell garage for information on the fishing and river conditions, or to be guided by him.

In the early 1970s, the Houston access to a favourite fishing and camping spot on the Morice was to be blocked by the forest company with the timber rights. Byman was instrumental in obtaining a new access at By-Mac, named by Karl Mausser by combining

Mist rising from the river and snow-capped mountains in the background greet fly-fishers drifting the Bulkley.

parts of two last names, Byman and MacKay. Max MacKay, the Houston postmaster, was Helge's fishing partner for a number of years. Byman passed away on August 2, 1990, but one of his legacies is the By-Mac campsite, probably one of the most well known and famous camping sites on the Skeena watershed. Learned from his mentor Helge Byman, Ray Makowichuk carries on the fly-fishing traditions and operates his fall steelhead guiding operation from By-Mac.

The world records of the early 1950s from the Kispiox brought attention to the area and fly-fishers from below the 49th parallel flocked to the Kispiox, Morice and Bulkley rivers. Most of British Columbia's early steelhead fly-fishing methods were based on British fly-fishing techniques brought to British Columbia by men like General Noel Money, Roderick Haig-Brown and Tommy Brayshaw. The influx of Americans into Skeena Country during the 1950s and 1960s had a profound influence on that area's fly-fishing. Short rods, shooting heads and American flies dominated the fishery.

Members of the Totem Flyfishers in Vancouver and Haig-Brown Flyfishers in Victoria reintroduced the double-handed rods (called Spey rods in the USA), Spey casting, and introduced the looping of sinking sections of line to a double-taper floater to steelhead fly-fishing in the early 1980s on the Dean and Thompson rivers.

When the two-handed rods made their comeback—they were standard fare on British Columbia rivers in the first half of the 20th century—the overhead cast was the norm. I remember well the day in 1984 that I looped a 16-foot-long home-made 185-grain sink-tip to the end of the double-taper fly line and sent that tip sailing about 75 feet over the water with a single Spey cast. I hooked seven steelhead that day using that combination of line, Spey cast and sunk-fly technique. I had about four tips of different densities and lengths at that time. I remember the phone calls to Bruce & Walker in England after others in the Totem Flyfishers had taken up Spey casting with sink-tips looped onto the end of their floating lines and were breaking rods. Tape the joints and use floating lines only was their advice after stating that they had never heard of anyone using that technique. Their rods were not designed for Spey casting with a sink-tip attached to a floating line, let alone sink-tips that were so heavy.

The popularity of the double-handed fly rods spread throughout the fly-fishing community into Washington State and Skeena Country in the late 1980s. Denise Maxwell, former Women's World Flycasting Champion for distance and accuracy and Mike Maxwell have been instrumental in promoting the double-handers on the Bulkley River. Mike, a former British Army soldier with his drill-sergeant approach to teaching, had produced videos and written books on Spey casting that have helped many fly-fishers learn the art and craft of double-handed-rod fly-fishing. With the re-introduction of two-fisted rods, steelhead fly-fishing is a blend of American, British and British Columbian fly-fishing styles, techniques, flies, and other equipment.

Through the 1950s and early '60s a number of American fly-fishers came to the Skeena and had lasting influences. Jack Horner, famous Californian fly tyer, visited the Kispiox in 1954 and introduced flies such as the Horner Shrimp, Burlap, Thor, Polar Shrimp and Comet. George and Ken McLeod from Washington State came

in 1955, introducing the Skykomish Sunrise, Purple Peril and later in 1962 the McLeod Ugly to the Kispiox. The McLeods took many *Field & Stream* prize-winning fish, topped by Ken's 29-pound 2-ounce world record taken on the Skykomish Sunrise in 1955.

In 1957, Karl Mausser journeyed north from his California home and fished the Kispiox River for the first time. Mausser came north in May and fished trout in the Babine. In August he moved to the Morice then moved to the Kispiox in early October for the remainder of his stay. He will be remembered in the world of steelhead fly-fishing for his 33-pound, fly-caught world record. A fixture on the Morice, Bulkley and Kispiox for many decades, he named many of the pools. One Kispiox run favoured by Karl bears his name. On September 4, 2000, Mausser's family and many of his angling friends celebrated Karl's life as a fly-fisher by depositing his ashes in the Morice River at By-Mac. About his world-record 33-pound steelhead and catch and release, in a January, 1989 letter to me Karl wrote that it:

> was 42 1/2" long and had a 24" girth—no one was with me at the time. It was formally weighed in [at] the back of Sargent's store in Old Hazelton and was witnessed by Polly Sargent and Drew Wookey. The fish weighed a bit more than 33 lbs. but, on a beef quarter balance scale the notches on the bar are at 8 oz. intervals or were at that time...
>
> I wrote a factual account that night at Wookey's camp and a few years later a chap named Trey Combs

A fly-fisher casting his line onto a smaller Skeena tributary.

Fly-fishing champion, Rob Brown and Pawsome.

was writing a steelhead book and contacted me and I let him use my story. It's there if you want it.

Part of the unpublished happenings are: I'd made the line myself based on a happening off Painter's resort some years before. And the fly which it took was something like a Skykomish and since I'd lost several to some sort of obstruction I felt when I tied it on having just lost another; that I didn't give a hoot if I lost it or not. Well the rest is history.

The fish was easy to capture. Maybe 10 minutes. One big problem; no gravel bar but it was so deep it [the fish] *stranded on a mound of rubble close to the bank and I was able to jam my whole hand in the gill and out the mouth.*

Of course these were the days with a 3 fish limit per day, nine in possession and catch and release wasn't even considered. We did release a lot but it wasn't a religion as it is today. I suggested to this [classified water and angling guide] *task force that they consider making the Skeena drainage entirely catch and release, all species!!!*

Through the 1960s others came to try to better first McLeod's then Mausser's record. With stars in his eyes and a lot of desire in his heart, a youthful Jim Adams of Berkeley, California made his

first trip in 1960. With four placing *Field & Stream* winners in the next few years, Jim, now a globe-trotting fly-fisherman, antiquarian book and used collector tackle dealer told me in September 2000 about some of the early Kispiox regulars such as the McLeods, Mausser and Forrest Powell. When Adams and Mausser were taking 30 to 50 steelhead a month from the Kispiox, Powell was catching considerably more fish. His secret was to rush from pool to pool and rip a Scientific Anglers "fisherman" or Wet Cel 1 through the water with a fast jerky retrieve. The big bucks in the Kispiox preferred a fly fished deep and slow and Powell's technique, although productive, was selective for female steelhead.

Bob Clay's youngest teen-aged daughter Kaili greeted me as I came into the yard. Her father and mother were down on the river fishing, which Kaili had fished earlier in the morning, taking her first-ever steelhead on the fly. A small 22-inch fish, not one to go into Kispiox record books, but after the first she took her second, a much better fish of about 10 pounds. First fish are precious, providing lasting memories. My only regret was that I wasn't there earlier to record Kaili's fish on film.

Bob Clay came to Kispiox Valley in the '70s, loved the valley and its fish and stayed eventually building a beautiful house overlooking the Upper Upper Potato Patch Pool. A guide on the river for years, he knows the river intimately. The day I arrived happened to be a day off from guiding for Bob and he suggested we try the river. But before he could fish he had to go to Hazelton and do some chores. He pointed me to the river saying that he would join me later.

Over the years when I saw Clay at Steelhead Society meetings or as he drifted with John Baigent and visited the Totems' camp on the Dean, Bob has extended numerous invitations to come fish the Kispiox. Years had lapsed since I had thrown a line in this famous river and I eagerly approached the top of the run. Spey-casting about 70 to 80 feet of line I sent the number-two Black General Practitioner on the end of my sink tip over the water and worked my way a pace or two at a time down the run. A fishy pool from which the Clay family had hooked half a dozen fish earlier, I was not surprised when my line stopped in mid-drift and I felt something solid when I stuck. Sometimes steelhead are slow to react, but from experience I knew it was a fish and not bottom. After an exciting struggle I slid a 31-inch female into shallow water. I had fished only 10 minutes. Bob joined me a little later and took a fish around 32 inches on his new experimental, Clay-built, double-handed bamboo rod.

Farm chores took Clay away from the river and again I was left to myself. The Kispiox was good to me that afternoon with six steelhead hooked and three landed. Sometimes luck plays a part when fishing. I had come from the Bulkley that morning more to see the river and Bob, but found excellent sport.

The early fly-fishers that fished the rivers around Hazelton, Smithers and Houston laid a solid fly-fishing foundation, which was built on through the late 1960s, '70s and '80s by Jerry Wintle, Harry Lemire, Martin Tolley, Mike and Denise Maxwell, Ray Makowichuk and many others.

Fly-fishing for the summer-runs on the glacial-fed Zymoetz (Copper) and Kitsumkalem rivers down near Terrace didn't have as many practitioners and didn't develop as quickly as on the clearer upper Skeena tributaries. Spin, spoon and float fishing were the favoured methods on these water. Starting around the mid-1950s, perhaps earlier, it did have a few fur-and-feather tossers who persisted, such as Fred Hall, Findlay Ferguson and Ted Rawlins.

Hall, a Lakelse trout fly-fisher, predates Ferguson and Rawlins. Findlay was converted to the fly by Rawlins back in the 1950s. He preferred the cutthroat river fishing on the Lower Skeena and tributaries, was one of the first to adopt the floating line—fishing it

Few coho felt the sting of a fly-fisher's hook, the commercial fleet had fished the coho to near extinction.

exclusively—and was one of, if not, the first to use black patterns for steelhead on the Lower Skeena tributaries.

Born on Vancouver Island in the fishy community of Parksville, Ted Rawlins learned to fly-fish as a boy on those streams around his hometown. Work at Columbia Cellulose brought him to Terrace in 1955 where he retired as a foreman in the late 1960s. He fly-fished the Copper, Kalum, Lakelse and Skeena for anything that swam but preferred steelhead and pursued them religiously with his Red and Polar fly. He influenced others to take up the fly. As the local fly-fishing expert, Rawlins was delegated the pleasant task of taking company dignitaries fishing on their visits to the area. Arthritis caused Ted to return to Vancouver Island after he retired. Some of the fish he caught from the Kalum and Copper were contenders in *Field & Stream* contests. That Rawlins had a lasting influence is evident. Three decades later, two pools—Rawlins Run on the Copper and Rawlins Riffle on the Kalum—bear his name.

That Hall, Rawlins and Ferguson were the Terrace area's fly-fishing pioneers, there is little doubt. However, fly-fishing needs champions and they got a master when Rob Brown moved to Terrace and took up the sport. In the mid-1970s Robert Brown, an enthusiastic, fresh-out-of-university teacher moved to South Hazelton where he remained for one year. During that year Brown spent many a day pursuing cutthroat in ponds and lakes. He became a steelheader the next year when he moved to Terrace, located about 100 miles upstream of Prince Rupert on the Skeena River. Already an ardent fisher, Brown found the waters of the Skeena tributaries—Copper, Lakelse, Kitsumkalem, and others—around his new hometown well stocked with wild steelhead. Soon Rob was looking for more aesthetically pleasing ways of catching these magnificent fish.

A trip to the local co-op department store produced a fly outfit that turned out to be totally inadequate for steelhead fly-fishing. The search for suitable fly gear took him to a small shop located on Highway 16 upstream of Terrace. He was served by three people—a tall one, professorial-looking, sporting a full beard and pipe, the other with short dark curly hair, and a woman. The tall fellow picked out an outfit and advised Rob about flies and lines and set up the equipment. Later, Rob got to know all three people very well. The shorter curly-haired man and the lady were Jim and Shirley Culp, the proprietors of the store. The professorial-looking gent was Peter Broomhall of the Totem Flyfishers and an annual visitor to the Terrace area.

Influenced by this chance encounter with Broomhall and his rapture with fly-fishing, Rob hung up his Silex gear. He was soon challenging steelhead on the fly and acting as an inspiration to a small group of like-minded anglers.

In those early years Rob and a small group of dedicated Terrace-area fly-fishers produced local fly patterns based on old favourites. However, it is the innovative, descriptive names, such as Tankallow, Lakelse Locomotive, Hassaler, Pink Dynk, A Touch of Blue, Crepescule, Riffle Cricket, Shirley's Fancy, Skinny Skunk, Polar Peril, Trick or Treat and Rob's latest, the Zymosedge, that Brown gave to these local fly patterns, that shows a man engulfed in fly-fishing lore.

It was shortly after Bob Garrett and Jim Culp founded the Northwest Chapter with Gene Llewellyn and Dave Dams that

Brown became involved in the Steelhead Society of B.C., locally and province-wide. Brown was one of the key members of the Northwest Branch and acted as chair of the Society's Skeena Valley-based but world-wide supported Wild Steelhead Campaign. Through his involvement in the Steelhead Society, the British Columbia Federation of Fly Fishers and as a journalist, representatives of industry and government bent on destroying fish habitat and over-exploiting salmon and steelhead runs have felt the sting of Brown's bite, both verbally and in print on many issues, locally and province-wide.

It is Rob Brown's skill as a writer that brings him distinction within the fly-fishing fraternity. He has a way with words that makes him stand out from other fly-fishing writers and outdoor columnists. Since the late 1980s, Rob writes under his Skeena Angler by-line weekly columns on a variety of environmental, conservation and fishing issues in the *Terrace Standard*. Besides his weekly column, Rob has written articles for *Field & Stream, Fly Rod and Reel, BC Outdoors, Steelhead Fly Fishing Journal, The Vancouver Sun* and *The Interior News* and he has written one book, *Steelhead River Journal: Skeena*. Furthermore, as the local fly tying and fly-fishing teacher, he has been and continues to be instrumental in persuading many to become fly-fishers.

The Copper and its magnificent runs of wild, free-rising, summer-run steelhead draws fly-fishers from around the globe. Partly through Brown's tutelage, Terrace has a growing core of fly-fishers. More and more steelhead, cutthroat and salmon on the Copper, Kalum, and Lakelse as well as other Lower Skeena tributaries and the mainstem river, are succumbing to fur-and-feather enticements.

Bob Clay came, saw, loved and settled in the Kispiox Valley in the 1970s.

"Rob, I would like to give the Clore a try today," I said. "I'd like that, it's been about 10 years since I fished it," he replied.

Rob's dog Pawsome lead the way through the game trail that would put us above the canyon. In some places, the path was fit only for a mountain goat. But this is not the first time I have bushwacked with Rob to go fishing. The Clore was flowing with maybe two feet of visibility.

We climbed down the canyon wall at the head of the dump in to the canyon pool. It looked fishy and on my first cast I took a 32-inch female steelhead. We found no others in that piece of water. Acting like mountain goats again, we clung and scrambled along the rock wall that blocked upstream waters, cautiously climbing an additional rock bluff so we were sure we could traverse a fast-flowing, turbulent branch of the river.

The right bank water on the next pool looked good, but we were on the left bank. A challenging wade chest high near the right bank, it was classic water and we were sure it was a good steelhead lie. Three fish came to our flies in the next hour with Rob christening his new 6-weight Grantham bamboo rod. The 32-inch fish was a good one for the Clore and it certainly put the Grantham rod to the test. It is nice to fish with well-made tools. Other pools and runs produced nothing and we began retracing the way down river.

We thought we might avoid a difficult climb by wading the fast-flowing branch a little lower. Rob was almost at the rock ledge we

were aiming for when he turned, looked at me and said something. I can't remember what he said but in an instant his footing gave way and he was floundering in water over his head. I scurried to the tip of the gravel bar where the branch joined the mainstem and wading as far as I could extended my wading staff. It fell six inches short of Rob's grasping hand as the main current pulled him away from me.

Aghast, I watched him struggle to swim and float in the 46-degree water. His head went under once as he struggled to the surface and said, "I can't fight it, I am going all the way through." I was relieved when he hit ground in shallow water at the end of a rock wall. It took me at least 10 minutes to get around the wall down to Rob. Still kneeling in the water from the cold water sapping his strength, he couldn't get up without help. A hearty soul, he emptied the water from his waders, wrung out his socks and we headed down river. The hike back to the truck helped Rob recover from the icy exposure. I am thankful he is okay and I will enjoy days to come fishing with a good friend. Discarded by Rob, his new bamboo rod, old Hardy St. George reel and a Bob Taylor-made wading staff were the only victims to the harrowing life-threatening experience.

The Skeena's salmon runs sustained the First Nations for millennia. In the early 1800s, explorers and fur traders of the Northwest

Company came and later, after they bought the Northwest Company, the Hudson Bay Company established trading posts in the Skeena watershed, partly because a reliable supply of salmon could be bartered from the Natives. Soon the silver fish attracted others intent on exploiting the riches of the river and, in 1878, the first fish cannery opened at the mouth of the Skeena. Many more followed and when the industry was at its peak, 18 canneries operated on the lower river. With the coming of an ever-increasingly efficient fishing fleet, steelhead—always an incidental catch of the fleet—were caught in a struggle to survive.

In the first half of the century there were few sport fishers. After the commercial fishing industry neutralized the Native fisheries, the lower river netters pretty well had the river and the fish to themselves. First Nations people of the Skeena River system

Rob Brown, The Skeena Angler,
chaired the Wild Steelhead Campaign.

Ray Makowichuk's ties of the Black Bi-Visible and Sofa Pillow.

traded fish and oolichan grease with other tribes, developed a culture based on the salmon and were the first commercial fishermen. In the early 1900s, reports of large Native catches of sockeye at Babine Lake outraged the commercial fishing industry. Using their considerable political influence, the cannery owners had laws passed which eliminated the Natives' selective weirs, traps and dip netting. At places like Moricetown Falls on the Bulkley River, First Nations people were forced to change from the efficient and selective methods to the destructive non-selective gaff fishery. Like the commercial netters at the mouth of the river the Natives were forced to use non-selective gillnets for their inland fisheries.

The inland Native fisheries were selective. The new laws allowed Natives to fish for sustenance, but bartering fish with others was outlawed. Those laws proclaimed by the stroke of a pen undermined the Native economy and destroyed a culture that had developed over many centuries.

After World War II, as access became easier and sportsmen had more time, they came in dribbles at first, then lured by reports in *Field & Stream* about world-record fish from the Kispiox and good catches in other tributaries, they came in ever-increasing numbers. The Skeena started to receive international attention. When anglers first come into a lightly fished area often the resulting good catches attract others. The Skeena and its tributaries became the destination for many sport fishers attracted by big fish and generous limits. From 1946 into the seventies, anglers could kill three steelhead a day and take home three days' possession limit, along with what they consumed during their stay. Through the 1970s into the late 1980s, daily limits were reduced from three to two to one fish a day, and from three to two days' possession limit. In the 1970s a yearly limit of 40 steelhead was imposed and this steadily declined through the 1980s until it was only one a year. In 1989 catch-and-release was imposed for the mainstem Skeena and tributaries above Cedarvale.

The sportfishing season was long. Most Skeena summer-run steelhead enter fresh water on their spawning migration through July, August and September. By early winter they have settled into holding pools, yet until the mid-eighties anglers continued to fish and kill them through the winter months, weather permitting. Regional Fisheries biologist and steelhead champion, Bob Hooton, closed the fishing for summer-run steelhead streams on December 31. He was determined that those fish surviving the commercial, Native and sport fisheries would not be harassed as they matured and depleted stores of body fat into roe or milt and that they would survive for the late-spring spawning.

More often than not, the few anglers who practiced some form of catch and release in the 1950s through the 1970s did so because the steelhead were too small. Indeed, they were searching for big steelhead to kill and, if that big dead steelhead was a world record or *Field & Stream* contender, perhaps glory. Catch-and-release did not have the large following it has today. With such generous

Pete Pedersen of Parksville has been
haunting the Skeena and tributaries for nearly 30 years.

limits, sport fishers took their toll. Their harvest when combined with the commercial catch that took on average 50% of the Skeena steelhead and a First Nations catch led to a situation where there were simply too many people killing too many fish.

However, as more fishing tourists came and the communities upriver grew, the sport fishery grew apace. More fish were killed. Fewer fish were available for the pan and fewer fish were making it to the spawning grounds. The incidental catches of steelhead by commercial and Native fishermen that took more than 50% of the steelhead run each year became the target of attention. By the mid-1970s, the conflict grew between the lower river commercial fishermen, the upstream sport fishers and Natives. The Natives just wanted to catch fish as they had done since time immemorial. The commercial fishermen assumed they had proprietary rights, while the people upriver saw tourism and sport fishing as the economy of the future. If their communities were to prosper, the number of intercepted steelhead had to be lowered. Conflict between the three groups grew.

The Skeena is home to all species of salmon, with historical runs of sockeye and pinks numbering in the millions; chinook, chums and coho in the hundreds of thousands; and steelhead in the tens of thousands. After nearly 100 years of commercial exploitation in the indiscriminate mixed stock fishery, all runs of salmon became depleted. The Department of Fisheries and Oceans (DFO) has, since its inception, catered to the canneries and the commercial fleet. More salmon was needed and vast sums of tax dollars were sunk into enhancement projects. Little did they know at the time that their success with enhanced sockeye projects, such as the Fulton River and Pinkut Creek on the Babine, would end up shutting down the commercial fleet at the mouth of the river. By the early 1990s, with close to 1000 commercial boats exploiting the enhanced run of sockeye near the Skeena's mouth, DFO was presiding over a driftnet fishery few fish could escape. The rate of coho and steelhead interceptions increased as did the conflict between user groups. But, change was in the wind.

In the early 1990s DFO pledged to reduce the commercial steelhead interceptions by 50% over a three-year period, i.e., 75% of the steelhead run would escape into the river. When this announcement was made, some commercial fishers threatened to retaliate and kill every steelhead brought aboard their boat. Others threatened to ignore the new regulations and fish closed waters. That the fleet was resistant to change is understandable: a way of life was threatened. Many grew up in commercial fishing families whose fathers and grandfathers fished from a gillnet boat. They were not about to change. New regulations such as area licensing and fewer fishing days, however, saw steelhead escapement increase from a low of less than 10,000 in 1991 to nearly 24,000 in 1996.

At the same time fisheries staff and conservation groups worked with upriver Native communities and they returned to selective-type fishing methods outlawed long ago by the government. This helped put more steelhead onto the spawning grounds. Also many recreational fishers had long ago adopted catch and release, but because the runs were in trouble, in 1989 total catch and release for upstream summer-run steelhead tributaries was implemented. The Steelhead Society of BC's Wild Steelhead

*With stars in his eyes, Jim Adams made his first trip
to the Kispiox in the early 1960s.*

Campaign, chaired by Rob Brown of Terrace, did yeoman's work in
the early 1990s to protect what was left of the diminished runs of
Skeena summer-run steelhead.

But another commercially targeted fish was to have a significant impact on Skeena River commercial fishers. "There are salmon
to be caught in the fast water of the Bulkley and upper Skeena,"
Pochin writes about the coho, once numbering in the hundreds of
thousands, in his 1946 book *Angling and Hunting in British
Columbia*:

> *During August and September when the cohoe run is
> on, it is possible to get a strike on every cast. Many
> will be hooked but few will be landed. Some will pull
> the scales down to eighteen pounds* (p. 120).

By the mid-1990s few coho felt the sting of a sportfishers hook
or swam into the lower river's nets, the fleet had fished the upriver coho stocks to near extinction. In 1998, David Anderson,

federal Minister of Fisheries, was determined that British Columbia
coho would not go extinct and DFO imposed severe restrictions on
the fleet, not just the Skeena's but coast wide.

DFO has operated a sampling station called the Tyee Test
Fishery on the Lower Skeena since 1956. From the numbers of
salmon and steelhead caught at Tyee, DFO extrapolates the abundance of steelhead for that year. From 1956 to 1997, Tyee records
show that the average escapement was about 20,000 steelhead,
with the lowest in 1957 of 8000. Included in the calculation of this
average are those strike years where the commercial fishermen did
not fish part of or the whole season; thus the 20,000 per year figure is a high average. Because of the coho's fight for survival, the
fleet has been severely restricted over the last three years. For the
first time in more than a century, the steelhead returned almost
unmolested to the Skeena with escapements of near 65,000 for
1998, 48,000 for 1999 and 55,000 for 2000 or an average of
52,000 fish per year.

Change is difficult for some to accept and some will go to their
graves still not accepting catch and release. With the 1998 returns,
a few residents in the Smithers area wanted to go back to the good
old days and kill steelhead. Accusations of elitism and two-tiered
fishery followed when many in the steelhead angling community
rallied against the kill fishery. It is noteworthy that when catch and
release was implemented, the same people wanted hatchery steelhead. These are the same people who complain about overcrowd-
ing and want preferred preference so they can have exclusive use
of a common property. When these people propose to eliminate or
restrict others from the fishery there is no mention on their part of
a two-tiered system.

You need to witness the crowding on hatchery streams like the
Kitimat, Vedder, Chehalis, Quinsum and Stamp rivers to appreciate
what crowding is. Hatcheries with their inferior products and ensuing crowds are the death knell of quality angling. The catch-and-
release Skeena steelhead fishery is world-renowned and even with
its increasing popularity—something that can and will be managed—it provides a quality fishery for wild fish, unknown to most
areas of the world. For the last three seasons, the same group lob-
bied aggressively for a return to a kill fishery. Peter Broomhall a
long-time steelhead fisher and conservationist says that:

> *it's time to separate angling and fish harvesting as sep-
> arate activities. Angling requires skill. Killing fish does
> not. Fishing can be sporting. Killing fish cannot.*

In the late 1980s and early 1990s, when the Pacific Stock
Assessment Review Committee (PSARC) established benchmark
escapements for Skeena salmonids, they established minimum
numbers needed to guarantee the survival of the species.
Accounting for the sex distribution necessary on the spawning
beds, that minimum for steelhead is 35,000. For three years now
the runs have exceeded that minimum of 35,000 and the coho
have rebounded as well. However, the steelhead, because it is the
least abundant species of salmonid, is the indicator species for the
Skeena watershed and needs special protection. The Skeena system, vast as it seems, is a small microcosm when you examine the
life and journey of steelhead in the North Pacific. Considering the
bigger picture, prudence dictates that we take a conservative

approach. Skeena steelhead are four to seven or more years old when they return on their first spawning run. Not taking into account habitat destruction from land use, to be on the safe side, it will take seven years of restricted commercial fishing to ensure that all steelhead stocks have had a chance to recover to anything close to approaching historic levels. However, the coho is a hearty fish and the Skeena stocks are rebounding. The skippers of the river-mouth boats idled during peak escapement times for three years, want to fish. DFO is currently considering moving from coho conservation to rebuilding the coho stocks and that change of emphasis means that there will be more commercial fishing. With DFO's

A Kispiox beauty.

25% steelhead interception rate, one thing is certain: as long as that amount of interception is allowed, the fleet will never change to truly selective types of fisheries and the weaker stocks of steelhead and coho will suffer.

Sport fishers along the Skeena and tributaries have plenty of opportunities to kill sockeye, pinks, chinooks and in places coho, as well as other game fish. The rebuilding of steelhead stocks has been a long and continues to be an ongoing struggle with sacrifices made by Native, commercial, and sport fishers alike. Summer steelhead are special creatures with a released fish providing many times more value to the local economy than a dead commercial, Native or sport-caught steelhead. Unlike our forefathers who viewed the animals and fish as creatures there solely for man's exploitation, our role now is one of stewardship. We are the only creature on this earth that has the option to give life over death. Catch and release of steelhead by commercial, Native and sport fishers is the only long-term viable solution for a fragile species that will continually be affected by man's encroachment on its environment.

Some of the Skeena's lower tributaries such as the Copper, Lakelse and Kalum provide winter fly-fishing opportunities for steelhead, but winter can be cold and it is usually not until March, April and into May—spring freshet permitting—that chucking fur and feathers becomes more appealing. Through the summer months, chinook are the main attraction. Few currently fly-fish for these large salmon, but they are attracting followers. Terrace guide Stan Doll's largest fly-caught chinook for the 2000 season tipped the scales at 53 pounds. In 1999, I sent Jim Yardley, Regional Director of the Ministry of Environment Lands and Parks a sample Black GP. "I just wanted to let you know that the dressing which you provided to me for the Black G.P. was very effective for Chinooks this season," Yardley reported in September, 2000. "I managed to land a total of 10 springs in July/August ranging in size from the low teens to the mid 40s including 7 on the Babine, 2 in the Skeena and 1 in the Kispiox. All fish were taken on the Black G.P."

But, the summer-run steelhead remain the main draw with most of the fishing for Skeena summer-run steelhead taking place during September to the end of October being the most popular part of the season.

Some rivers fish earlier in August and some will fish longer than October 31 if the weather is agreeable, but most who journey to Skeena Country in the late summer and early fall do so in those two months. In 1998, with the mild fall, local fly-fishers enjoyed fishing well into December. However, that is not usual. Usually around mid-September the frosty mornings of fall arrive, turning the aspens brilliant yellow and cottonwoods rustic orange. Any time in and around mid-October temperatures may stay around the freezing level all day. Frost-filled days can happen even earlier on high-elevation rivers such as the Sustut and Babine. Around the end of September, snow is not that uncommon, especially at the higher altitudes.

The Skeena steelhead runs start entering the river at Prince Rupert as early as late June and continue through early September with the bulk of the run going through in mid-August. However, on average, it takes about 3 to 5 weeks for steelhead to journey from tidewater to their natal stream.

The Copper and Kalum rivers at Terrace, both heavily glaciated streams, have steelhead from July through until the cold or the snows of late fall drive fishers from the river, usually mid to late October. Both rivers' steelhead are of a good average size and have some fish in the 20-plus-pound range.

The Kispiox River has some fish arriving in late August, but the bulk of the run arrives later in September and October. Of all the Skeena watershed rivers, the Kispiox has a higher proportion of larger fish with fish of 15 to 25 pounds quite common. And with some steelhead going into the 30-pound-and-larger range, this river provides the angler with chances at huge fish, but because of its accessibility it is often very crowded.

Bob Clay with a Kispiox River steelhead.

The Morice will fish through August and go into late October or later, depending on the weather. The Morice has a large number of small fish of around 5 pounds. Although the Morice has some fish in the 15- to 20-pound category, fish of 20 pounds are rare and a 15-pound steelhead from the Morice is a good one.

The Morice flows into the Bulkley at Houston and all Morice fish travel through the Bulkley to the Morice, for that reason there is steelhead fishing through August if water conditions are favorable. The bulk of the fish homing in on the Bulkley arrive through September and October. The Bulkley fish are of a higher average size than Morice fish, with those in the 8- to 12-pound range quite common and there is always a chance of larger fish. The Bulkley's character makes it an excellent fly-fisher's river.

The Suskwa, entering the Bulkley upstream of Hazelton, doesn't have a big run of steelhead but it does have some large ones that push the scales above the 20-pound mark. Suskwa fish can be found in the river as early as mid-August. It is one of the Skeena's smaller tributaries and best fished as it drops after a good rain.

The Babine fishes best from mid-September through October but has some fish showing as early as late August. Aside from the Kispiox, the Babine has the next largest average size steelhead with many fish in the 20-plus-pound range and some going into the 30s.

The Sustut has some early fish running through August that are heading to the upper part of the Sustut watershed. The lower Sustut fish migrating into the river below the Bear River confluence usually arrive through September and October. Although the run is not as large as other Skeena tributaries, the river has a good average size with a reasonable number of fish in the 20-plus-pound range.

As the steelhead make their way up the Skeena, and if the mainstem clears enough, there are fishing opportunities on some of the Skeena bars, mostly in the Kitwanga to Kispiox area, but even those lower down towards Terrace produce steelhead. However, the river water must have reasonable visibility. Rain frequents this watershed during the fall and it can be intense with all the rivers going out. The Skeena is probably the last to go, but it will also be the last to come back in after a big storm. But the angler who is there at the right time can experience catching some large fish in huge pieces of water. A thrill in itself.

A characteristic of Skeena watershed steelhead is their enthusiasm for rising to flies fished on or just below the surface in much lower water temperatures than on other steelhead waters. River temperatures vary through the season. In general you will find temperatures on many Skeena rivers in the mid to low 50s F. in the early part of the season and decreasing to about the mid 40s F. by mid-October, but sometimes earlier on the higher-elevation streams or if there was a cold fall. Perhaps that free-rising phenomena can be explained by the multi-year fry-to-smolt residence in fresh water and a short freshwater growing season where every feeding opportunity is taken, including the late-hatching Diptera flies common to most streams. Whatever the reasons, fly-fishers can consider themselves fortunate, because there are few more thrilling experiences in steelhead fly-fishing than presenting a fly on or just below the surface and having a fish rise and take that fly.

As night turned into dawn, the early morning became still. It was the silence that accompanies snow and when I looked out from the camper, flakes were fluttering to the ground. Working my way back up the Skeena Valley from Terrace on my way home, the snow followed me almost to Smithers. Not eager to wet a line this morning, I'd had a good trip, and today would be my last day to fish. I wanted to take one more steelhead from the Bulkley and christen my McVey bamboo rod with a summer-run.

In cold showers with a biting wind blowing, I worked my way down the run waking a Skeena Bee. If I wasn't watching the fly cross the current throwing its wake, I would have missed the surface disturbance as the fish came to fly. But it didn't take so I tried my usual changes of flies and when they produced no response I backed up and worked my way down using a smaller #10 Skeena Bee. Sometimes a steelhead will respond to a fly of different size— sometimes larger, sometimes smaller works. This time it was a smaller one that the steelhead took and after a good scrap I released a 25-inch male. I took my first winter-run steelhead on the McVey rod in April from the Lakelse and it was fitting that my first summer-run steelhead on the McVey rod came from Skeena waters too.

I liked the water and carried on fishing towards the hanging spruce tree. There I would call it a day. The #8 Woolly Bear Bomber waked across the surface and I saw and heard the boil. I knew from the noise and surface disturbance that this fish was much larger than the 25-incher just landed. It made no mistake on the next cast. I witnessed the fish shoulder through the surface taking the fly as it went down. A strong fish that taxed my rod as it ran and jumped, going into the backing a number of times. I was pleased when I slid the hook from the 35-inch male. Yesterday, my last fish from the Copper was a 35-inch female, which rose to the surface and took the same pattern in 40 F water, today the Bulkley was 43 F. What a river system and what fish!

References

Combs, Trey. *Steelhead Fly Fishing and Flies.* Portland: Frank Amato Publications, 1976.

Fennelly, John F. "Steelheading the Morice." *Northwest Sportsman*, July (1956): 8-11.

___. *Steelhead Paradise.* Vancouver: Mitchell Press, 1963

Large, G. Geddes. *The Skeena: River of Destiny.* Vancouver: Mitchell Press, 1957.

Pero, Tomas R. "Splendid Skeena." *Trout*, 31, 4 (1990): 22- 49.

Pochin, W. F. *Angling and Hunting in British Columbia.* Vancouver: Sun Directories Limited, 1946.

Railton, Jim. "Steelhead Grow Big." *Northwest Sportsman*, January (1955): 6-7.

Williams, A. Bryan. *Rod & Creel in British Columbia.* Vancouver: Progress Publishing Co., 1919.

___. *Game Trails in British Columbia.* New York: Charles Scribner's Sons, 1925.

___. *Fish and Game in British Columbia.* Vancouver: Sun Directories Ltd., 1935.

CHAPTER
13

The Thompson River

Greg Gordon knows it's easier to catch trout in shaded waters on the sun-baked Thompson.

THE YEAR 1969 WAS A MEMORABLE ONE. IT WAS THE YEAR in which I caught my first Thompson River steelhead. Some experiences are etched forever in a fisherman's mind and I remember vividly Jim Dobie, Joe Kambeitz and I fishing one weekend in late November, 1969. On Joe's recommendation, Jim and I had gone up river to a spot we had never fished before and Jim took a nice steelhead. I returned to that spot many times over many years but, although it is a good spot, I never managed to hit it right.

I needed a break from book writing and decided I would spend the last few days of the year on the Thompson. I arrived late on a Wednesday afternoon. On the afternoon I arrived, a quick fish from the Graveyard Run made my trip worthwhile. On December 29, 2000, I decided I would walk to that spot where Dobie had caught that steelhead so many years ago. With the river flowing cold at 39 F. I put on a three-inch-per-second, sinking tip with a Black Marabou General Practitioner, casting and doing a two-step through the run. The fish took me by surprise and I was pleased to

end the 30-year drought as I slid the hook from a 34-inch female. Life is good. Contented, I worked my way down river fishing likely spots. In just over two hours that morning I hooked and landed three steelhead, all females, all between 32 and 34 inches long, and all on the same fly. For a steelheader, what a climax to a 30-season dry spell—Thompson River steelhead season, the year 2000, the 20th century, the second millennium.

A river bed full of slippery cobbles, steep granular walls with hoodoos sculptured by the elements over thousands of years, and locomotives speeding along pulling mile-long trains on both banks are some of the sights that greet the fly-fisher as he sends his feathery creations over the crystal-clear waters of the mighty Thompson River. Warned by Greg Gordon that the trout had been fished hard for most of the summer and the fishing may be tough, we set off from our base camp at Savona on the late August day.

I sent my dry fly—a simple stonefly imitation consisting of bunches of deer hair stacked along the size-six, long-shanked hook with a hackle wound around the head—onto the water at the head of the run. Greased with dry-fly dope, it floated well, but the water reflecting the sunlight glistened, making it difficult to see the fly. My Polaroid sunglasses helped offset the intensity of the glare in the trying light conditions and, despite this, I lost sight of the fly but I followed the drift of my floating line. A tell-tale boil of a fish about where my fly should have been provoked my strike and I felt the weight of the trout. My Hardy fly reel singing, in seconds the trout had all my fly line and was well into the backing when it ended its run with a jump. Thompson River rainbows are grand fighters and because they show their mettle when hooked they have been a highly regarded fly-fishers' fish for well over a century.

Simon Fraser, the famed Northwest Company explorer, named the Thompson River after David Thompson, another company explorer and topographer. When Fraser made his epic journey to the Pacific Ocean down the Fraser, he camped at the forks of the Fraser and Thompson, a place the natives called *Cumshin*. On June 20, 1808, Fraser recorded in his diary that, "*We gave it the name of Thomson's* [sic] *River.*"

After the explorers and fur traders came prospectors in search of gold, and they were followed by Canadian Pacific Railway surveyors and engineers who trekked along the river's banks seeking a route for a trans-continental railway. Built in the 1880s, the line wound its way down the Thompson River and through the Fraser Canyon to the coast.

Seeking adventure with rod and gun on waters near the rail line, British sportsmen soon followed. H. W. Seton-Karr was one of the first to wet a fly for Thompson River trout. In "Letter XI., An Angler's Eden" of *Bear-Hunting in the White Mountains or Alaska and British Columbia Revisited,* he writes in July, 1890, he "*went eastwards, by the Canadian Pacific Railway, in search of 'angling adventures' on the almost unknown waters of the upper Thompson River* (p. 110)." He stayed at Spences Bridge and fished one evening, and says:

> *Some persons connected with the survey of the* [CPR] *line were camped here, and informed me that they had angled with natural fly every evening, but had never succeeded in capturing more than one trout apiece. However, with artificial fly I took eleven, the largest about a pound in weight; on the only evening I was there.* (p. 114)

Later, he writes:

> *The result of my visit to Spence's Bridge was to show that fair bags of trout can be caught with fine tackle and small fly (people in this country are in the habit of fishing with very large artificial flies compared to those we use in Europe) in the afternoon in those parts of the South Thompson* [This is the Thompson River, the South Thompson joins the North branch at Kamloops, miles upriver.] *which are rocky and not too swift, but not so much where the current is deep and rapid and the bottom smooth.* (p. 118)

With those observations about afternoon fishing, smaller flies, and types of water, Seton-Karr hinted at some things an angler needs to keep in mind when fishing the Thompson. The runs are huge and the trout can be very difficult to find. Also, they are more difficult to entice to a fly in bright sunlit waters than in the shaded waters of afternoon and evening.

A prime Thompson River rainbow.

The Thompson has good stonefly populations.

Two years after Seton-Karr journeyed through the Interior looking for sport with fly rod, Dr. T. W. Lambert came to British Columbia. Dr. Thomas Wilson Lambert, a native of Yorkshire, after graduating from Cambridge University in 1889 and holding house appointments and studying medicine at St. Thomas's Hospital, became a practicing physician in 1890. The Royal College of Surgeons of England has Lambert listed in their Medical Registry up to 1891 then his name disappears for a number of years. Soon after becoming a practicing doctor, Lambert emmigrated to British Columbia and in early 1892 became a partner of Dr. Furrer of Kamloops. Lambert remained in British Columbia for almost 12 years. During his practice in British Columbia he was appointed medical officer to the Western Division of the Canadian Pacific Railway and Royal Inland Hospital, and vice-president in 1897 and president in 1898-1899 of the British Columbia College of Physicians and Surgeons. In the early 1900s he returned to England, completed writing his only book, *Fishing in British Columbia*, published by Horace Cox in 1907.

When Lambert came to British Columbia, the Canadian Pacific Railway was the main link between the coast, Kamloops, and points east. Adventurers wanting to sample the fishing used rail to get as close as possible to their destination then either walked or rode horses into the backwoods. Combining personal experiences and reports from knowledgeable sources, Dr. Lambert documented the fishing available along the CPR line and other well-known British Columbia hot spots. Lambert was enamoured with the rainbow trout fishing in the Thompson River from that section of river paralleling the Canadian Pacific Railway's mainline from Savona to Spences Bridge.

The Canadian Pacific Railway wanted sportsmen to travel by train and stay at their hotels and lodges so they promoted the sport available in British Columbia and across Canada. In 1888, the first

of their many-paged guide-book, *Fishing and Shooting on the Line of the CPR*, appeared, and about thirty editions were produced, the last around 1918. Of course, the guidebooks promoted the fishing around their luxury hotels in the Rocky Mountains and not the Thompson River.

Contrary to what the railway guide books claimed about the fishing in the mountains, the Thompson's trout fishing was better. Of the rainbow fishing opportunities that British Columbia offered the sportsman of the day, and specifically those of the Thompson, Dr. Lambert offers this advice to British travelers contemplating a trip to British Columbia:

> *The streams and lakes in the mountains are too turbulent, and fed by too much glacier and snow-water, to make the best fishing grounds. The guidebooks of the railway speak highly of the fishing through the mountains, but there is better to be obtained lower down, and my advice to the traveler is to make no stop for fishing purposes until Sicamous is reached, at the head of Shuswap Lake where the Eagle River enters it. The Thompson River flows out of the lake at the other end, and the Shuswap Lake and Thompson River constitute the best fishing district of British Columbia....(pp. ix-x)*

The Thompson River trout fishing impressed Dr. Lambert and his description of the fish and the river is one of the reasons why, even today, many anglers travel considerable distances to challenge the river and its fish:

> *On the whole there is probably no fishing river in British Columbia to beat this one for the size and quality of the fish, though it does not afford the large bags that can be obtained on the Kootenay. It is a very*

sporting river, owing to the strength of the current, for a big fish is hard to hold if it once gets out into the main current, away from the side eddies. Mainly owing to this is the fact that there seems to be no record of fish over about 4lb., for a larger fish can get into the main stream, where the force of a ten-mile current drags on it and the line to such an extent that there is no chance of holding it. Such large fish are rarely met with, but every fisherman on the Thompson has stories of them, and they are all the same and coincide with my own. It was only once my luck to hook a really large fish. He jumped out of the water twice close to me, and I had a splendid view of him, and judged him to be about 8lb. He headed for the opposite bank, and just as a break was inevitable the fly came back. Other men have told me the same story, but such large fish are hooked so seldom that it is not worthwhile using a stronger rod and tackle. Though very large fish are undoubtedly plentiful, they seldom take either fly or any other bait, and perhaps deep live baiting would be the only means of success-fully fishing for them.

The average fish is from 1/2lb. to 4lb., but much larger fish are in the deep pools. I once was shown at Spence's Bridge three supposed salmon in the winter which had been speared and sold by the Indians for two shillings apiece. I noticed their perfect condition and bright red side stripe, and, on examining them more carefully, pointed out to an experienced fisher-man who was present, and to the proprietor of the hotel and others, that these fish were large rainbow trout. The largest weighed 15lb., the two others 12lb. apiece. This incident happened at Spence's Bridge, on the Lower Thompson. On another occasion of a visit there, the bar-tender of the hotel, who happened to be a young Englishman, told me that the angling editor of an American sporting paper had stayed off there and proposed to try with spoon and minnow for large rain-bow trout, which he had heard could be got. The next day they went to where the Nicola River, a large stream, flows into the Thompson about half a mile from the hotel. The angling editor was provided with strong spinning gear and rod, and much to the bar-tender's surprise, very soon got into a fish of most sur-prising strength and dimensions, for they saw him several times, and estimated him at the unbelievable weight of over 30lb. The fish took them rapidly down to some impassable rocks, and went away with every-thing but the rod. (pp. 14-16)

The last paragraph of the preceding Thompson River trout-fish-ing citation is the first written record of a steelhead played and lost on this magnificent river. However, from the 1890s to the mid-1940s, it was opined that steelhead were not strong enough to swim the fast-flowing, turbulent water of the Fraser Canyon. Our angling doctor was skeptical about this, but he reported what was

determined by the fisheries' scientists of the day: that steelhead abounded at the mouths and lower reaches of rivers. And in the case of the Fraser River, the fish found above Hell's Gate were rainbow trout, below steelhead.

Fellow Totem Flyfisher Bob Taylor has fished many years and claims that all expert fly-fishers are good observers and do question concepts that don't quite gel in their mind. Lambert, an astute observer and a knowledgeable, experienced fisherman, questioned the Hell's Gate steelhead/rainbow trout hypothesis:

It is hard to say how far the steel-head may run up the Fraser—probably at least as far as the Coquehalla [sic] at Hope, for up to this point there is nothing in the strength of the current to prevent it; but above, in the Fraser Canyon, the tremendous difficulties of the ascent may well stop its further progress. The steel-head has not developed the powerful tail and anal fin of the Pacific salmon, which must be a great aid to it in passing through such strong water for such immense distances. It may well be that the smaller tail

Thompson River summer-run steelhead are one of hardest fighting in the world.

Brilliant colours greet the fall steelheader.

of the steelhead renders it unfit for the effort. Otherwise, there would be no reason why it should not travel up the rivers as far as the salmon, just as the sea-trout does in European rivers. This is apparently not the case. The Fraser canyon appears to be impass-able to them, and they are only found in the lower tributaries of the Fraser and shorter coastal rivers. (pp. 68-69)

Once it was recorded that steelhead weren't strong enough to swim the Fraser, the myth about the impassability of Hell's Gate to steelhead lasted for about 50 years. However, at the time of the writing of Lambert's book, steelhead had been caught off the mouth of the Nicola River. The time of the year is October and the fish described in Lambert's passage are undoubtedly steelhead:

Mr. Inskip has within the last year or two written some letters to the Field describing the capture of a number of silver fish up to 10lb. weight near Spence's Bridge, at the mouth of the Nicola River, where it joins the Thompson. He believes these fish to be salmon, and it is possible that his view may be correct. But it is also possible that they may be silver trout or steel-head trout; the evidence is not yet complete. No salmon have ever been taken in this way with spoon or minnow above this point, in spite of the number of years that fishing has been carried on in these waters. The Indians never catch salmon by trolling with the spoon, though they troll persistently for trout, the line

being fastened to the paddle of their canoe.

Mr. Inskip states that these fish never take the fly, and he has only caught them in October. There is, of course, no doubt of the truth of his statement, and a possible explanation might be that the steelheads run up as far as this point, and go up to the Nicola River. It has never been thought that the steelhead runs as far as Kamloops Lake, and I have never heard of any-one who claimed to have caught one; it is, however, quite within the bounds of possibility that some of these fish may come up with the salmon. The problem can be easily solved by counting the rays in the anal fin; in the true trout these rays only amount to about nine, in the salmon there are fourteen to sixteen well-developed rays. (pp. 42-43)

Even though Lambert wrote these words about the Thompson River steelhead, the fish wasn't discovered until 1948 when *The Vancouver Sun* reported that the large rainbows that locals thought dropped down out of Kamloops Lake were in fact steelhead, return-ing from the sea to spawn. Lambert's book is a jewel, and packed with information on the Thompson River.

The best of the trout fishery takes place after the spring freshet has peaked in mid to late June and subsides during the months when it is hot. This is desert country with summer temperatures in the 80- to 100-degree range and sometimes higher. To enjoy trout fishing on the Thompson you should enjoy the heat. But during the fall when the temperatures are more comfortable and later often very cold, the steelhead return to the river and are the big attraction.

Most steelhead fishermen know that steelhead range in size from about three to over 30 pounds. Some rivers have races of steelhead of small average size, and some of large average size. Some steelhead run up short, coastal, low-gradient rivers, while others travel a couple hundred miles into inland drainages, often through turbulent, high-velocity sections of water passable to the fish only at certain times of year.

The Thompson steelhead are a race of superb, large-average-sized, summer-run fish. They start their migration through the Fraser River in late August, and the run continues through September into October and early November. The leaders of the Thompson River stocks show up in the Spences Bridge area in late September, with the bulk of the run arriving in October and November. They winter in the mainstem Thompson below Kamloops Lake and, in May, start into the tributaries for the June spawning.

On a trip with Roderick Haig-Brown, the legendary Tommy Brayshaw took the first on-record, fly-caught steelhead from the "Y" Run on November 13, 1953. Since then, the numbers of fly-fishers plying the waters have steadily increased, and now about a third of the rods chuck fur and feather. Thompson steelhead respond well to the fly, particularly those on floating lines, includ-ing "skaters" or "waked" flies. Bringing steelhead to the surface has its appeal, but many steelhead are caught using a deeply-sunk fly on the traditional down-and-across swing. Nonetheless, when you combine big, strong fish that respond to a well-presented fly with a big river, you have the makings for some spectacular sport. The great Thompson steelhead fly-fishing attracts anglers from all over the Pacific Northwest, Canada, the USA, and other parts of the world. However the river's size and the difficulty in reading its water, sends many home with tales of failure. Those who have learned the river's secrets, and are willing to work hard, have memories of a lifetime. More so if you happen to encounter some of the famous Thompson River "screamers."

There are rivers and there are "Rivers", and there are steelhead and there are "Steelhead." When the two unite, you have some of the most exciting fishing on earth. It takes a specific combination of river and fish before a truly exceptional fishery exists, at its best. Over the past 30-plus years of wandering, I have sampled over three dozen steelhead rivers and caught steelhead from most of them. Only one has drawn me back, year after year. This "River" is home to sleek large fish, is large, and the fish have plenty of room to show their mettle when hooked. That river is the mighty Thompson.

Steelhead runs are cyclic, the size of the run varying from year to year. Runs all up and down the Pacific Coast have suffered during the 1990s. In the past, commercial and Native interceptions took a good share of the run, but fisheries' managers have worked with both these groups to allow more steelhead to return to the river. However, ocean survival, habitat destruction and water extraction on the Nicola, Bonaparte and Deadman, the main spawning tributaries, all have had cumulative detrimental effects on the run. With only 850 fish on the spawning beds from the 1999 run, there was real fear that the mighty steelhead of this great river were in very serious trouble. However, in the fall of 2000 the early fishing through mid to late October, as well as the steelhead taken in the Albion Test Fishery, show a substantial increase in the run for this year. Catch-and-release regulations ensure that most of the fish that make it into the Thompson will make it to the spawning grounds as well as providing about twice the angling experiences per fish. Creel surveys show that the number of fish reported caught is about twice that on the spawning beds.

The Thompson trout and steelhead are quality fisheries even though they are anything-goes fisheries, with bait fishing allowed below Martel. A day's trout fishing can produce some fine fish, but certainly not great numbers. Steelhead fly-fishers have to work hard and will usually spend a number of days per fish, but every Thompson steelhead is a prize. There are also a number of fish and most seasoned pros who have fished the Thompson for a number of years, I think would agree, that about 25 percent of the fish hooked (usually females) have that little extra that puts them in a class of their own—the heart-stoppers. With the heart-stoppers, one moment you are swimming your fly through a lie, the next you have been stricken by a bolt of lightning. All your fly line and 100 yards-plus of backing are taken and you are scurrying out of the water to follow the torpedo downstream.

In January, 2000, I retired and through that year have many fond memories from my wanderings around the Province fly-fishing for trout and steelhead. Fresh on my mind though is an evening fishing for Thompson River trout with Greg Gordon. We had worked our way down river almost to Ashcroft and had reasonable sport, with Greg's lovely 22-incher the largest of the day. As the sun dipped behind the mountains, shading the river, we had time to fish one more run. I walked up to the top of a likely looking spot and sent my stonefly imitation onto the water. No sooner had it landed when a fish grabbed it. I landed it a little down river but because time was short I resumed fishing where I landed the trout. The fish went nuts over the fly and when I had finished the run, nine beautiful, hard-fighting 16- to 18-inch-long trout had pounced on that fly. Yes, magic things can happen on that river.

On October 25, 2000, I returned to the Thompson River. On my first day I found two fish and managed to yank the fly from the mouth of both fish. Steelhead encounters are hard earned on this river and one cannot make stupid mistakes. I wondered what kind of trip it would be. The next day I didn't make any silly goofs. I fished hard but didn't get a sniff. The third day proved better and half a dozen fish found my surface-presented flies appealing. But certain fish are remembered and often it is the first of the season. I was near the end of my pass through the run when the fish lunged and took my size-8 Bomber. In an instant the fly, fly line and considerable backing disappeared from my reel and a good steelhead cartwheeled from the water. Three or four times it took line and sent spray over the water surface as it jumped. As I slid a rosy-cheeked, pink-sided steelhead into shallow water, I thought to myself: this gorgeous creature is why I have returned to the river for 31 seasons.

As I get older, the cobbled banks and slippery wading become more challenging, and eventually I will have to give up wandering the banks of this mighty river. But may the steelhead and trout prevail so that future generations of fly-fishers can enjoy the thrill of line speeding off the reel from a magnificent Thompson River trout or steelhead.

References

Lamb, W. Kaye, ed. *The Letters and Journals of Simon Fraser 1806-1808*. Toronto: The MacMillan Company of Canada, 1960.

Lambert, T. W. *Fishing in British Columbia*. London: Horace Cox, 1907.

___. *Fishing in British Columbia*. White Rock: Pices Press, 1997 reprint.

Lingren, Arthur James. *River Journal: Thompson River*. Portland: Frank Amato Publications, 1994.

Seton-Karr, H. W. *Bear-Hunting in the White Mountains or Alaska and British Columbia Revisited*. London: Chapman and Hall, 1891.

14

The Tlell River

The coho is a grand game fish.

THE TLELL RIVER IS LOCATED ABOUT HALF WAY UP THE east side of Graham Island, the largest island in the Queen Charlotte archipelago. This group of islands is also known as Haida Gwaii, homeland of the Haida people. Tlell is a corruption of an ancient Haida word with numerous meanings: "land of plenty, land of berries or place of the big surf," writes Kathleen Dalzell in *The Queen Charlotte Islands* (1968).

The river flows tea-coloured. The river's tannin colour owes its origin to thousands of years of decaying vegetation in the cedar and spruce forest. At first glance you wonder how fish can see a fly, but the colour is deceiving and the water is really quite clear.

From about 1920, the Tlell has been known for its excellent cutthroat trout and coho salmon fly-fishing. Lee Richardson, from Seattle and no connection to the Eric Richardson family, in his book *Lee Richardson's B.C.* (1978) reports that George Shafer's 23 1/2-

pound coho and George Henrye's 5 1/2-pound cutthroat are the Tlell's largest fly-caught fish, large fish indeed.

"I caught a three-pound cutthroat," said young Dane Richardson to Bob Crooks as we drove into Richardson's Ranch located on the banks of the Tlell River. Crooks is teaching Dane to fly-fish and replied, "That's a good trout, I hope you caught it with a fly." "Yes," replied the eager young voice.

The Richardsons came to the Tlell in 1919 and, including Dane, six generations have lived on the property and five generations of Richardsons have cast lines into the Tlell. Dane's great, great grandfather was Eric Richardson. Of English ancestry, he farmed on the prairies and came to the Islands after he was advised by his doctor to seek a more moderate climate. On the first night at his new ranch, while eating dinner, he could hear a splashing coming from the river. When told it was salmon making the noise, he looked for himself and sure enough "the whole half-mile stretch of river was a solid mass of jumping fish."

Eric's grandson and current patriarch of the Richardson clan, Doug Richardson says that "his earliest memories of his grandfather was that of a man with a fly rod and cast of three trout flies." The ranch Eric Richardson bought had been worked for about a dozen years previously. But Eric Richardson was a fly-fisherman and was probably the first to cast a fly for the river's cutthroat, coho, steelhead and Dolly Varden. The Richardson Pool located in front of the main farm house remains one of the best on the lower river.

The Richardsons have provided room and board for fishermen coming to the area since about 1950. They also leased property to groups, such as the Tlell Anglers Club, whose members journeyed to the Tlell for decades. Since Eric Richardson first cast his flies on its waters, the Richardson's have been an integral part of the Tlell's fishing history.

Another family, the Nelsons, planted roots on the Tlell decades ago and added to the river's fly-fishing history. In the 1930s, Norman Nelson, of Nelson Bros. Fisheries, purchased a 160-acre homestead fronting the river from the highway, along and down to the foot of Beitush Road. In 1949 they replaced the old house and built a log fishing lodge that was used by family and friends until they sold it in the early 1990s. The Nelsons made two trips a year, one in May for cutthroat and another in mid-September for cutthroat and coho. About the fishing and popular patterns, Bill Nelson, nephew of Norman, says that, "the Tlell had excellent cutt and coho fishing and that the Mickey Finn, Mallard & Silver and Umpqua flies were favourites." Since he and his group introduced it to the Tlell in the 1960s, the Umpqua has earned high praise as both an excellent cutthroat and coho fly and remains the fly of choice for many to this day.

Near the end of the open meadow, close to where the Tlell's wooded banks start at the end of Richardson Road, you will see one of the quaintest structures on the island: Noel Wotten's tree house. Noel laboured to get the huge cedar stump from the forest and onto his property. Then, using his skill as an artist, he transformed the old stump into a fairy-tale cottage. Noel Wotten and his wife Barb Small provide lodging and also have an artist studio where they sell Wotten's art work and other local arts and crafts as well as books and fishing flies.

An ardent and expert fly-fisher, Wotten, wearing his French beret cap with his dogs in tow, is an unmistakable figure on the river when the cutts, coho or steelhead are in.

Bryan Williams' books are jewels of early information on British Columbia fly-fishing. In his first book *Rod & Creel in British Columbia* (1919) there is no mention of the Tlell or any other Queen Charlotte Island stream for that matter. That is understandable, Eric Richardson had just moved to the island the year it was published and had not explored the fly-fishing opportunities to a great extent. In Williams' 1935 book *Fish and Game in British Columbia*, the Tlell is the only Queen Charlotte Island river mentioned and it receives high praise. About the Tlell's fly-fishing, Williams writes:

> *Fly fishing for salmon, Steelhead, Cut-throat and Dolly Varden trout. Best time, June 1 to August 31. Boats available from hotel at Tlell.*
>
> *It is unquestionably one of the best Steelhead rivers in the province. They can not only be taken by spinning and with bait, but they take the fly freely also.*
>
> *There are three runs of Steelheads on this river. There is the usual winter run, then another in April, a small run somewhere about October. The time of these runs varies somewhat. The April run is the best for fly fishing.*

Noel Wotten's quaint cottage.

> *This river also has a good run of Cohoes [sic] in the fall, and they, like the Steelheads, will take the fly freely.*
>
> *Boats go from Prince Rupert to Queen Charlotte City every two weeks.* (p. 135)

A glowing report indeed. In his fly-fishing for salmon section in *Fish and Game in British Columbia,* Williams recommends a bucktail fly, popular to this day. Bob Crooks prefers the Umpqua and the Muddler Minnow for his fishing, but says that pink-coloured streamers and bucktails are popular for coho.

Francis Whitehouse, hearing about the fishing on the Tlell, spent six months in 1946 sampling the sport with rod and reel. In *Sport Fishing in Canada* (1948), he writes about the cutthroat:

> *There are three distinct phases (a) A run of fish to some four miles upstream to meet the humpback salmon fry coming down the river. This commences about the 3rd week in April and lasts well into June- the trout gradually dropping downstream. These cut- throats are very numerous but they average rather small. The lightest tackle will suffice. (b) A light run of cut-throats in July of better size in the lower reaches of the river. These apparently come in with the tide, following the sand launces. (c) A final run from mid- August of cut-throats anticipating or accompanying the humpback and coho salmon spawning runs. These trout usually have sea-lice around the anal fin, and in size run 1 1/2 to 2 1/2 pounds; the largest seen being 4 pounds 12 ozs., length 23 1/2 inches, girth 12 1/2 inches.*
>
> *For flies the common cut-throat patterns will serve. The "Tl-ell [sic] River bucktail" series as tied by John Slagboom... cannot be bettered. (p. 37)*

Later, in the same treatise about the Tlell's coho fly-fishing, he writes:

> *This river from September 10th to October 10th provides excellent coho fishing...Fly Fishing: rod stiff enough to cast popular streamers or bucktails, as large conspicuous flies are best, though they will take small flies. These river cohos [sic] will sometimes take a fly or spinner so close to the wading fisherman's knees, that as they feel the hook and leap in response, he gets well splashed.*
>
> *At the river's mouth and along the sea-shore in the vicinity—period end of August to mid-September—fly*

Dane Richardson casting his fly onto the Tlell's Richardson Pool.

A Tlell River cutthroat.

fishing in the surf offers fine sport. The fish are right inshore feeding upon sand launces, so the fisherman has but to reach them with his streamer fly...In the annals of salmon fly fishing anything more unique than wading in the surf and taking silver cohos of 10 to 15 pounds on a fly is hard to imagine. (p. 170)

Another testimonial to the Tlell and its fish is provided by Clark Van Fleet. In his book *Steelhead to the Fly* (1954):

> *This volume was to be confined to streams within the borders of the United States: but there is one unique, if relatively small, river which for those who have fished it can never be forgotten, and which deserves to be extolled. Along its reaches are to be encountered six salmonid fishes that come with a rea- sonable degree of readiness to an artificial fly. Thus you can experience almost every approach to the lure that you will encounter anywhere in wet-fly fishing for either trout or salmon. (p. 228)*

In the few pages he devotes to the Tlell, Van Fleet provides vivid accounts of battles with cutthroat and coho during his stay at The Dunes hotel. The hotel was built in 1926 by Madame Rajout, which she and her family operated for many years, selling it even- tually to John Slagboom. The hotels' amenities, setting, remoteness and the excellent trout and salmon fishing nearby in the Tlell River attracted well-to-do fishermen. In the early 1950s a group of wealthy fly-fishers offered Slagboom a deal he couldn't refuse. The syndicate who bought the property turned The Dunes into a private fishing club.

The Dunes was loved by the guests but, after it was sold to the syndicate, it caused some resentment in the community. The syn- dicate attracted local ire when they attempted to make the Tlell their exclusive fishery. They bought up land along the Tlell and restricted access to non-members, some of whom had fished those waters for decades.

During The Dunes' club heydays throughout the late 1950s into the 1960s, the daily limit was 15 trout a day and three days possession limit. Like most fishermen of the day, club members and others killed the larger cutthroat, releasing the smaller ones. With such generous limits those two- to four-pound, 5-plus-year-old cutts that made the Tlell cutthroat fly-fishing famous became fewer. With improved access to the island by ferry, an improved highway to Masset and air travel, more fishermen came and in the early 1970s the syndicate sold The Dunes to the Provincial government. In 1973, Naikoon Provincial Park was established and The Dunes became park headquarters.

Bob Taylor, spotting a dark fly-like object in the river mud, stooped down and after he washed it saw that it was a Purple Spey fly. Too large or not a colour that suited his preference he offered it to Ron Schiefke, one of our Tlell River fishing companions. Schiefke put it on his vest for drying and then away in his box.

Bob Crooks, the Tlell River Man.

After a late start, we had one hour before the morning tide started to flood the Picnic Pool water. I was having good success with my Black GP fished on a floating line, but this morning the fish didn't like Schiefke's flies or presentation. The truck on the opposite bank, we were going to wade the tail of the Picnic Pool before the tide's inflow trapped us on the river's left bank. When the tide starts running up the Tlell estuary it will back the river up for about five miles on a good high tide.

When the fish don't cooperate, sometimes changing flies keeps you fishing longer and instills hope. Looking in his fly box, Schiefke spotted the large Purple Spey given him by Taylor a day or two before and tied it to the end of his leader. Usually, we preferred to fish the outflow but, by this time, the tide was flooding well. If someone totally unfamiliar with the Tlell came, they would have thought that the river flowed north to south rather than the opposite.

Schiefke made one cast allowing the fly to work its way around to where the river's flow became quiet at the edge of the rip. The fish lunged at the fly and the next thing I witnessed was Schiefke's rod in full bend and a large coho breaking water. Coho are a fine game fish and this one showed its fiber with the runs and jumps typical of the species. Minutes lapsed before Ron edged it to shore. Using a mathematical formula to calculate its weight, Ron's coho would have pulled the scale's needle down to about 18 pounds.

Schiefke and Taylor have fished together for many years and I think through close friendship some unexplainable force influenced Ron to extract that fly out of his box and tie it to the end of his leader. None of us had ever used a purple fly for coho before and none of us had ever used a Spey fly for coho either. That fish not only turned out to be the largest of the 10 we beached that day, but the largest of the 12-day trip.

No treatise on the Tlell is complete without some words about the Tlell River Man. Let your imagination drift to a year many centuries in the future. Man through the third millennium wreaked such havoc on the earth's environment that he destroyed his civilization. After a long healing process, the few survivors re-colonize the earth and are exploring past civilizations.

On the banks of a river known long ago as the Tlell, archaeologists unearth a skeleton under a towering aged spruce tree. The skeleton, in odd-looking clothing, had funny-looking black shoe-type things up to its knees and an odd peaked cap on its skull. Buried alongside the skeleton was a nine-foot-long skinny rod made of a carbon substance with a round object fixed near the bottom carrying a green cord. A curved slender metal object with claret-and-golden body was fixed to the end of a nine-foot clear nylon string. Wrapped up its shank was a shiny material and a hair-type wing on top. A couple of metal boxes were also found with many of the same odd-looking furry things in clips. The archeologist dubbed the find "The Tlell River Man" and carbon dated it to sometime in the 21st century.

From books that had survived this long-destroyed civilization, they determined the skeleton belonged to man who, for a pastime, waved the long skinny rod in the air and threw the fur and feather contraption into the water to catch a fish. Even though burial of this kind were not allowed during the 21st century and before, further research revealed that the "fisherman" was secretly buried under the tree by his wife at his favourite fishing spot known as "The Meat Hole."

Those fly-fishers fortunate enough to have fished the Tlell any time in the past quarter century would know that Bob Crooks is The Tlell River Man. Crooks grew up in Surrey learning his fly-fishing skills on the Little Campbell River. He moved to Terrace, living there for a while. In 1974, looking for less crowded fishing waters, he came across to see what the Islands offered. Seeing the Tlell, it was love at first sight and he settled on a Hecate Strait property about a mile from the river. Even after 25 years of fishing the Tlell, Crooks still feels passionately about the river. He can be found on the river about 150 days a year, in his black gumboots, sporting his baseball hat, and waving his nine-foot rod with a claret-and-golden Umpqua on the end of his cast. Other days he visits the river just for a look-see and is involved in many watershed stewardship activities. It is his fiefdom, and he the river's master fly-fisher.

This morning I had caught a small coho, a number of cutts and Dolly Varden in the estuary. With my spring trip to the Islands nearly over, I wandered into the wooded section of river for the last afternoon of fishing. Bob Crooks and I had fished it a couple of days earlier and found eager cutthroat. As I worked my way down the run, I had a take from a fish that felt heavier than the cutthroat normally found in this part of the river. It didn't come back to my Muddler Minnow. I continued working my way down river.

Before I felt or saw the fish I knew the take was that of a steelhead. I can't describe why. This was April, the water was 46 degrees and winter steelhead don't rise to the surface that often to take a fly. But the surge of power in its first run and then its jump proved me correct. How many minutes I played that fish in the log-infested waters I don't know. The minutes seemed like hours as the bright sea-run steelhead ran and jumped through the still waters. Set up with my number-five Thomas & Thomas rod and eight-pound leader I experienced a long and exciting fight. With a jumbled mass of branches below I couldn't bring the fish to shore there. My only option was to coax the fish up river to a small uncluttered gravel patch just barely out of water, and even then to get it through the sticks and twigs common on the upper Tlell without the fish snagging something, would be a chore. The fish showed signs of tiring. I was edging it towards the landing spot when I noticed a loop of fly line protruding from the reel. The fish holding still in the river,

I stripped line from the reel to remove the loop. I was surprised when the line jammed, but not too concerned. I had played the fish for some time and had it to shore a couple of times. I thought there was ample line to play and land a tired steelhead. All I needed to do was land the fish and then work on the tangle. When I retrieved the line after one of the fish's many runs, the line had built up on one side of the reel and then collapsed over later-wound coils causing loose coils and a snarl.

No sooner had I made that decision when the fish decided to continue its upstream journey and took another run. Not the tired fish I thought, I watched in horror as the line flew from the reel. I was already knee deep in the tea-coloured water and wading deeper with the woody debris in the water was not easy. Suddenly, the fish had run the line tight against the jam and my tugging didn't free it. Hoping it might turn, I stretched my arm and bent as far forward as I could, but the fish increased its upstream effort. Disappointment comes in many forms. When the leader broke and line went slack I was disgusted with myself for losing a fish this way. With my fishless floating line trailing in the water, I gave the fly line a firm yank and the line freed. If only I had yanked harder!

It seemed forever, but when I looked at my watch only 10 minutes had lapsed. I tied on a Black GP, made a couple more casts and caught a 19-inch cutthroat, my last fish from the Tlell.

For those who had the time, from its earliest days the Tlell offered good fishing, but, until plane travel and the much-improved BC Ferries schedule, access has always been difficult. Through the last couple of decades, the excellent cutthroat and coho fishing has suffered. The decline in the coho runs was a direct result of too many commercial and sport fishermen taking too many fish. The Tlell coho spent much of their lives in Hecate Strait and have been exploited for years. Through the late 1980s the coho runs suffered but through the 1990s they plummeted all along the coast.

The coho is usually a three-year-old fish when it returns to the river, spending its first year in fresh water followed by two years of

"Place of the big surf," is one of the meanings for the word Tlell.

Charles Lingren's goal: to catch a coho on the cast fly.

sea feeding where it grows large. The sea-run cutthroat, typical of the Tlell River, however, spends much of its life in fresh water. Sea-run cutthroat, even in their saltwater forays, do not wander too far from their parental stream and often return to feed in the brackish waters of the Tlell estuary. It takes about six years to grow a 20-inch cutthroat weighing about three pounds.

A targeted sport fish for nearly three quarters of a century, the large cutthroat that Eric Richardson and Francis Whitehouse enjoyed are scarce now. In the 1980s and early '90s with coho in short supply anglers wanting something to eat took cutthroat. With most of the big cutts already gone, the 13- to 15-inch cutthroat population suffered. In the early 1990s, catch and release for cutthroat was implemented in the river and estuary.

After the disastrous 1997 coho season that resulted in a closure of the Tlell for coho fishing, commercial fishing for coho was curtailed all along the BC coast. With the implementation of catch and release for cutthroat and the curtailment of commercial fishing for coho, the job of rebuilding the stocks to the Tlell has begun. The Tlell River watershed, with marginal encroachment by landowners and with only 3-mile and Survey creeks being logged, is healthy. Time will tell whether stewards of the river such as Bob Crooks and Noel Wotten will see the three- to five-pound cutthroat and historic runs of coho, estimated to be about 20 to 25 thousand, return to the Tlell River. And as Francis Whitehouse in *Sport Fishing in Canada* said as he closed his chapter on coho: "May their numbers never grow less (p. 170)!" so future generations can enjoy catching coho on the cast fly.

My son Charles was starting his second year at the University of Victoria in early September. When I left Vancouver on my 1000-mile road and ferry journey north to the Islands, C.T. said, "Dad, I want to come to the Charlottes so I can catch a coho on the cast fly." A positive statement, perhaps too positive. Usually, we attempt to do something with never any guarantees. I said I would pick him up at the airport on that Thursday.

Just before 10 a.m. Friday morning we drove down Beitush Road, paralleling the Tlell River, parking at the wide spot in the road with the river about 100 feet away. We looked at the water, discussed where to start fishing and C.T. headed down. Three casts later a scrappy coho took his red-and-white bucktail fly. He was one proud young man when he slid the nine-pound coho on the beach. He came, he saw, he caught and he would return to school achieving his goal.

As soon as he landed the fish, a tall distinguished-looking fly-fisher was asking him questions. It turned out the man was from Germany and on a fly-fishing holiday. He told C.T. that he watched us pull up to the river, get out of the truck, walk to the river, cast the fly onto the water and catch a fish. He had fished two full days without success and wanted to know the secret of C.T.'s success. My son directed him to me and I told the fellow that C.T. used a sparsely dressed bucktail fly and a floating line, which suited the water and light conditions. And he worked the water, moving downstream after a cast or two through the run. The German was using a sink-tip and large gaudy fly. I am not sure how experienced he was but, set in his ways, he didn't change. For the next few days we often saw him fishing, I thought, not the best of water and not moving. While our group was catching coho quite often, he drew blanks. His trip nearly over, one day he proudly came over to me and said that he had finally caught his first coho that morning. Reward is often the result of perseverance and hard work. I wonder though how his trip might have turned out if he was a little more receptive and tried a sparser fly on a floater and fished more productive water. But like C.T. he did go home achieving his goal of catching a scrappy coho on the cast fly in the area of big surf.

Hopefully, the Tlell will remain unspoiled and the runs will increase so that future generations can enjoy the thrill of catching a cutthroat or coho in the river of plenty.

References

Dalzell, Kathleen E. *The Queen Charlotte Islands 1774-1966.* Terrace: C.M. Adams, 1968.

Richardson, Lee. *Lee Richardson's B.C.* Forest Grove: Champeog Press, 1978.

Van Fleet, Clark. *Steelhead to a Fly.* Boston and Toronto: Little, Brown and Company, 1954.

Whitehouse, Francis C. *Sport Fishing in Canada.* Vancouver: Privately printed, 1948.

Williams, A. Bryan. *Fish and Game in British Columbia.* Vancouver: Sun Directories Ltd., 1935.

15

Other Waters

The Pennask Lake Lodge was built by James Dole in the late 1920s.

IN A NEW LAND AND NEW WATERS, EARLY BRITISH Columbian fly-fishers were treated to a bounty of fish. Some great waters with good stocks of fish permitted skilled fly-fishers to blossom, producing famous fly-fishing waters. Scattered throughout the province are other waters that fly-fishers have enjoyed casting their flies on for decades. Present-day guide books list thousands of locations. This last chapter sums up a few other waters that have at least a half century of fly-fishing history.

Of the five waters featured in this chapter, the Stave is a meager remnant of a great river and has suffered the most by man's presence. The Pennask, on the other hand, with the protection it enjoys because so much of the surrounding lands are privately owned, has suffered the least.

Stave River: On old maps of the upper Fraser Valley near Stave Falls Dam about eight miles from the Fraser River, a dot marks the community named Steelhead. Years ago, curiosity got the best of me and I made the journey up to Stave Falls and looked around but

found nothing to indicate a settlement existed. I thought it must have been a grand river, with perhaps a run of summer-run steelhead that migrated above the falls, why else would they name a community Steelhead? However, early in the 20th century, the Stave Falls hydroelectric dam was constructed, blocking access to the upper river.

If there was a summer-run of steelhead above the Falls they were lost when the dam was constructed. Below the falls though, the remaining eight miles of river supported a fine winter-run of steelhead. About the river and its fish Bryan Williams, in *Rod & Creel in British Columbia* (1919), writes:

> It is one of the finest steelhead rivers in the Province for a man who has grit enough to fish in cold weather. To get the best steelheads you should fish in January and February: they run in March also, but only in limited numbers and many you catch would be out of condition.
>
> It is a good river to fish steelheads with a fly. Use one [of] either a Grouse and Claret or Jock Scott.
>
> In July and August some good fly fishing can often

be had. *The best flies are Tippet and Yellow, Tippet and Green, Royal Coachman, Teal and Green, Cow Dung, and Blue Doctor; sometimes also the Stone Fly.* (pp. 109-110)

Paul Moody Smith fly-fished the Stave before World War I and recorded some of his experiences in his journal. After journeying to the Stave from Vancouver, for Sunday, February 22, 1914, he writes:

Walked to the river in the morning. I went up and they went down. Caught three dollies going up, in Davis Pool. Went on up to Hinch's Pool and there caught 2 dollies over 9 lbs. and 4 steelheads, the largest about 19 or 20 lbs.

Total bag   4 steelheads
and   7 dollies
Approximate weight 80 lbs.
Burns and Sage caught 7 dollies and 1 steelhead.

What a day's sport! In 1929, the Ruskin hydroelectric dam was built five miles down river from the Stave Falls dam, eliminating the spawning water used by most of the winter steelhead. In the three miles of remaining river, fly-tossers chuck their creations year round for a few wild trout and salmon. Mostly though, they are after the hatchery runs of salmon, trout and steelhead. Long gone are the halcyon days of pre-hydroelectric development and the great catches of large wild steelhead, cutthroat and dollies from this once magnificent river.

Vince Sweeney cooking up some trout for lunch.

At 88 years old, Tom Brown is still casting his flies to Pennask trout.

Pennask Lake: A trip to the Pennask Lake Club is like going back half a century in time. Doc Spratley, Lioness, Carey Special and Pennask Lake Special fly patterns are favoured by the fly-fishermen. Because Pennask Creek provides ideal spawning habitat, the fish are plentiful, but not large. A fourteen-incher is often the catch of the day and an eighteen-incher a trophy fish. However, there are some smaller more difficult-to-get-to lakes not too far from Pennask that provide the ardent, agile angler with larger quarry.

Pineapple baron James Dole founded the Pennask Lake Club back in the late 1920s and all the original members were from the USA. Dole and other shareholders enjoyed the pristine setting and their journeys to Pennask for 20 years. Eventually, in 1949 the club was sold to a group of Canadians who formed a Society under the BC Societies Act called The Pennask Lake Fish and Game Club. Since its inception those that came fly-fished. Fly-fishing-only regulations did not exist in the province, but club members permitted no other method for members and guests. In 1970, British Columbia fly-fishers from Kamloops, Vancouver and elsewhere recommended that British Columbia introduce fly-fishing-only regulations to some of the province's waters. Three Interior lakes:

Peterhope, Salmon and Pennask became the province's first artificial-fly-only waters. Peterhope lost its special status as artificial-fly-only a few years back, but the regulation remains in effect on Pennask and Salmon. That restriction has been introduced to other waters as well.

It was a cold June day with fresh snow still evident on the road as we drove down the pine tree-lined gravel track to Pennask Lake Lodge. One member in his 90s had to bow out of his annual trip and I was asked to join the group as a replacement for the four-day trip. I joined Ted Wilkinson and Tom Brown, both shareholders in the club, and guests, Charlie Brumwell, Vince Sweeney, and Herb Randal. We fished usually two to a boat and rotated partners. Because this was my first time to the Pennask my companions made sure I fished all the popular spots. The cold, windy spring weather didn't improve. With few insects hatching, flies fished on sink-tip lines produced the best results.

I remember well the one morning Herb Randal and I went to Hancock Point and found fish eager to take our sinktip-presented

The sun sets on one of the many Interior waters favoured by fly-fishers.

flies. With about 30 fish landed in two hours, we had a good morning. The lunchtime cookout with warming camp fire proved a welcome respite from the biting wind. The fishing was on and off for the four days. Tom Brown, who was 88 years old and as enthusiastic as a youngster was my partner on the last day. The fishing was not good, the wind never abated and we had to fish sheltered spots rather than hot spots. We worked hard all day for the trout we managed to catch. As we were headed in for the day, Tom suggested we try Mitzi Island. In the lee of the island out of the wind I decided to try a size-14 Halfback fly and on four casts I took four nice trout. A most suitable ending to a pleasant trip with fine angling companions to a historic British Columbian fly-fishing spot.

Babine's Rainbow Alley: Near the western end of Babine Lake, the lake sides slowly narrow and then the water flows gently though wooded banks for three to four miles before it widens, forming Nilkitwa Lake. This section of slow-moving river with its gravel bottom abounds with stonefly, caddisfly and mayfly nymphs. But it's also the spawning grounds for some of the salmon running into the Babine.

In the spring, usually mid to late May, the salmon fry wiggle out of their gravely wombs and into the mouths of rainbow trout. So many rainbow trout have massed to reap the benefits of Nature's bounty that this section of river became known as Rainbow Alley.

Rainbow Alley has attracted fly-fishers to its banks for more than half a century. John Fennelly fished it in 1951 and in *Steelhead Paradise* (1963) claims that the Babine was already well known as a trout fishery because of the ease of landing float planes and the availability of hiring fishing boats from the First Nation's people at Babine. Flying to remote waters was a post World War II phenomena. Many fly-fishing explorers discovered productive waters, some by just flying over them and looking for fish in crystal-clear streams.

Rainbow Alley enjoys a fly-fishing-only, no-bait, single-hook-barbless regulation. The fly-fishing season begins with the salmon fry in May, and the fly-fisher has a myriad of silver-bodied fry patterns from which to choose. The "fry hatch" is followed by hatches of stoneflies, caddisflies and mayflies through June, July and August, with trout rising freely to a well-cast dry fly. In September, the salmon start spawning and the trout gorge on salmon eggs, with a single-egg pattern often doing the trick. This is a fine wilderness fishery.

Big Bar Lake: Back in 1919 when Bryan Williams *Rod & Creel in British Columbia* was released, Clinton was the northern terminus of the Pacific Great Eastern Railway. Originally called the Junction, Clinton came into existence in 1862 because it was located at the junction of the Douglas Trail and Cariboo Wagon Road. There are a number of good lakes in the area, "*the two best lakes are probably Big and little Bar,*" said Williams. In those lakes, the fish ranged from a pound to five pounds and "*almost any flies will do.*"

In *Fish and Game in British Columbia* (1935), about Big Bar,

Rear: Vince Sweeney, Ted Wilkinson, Tom Brown. Front: Charlie Brumwell, Herb Randal and Art Lingren.

which "*is essentially a fly-fisherman's piece of water*," Williams writes:

> *Fishing is to be had practically the whole season. Fly fishing is at its best from the middle of May until well on in July, then again later on when the water cools off. In early July there is usually a hatch of duns, that have a very light bluish-grey colored wings, with almost transparent pinky-tinged bodies. The trout feed on them ravenously; but as the hatch is confined to parts of the lake, wet fly fishing is always successful.* (p. 73)

In the same book, Big Bar Lake Lodge advertised that they give a "*special rate to business girls during July and August*" and that it was special place for fishing, boating, swimming and horseback riding. This lodge was the forerunner of the dude ranch.

The mayflies still hatch and provide good sport with a dry fly if you hit it right. And some fish grow large, with a few each year pushing the scales down to between 5 to 10 pounds. A popular summer vacation destination with a Provincial campsite, there are unfortunately no restrictions on this lake. Nonetheless, its clear water with marl shoals supports prolific insect populations and, for skilled fly-fishers, good sport.

Stellako River: Fraser Lake is not far from Francois Lake and these two large lakes are joined by the Stellako River. Arthur Bryan Williams in *Rod & Creel in British Columbia* (1919) reported that

the best way to fish this river, which has excellent fly-fishing for trout that run from one to three pounds, is to go and camp out and that the best fly-fishing is at the outlet of the lake in the Stellako River.

For many years, the river produced good fly-fishing, but like many British Columbian streams it had few restrictions and generous bag limits. As industrial activity increased, bringing more people to the area, the trout populations suffered badly. About a decade ago, it became one of the province's classified waters. Through a progressive management regime—with its June 1 to November 14 season, rainbow trout release, no power boats from the lake down to the falls and fly-fishing-only for the upper 2.5 miles—has once again become a blue-ribbon trout stream.

References

Fennelly, John F. *Steelhead Paradise*. Vancouver: Mitchell Press, 1963.

Read, Stanley, E. *A Place Called Pennask*. Vancouver: Pennask Lake Fishing and Game Club, 1977.

Williams, Andrew. "At the End of the Rainbow," *The Canadian Fly Fisher*. 2, 3 (Fall 2000): 16-20.

Williams, Arthur Bryan. *Rod & Creel in British Columbia*. Vancouver: Progress Publishing, 1919.

___. *Fish and Game in British Columbia*. Vancouver: Sun Directories Limited, 1935.

Appendix

Field & Stream Fishing Contest, Western Trout Fly-Casting Category

Field & Stream ran fishing contests for 67 years, starting in 1910. These are the prize-winning British Columbia fish extracted from records that I found or have in my possession. There are many gaps, especially in the first 35 years.

Year	Date	Angler's Name	River or Lake	Weight	Placing	Fly Name
1933*	?	Unknown	Okanagan Lake	15 1/2 lb.	second	Not given
1933*	?	Frank Darling	Capilano River	14 lb.	third	Not given
1933*	?	Not given	Capilano River	?	fourth	Not given
1933*	?	Frank Darling	Capilano River	12 1/4 lb.	fifth	Not given
1945	June 17	Heber Smith	Peterhope Lake	16 lb.	third	Home-tied
1947	August 7	J. Aldington	Somass River	16 lb. 11 oz.	sixth	Jungle Cock
1949**	July	Paul Moody Smith	Capilano River	15 lb. 12 oz.	sixth	Whiskey & Soda
1950	October 25	Eric S. Martin	Bulkley River	15 lb. 12 oz.	first	Harkley & Haywood pattern
1951	February 18	W. Jeff Germaine	Chehalis River	16 lb. 2 oz.	third	Optic
1952	December 14	Frank Vine	Allouette River	15 lb. 1 oz.	sixth	Lioness
1954	September 22	W. W. Thompson	Hazelton (Skeena or Bulkley?)	20 lb. 8 pz.	first	Skykomish Sunrise
1954	September 19	Bertram H. Woodruff	Kispiox River	19 lb. 8 oz.	second	Shrimp
1954	November 12	David H. Maw	Thompson River	19 lb. 3 oz.	third	Colonel Carey
1954	September 21	Louis Roux	Kispiox River	15 lb. 8 oz.	sixth	Carson
1955	October 6	George W. McLeod	Kispiox River	29 lb. 2 oz.	first (World Record)	Skykomish Sunrise
1955	September 24	Thomas E. Jacob	Kispiox River	26 lb. 9 oz.	second	#4 Georgetta Coachman
1955	October 10	W. W. Thompson	Kispiox River	25 lb. 10 oz.	third	Skykomish Sunrise
1955	September 17	Ralph Wahl	Kispiox River	16 lb. 12 oz.	sixth	Yum-Yum
1955	September 16	Enos Bradner	Kispiox River	15 lb. 12 oz.	eighth	Red Dragon
1955	April 27	Thom. H. Olin	Bella Coola River	15 lb.	tenth	Mop Fly
1956	September 19	Henry W. Perrott	Kispiox River	23 lb. 15 oz.	first	Fall Favourite
1956	September 13	Donald V. Redfern	Kispiox River	21 lb. 8 oz.	second	Marletta Special
1956	September 20	Dr. Charles B. Mincks	Kispiox River	16 lb. 4 oz.	fifth	Red Hackle
1956	September 27	Ralph L. Ward	Babine River	16 lb. 1 oz.	sixth	Grey Hackle
1956	September 17	Al Knudson	Kispiox River	15 lb. 4 oz.	eighth	Al's Special Spider
1956	September 8	Lowell S. Johnson	Skeena River	14 lb 15 oz.	tenth	Skykomish Sunrise
1957	September 21	Thomas E. Jacob	Kispiox River	28 lb. 4 oz.	first	Skykomish Sunrise
1957	October 9	Ken McLeod	Kispiox River	23 lb. 14 oz.	second	Skykomish Sunrise
1957	September 20	C. W. Johnson	Kispiox River	22 lb. 12 oz.	third	Skykomish Sunrise
1957	October 7	George W. McLeod	Kispiox River	21 lb. 9 oz.	fourth	McLeod Sunrise
1957	September 26	Buzz Fiorini	Sustat River	21 lb. 8 oz.	fifth	Home-tied
1957	October 29	Dr. W. A. McMahon	Bella Coola	14 lb. 15 oz.	eighth	Mop Fly
1958	October 20	W. A. McMahon	Kispiox River	14 lb.	third	Marletta
1959	October 6	Ken McLeod	Kispiox River	22 lb. 8.5 oz.	first	McLeod Bucktail
1959	October 2	Kay Brodney	Kispiox River	20 lb. 12 oz.	second	Fall Favourite
1959	October 13	John P. Walker	Kispiox River	19 lb. 8 oz.	fourth	Skykomish Sunrise
1959	October 12	George W. McLeod	Kispiox River	17 lb.	sixth	Skykomish Sunrise
1959	September 29	Donald V. Redfern	Kispiox River	13 lb.	ninth	Marietta
1959	October 1	A. W. Hempleman	Kispiox River	11 lb.	tenth	Marietta
1960	November 4	James R. Adams	Kispiox River	20 lb. 4 oz.	first	Red Comet
1960	August 24	Otis Hart	Kispiox River	20 lb.	second	Loon Fly
1960	October 20	Ken McLeod	Kispiox River	17 lb. 3 oz.	third	McLeod Bucktail
1960	October 24	John P. Walker	Kispiox River	16 lb. 13 oz.	fourth	Skykomish Sunrise
1960	October 13	George W. McLeod	Kispiox River	16 lb. 3 oz.	sixth	Skykomish Sunrise
1960	September 20	Donald V. Redfern	Kispiox River	16 lb.	seventh	Marietta
1960	September 17	Robert M. Levison	Kispiox River	15 lb. 4 oz.	eighth	Royal Coachman
1961	October 1	R. E. Young	Skeena River	20 lb. 4 oz.	first	Marietta

1961	October 2	George McLeod	Kispiox River	19 lb. 8 oz.	second	Skykomish Sunrise
1961	April 15	E. H. Rawlins	Kalum River	18 lb. 2 oz.	third	Home-tied
1961	October 7	Ken McLeod	Kispiox River	17 lb.	fourth	Skykomish Sunrise
1961	October 1	Elmore J. Wilson	Skeena River	16 lb.	sixth	Home-tied
1961	September 27	Donald V. Redfern	Kitwanga River	16 lb.	seventh	Marietta
1961	September 13	Adel Lockhart	Kispiox River	14 lb. 8 oz.	ninth	Home-tied
1962***	September 5	Lee Straight	Takla Lake	10 lb. 4 oz.	first	Coronation Streamer
1962***	October 8	Karl Mausser	Kispiox River	33 lb.	first	Kispiox Special
					(World Record)	
1962	September 8	Forrest R. Powell	Kispiox River	23 lb. 8 oz.	second	Royal Coachman
1962	October 13	Johm P. Walker	Kispiox River	22 lb. 12 oz.	third	McLeod Ugly
1963	September 5	Cecil V. Ager	Kispiox River	26 lb. 4 oz.	first	Home-tied
1963	October 14	Stephen E. Keough	Kispiox River	26 lb.	second	Mausser Special
1963	September 20	Lawrence Lovelace	Kispiox River	25 lb. 8 oz.	third	Skykomish Sunrise
1964	May 19	Arnold Cummings	Kootenay Lake	12 lb. 9 oz.	second	Black Ant
1964	September 21	Alf. E. Sealey	Kispiox River	23 lb. 2 oz.	first	Skykomish Sunrise
1964	October 17	Forrest R. Powell	Kispiox River	21 lb. 4 oz.	second	Royal Coachman
1964	October 2	James R. Adams	Kispiox River	18 lb.	third	Fire Orange
1965	October 12	Karl Mausser	Kispiox River	25 lb. 1 oz.	first	Kispiox Special
1965	August 15	Elizabeth W. Stokes	Dean River	24 lb. 8 oz.	second	Mop Fly
1965	August 16	Forrest R. Powell	Skeena River	22 lb. 10 oz.	third	Royal Coachman
1966	October 19	Andrew Jordan	Kispiox River	30 lb. 2 oz.	first	Skykomish Sunrise
1966	September 25	Karl Mausser	Kispiox River	27 lb. 2 oz.	second	Kispiox Special
1966	September 25	Kenneth B. Anderson	Kispiox River	26 lb. 8 oz.	third	Skykomish Sunrise
1967	October 22	Forrest R. Powell	Kispiox River	25 lb. 6 oz.	first	Sam 'n Daisy
1967	July 20	Denton E. Copple	Dean River	23 lb. 12 oz.	second	Home-tied
1967	October 20	Elmore Wilson	Skeena River	23 lb 4.5 oz.	third	Home-tied
1968	November 8	John P. Walker	Kispiox River	27 lb. 10 oz.	first	Thor
1968	September 7	Jack M. Jones	Babine River	27 lb. 8 oz.	second	Double-Egg
1968	October 31	Forrest R. Powell	Kispiox River	27 lb. 3 oz.	third	Royal Coachman
1969	October 28	Forrest R. Powell	Kispiox River	26 lb. 10 oz.	first	Royal Coachman
1969	August 4	Joseph E. Sladen	Dean River	24 lb. 8 oz.	second	Hand-tied
1969	October 17	Troy J. Ceschi	Kispiox River	23 lb. 12 oz.	third	Hand-tied
1970	October 24	Karl Mausser	Kispiox River	27 lb. 8 oz.	first	McLeod Ugly
1970	September 21	Floyd L. Griesinger	Kispiox River	27 lb. 8 oz.	second	Babine Special
1970	October 23	Ken McLeod	Kispiox River	27 lb.	third	Gray Ugly Fly
1971	October 11	Donald D. Larson	Kispiox River	27 lb.	first	Skykomish Sunrise
1971	September 23	Lorraine Ruggiero	Sustat River	22 lb.	second	Skunk
1972	September 25	Lawrence Lovelace	Kispiox River	26 lb.	first	Skykomish Sunrise
1972	November 15	G. Hetherington	Babine River	23 lb. 2 oz.	second	Fire Fly
1972	September 22	F. W. Brandenberger	Kispiox River	22 lb.	third	Royal Coachman
1973	August 23	Willis C. Barnes	Kispiox River	25 lb.	second	Home-made
1973	October 11	Donald D. Larson	Kispiox River	24 lb. 10 oz.	third	Lorain
1974	November 1	Frederick H. Boyle	Kispiox River	32 lb. 4 oz.	first	Home-tied
1974	September 15	Karl H. Mausser	Kispiox River	26 lb.	second	Kispiox Special
1974	August 7	Jerry L. Schroeder	Dean River	25 lb.	third	Pete's Special
1975	September 14	Floyd L. Griesinger	Kispiox River	21 lb 4 oz.	first	Babine Fly
1975	June 2	R. J. Billado	Trappers River	16 lb. 3 oz.	second	Peril Fly
1976	March 29	Gary W. Miltenberger	Bella Coola River	25 lb. 2 oz.	first	Morning Magic
1977	September 18	Vern L. Gurnsey	Babine River	28 lb. 8 oz.	first	Gurnsey Guru
1977	June 2	Don Erickson	Vancouver Island	16 lb. 6 oz.	third	Polar Shrimp

Notes

1. * 1933 prize winners information from a 1934 letter from Frank Darling to Jim Carlson.

2. ** 1949 PM Smith prize winner information from Smith's July 22, 1949 letter to *F&S* editor Mike Ball.

3. *** In 1962 the Steelhead Trout fly-fishing Category was introduced. In 1966, after four years the Steelhead fly-fishing Category was discontinued and entries reinstated in the Western Trout fly-fishing Category. In addition, starting in 1962 *Field And Stream* published only the three top prize winning fish.

Resources

Province of British Columbia

Tourism British Columbia: They produce a wide variety of tourist-related publications, including freshwater destinations. They can be contacted through writing to Tourism BC, Box 9830, Stn. Prov. Govt. TG, Victoria, BC, V8W 9W5 or toll free in North America 1 800-663-6000.

Fisheries Branch: The province is divided into 8 regions and each region has personnel who job is to manage the fisheries. They will provide or clarify fishing regulation but do not offer advice on fishing opportunities. Regional office's address and phone numbers are listed on the first page of the *Freshwater Fishing Regulations Synopsis*, available at all fishing shops or government agents' offices, in addition some information is available through the BC Fisheries Internet site at www.bcfisheries.gov.bc.ca.

BC Parks: Information on Parks Services can be obtained by writing BC Parks, 2nd Floor, 800 Johnson St., Victoria, BC, V8V 1X4 or through the Internet at www.env.gov.bc.ca/bcparks.

Fishing Adventures

Many freshwater fishing resort owners belong to the British Columbia Fishing Resort and Outfitters Association. A copy of their booklet can be obtained by writing them at Box 3301, Kamloops, BC, V2C 6B9, phone 250 374-6836 or by visiting their Internet site at www.bcfroa.bc.ca.

The Internet site called BritishColumbia.com offers information on fishing adventures as well.

Index

About the Author

KARLA WOODE

RECENTLY RETIRED, ART LINGREN HAS LIVED ALL HIS LIFE IN Vancouver and spent 37 years of his professional life supplying water and collecting and treating wastewater for the lower mainland's member municipalities. However, in his life away from work and through most of his adult life, Art has had an ever-lasting love affair with fishing steelhead and other British Columbia game fish. In that pursuit, he has traveled throughout British Columbia.

With a mound of experiences from these travels to call upon and his passion for the history of the sport, he has authored *Fly Patterns of Roderick Haig-Brown, Thompson River Journal, Fly Patterns of British Columbia, Irresistible Waters* and *Steelhead River Journal: Dean*. In recognition of those literary endeavors, in 1999 the Federation of Fly Fishers awarded Art with the prestigious Roderick Haig-Brown Award.

For many years, Art has been actively involved in fishing conservation groups, serving on the executive of the Steelhead Society of British Columbia, the Totem Fly Fishers, and the British Columbia Federation of Fly Fishers. When not involved in fisheries' issues, spending time with wife Beverley and son Charles or writing about his passion, he is usually planning his next trip.

About the origins of fly fishing in British Columbia, *Famous British Columbia Fly-Fishing Waters* is his sixth book In it Art provides an insight to the sport of fly fishing on those special waters where the sport developed and the fly fishers who laid the foundation for the fly fishers who came after. Some of British Columbia's waters became so well known, they attracted fly fishers from England, America and other parts of the globe. Some waters have suffered seriously from man's presence while others have been less so affected and remain world-class fly-fishing destinations.

More Excellent Fly-fishing Books!

FLY PATTERNS OF BRITISH COLUMBIA
Art Lingren

Lingren captures the allure of this region, providing us with a look at its fascinating history, as well as plenty of useful information on techniques and flies. In this beautiful all-color book, Lingren shares the patterns you will need to satisfy all of your B.C. fishing needs. 8 1/2 x 11 inches, 104 pages.

SB: $29.95
HB: $39.95
ISBN: 1-57188-068-2
ISBN: 1-57188-069-0

THOMPSON RIVER
Art Lingren

EACH RIVER JOURNAL TREATS IN-DEPTH ONE FAMOUS NORTH American fly fishing river on gloss paper with dramatic all-color photographs showing the river and its fishing in its different moods throughout the year.

Each book is authored by one experienced writer/angler; color photographs are contributed by professionals. Helpful area maps provide access information for anglers including river drifting, campgrounds, boat launching, shuttling, etc. There is insider fly-fishing help including timing of insect hatches, matching flies, lodging, guide and fly shop services, additional bibliography, map sources, phone numbers and addresses. *River Journals* provide traveling anglers an in-depth experience of one river per book and its fish and fly fishing

Thompson (B.C.) ISBN: 1-878175-47-5   14.95

DEAN RIVER
Art Lingren

Steelhead River Journal is a book series with each issue featuring one famous steelhead river in full color, authored by one writer who knows the river well. Color photographs show the river in all its seasonal moods. The angling history of the river is included as well as a fly plate showing the most productive patterns. A color map assists the reader in finding specific locations. Included is information about techniques, steelhead seasons, lodging, guides, tackle shops, and other sources of information for visiting anglers. Each book is printed on high-quality, 80-pound gloss stock, stitched and bound in a large 8 1/2 x 11-inch format.

Dean (BC) ISBN: 1-57188-116-6 $15.95

HATCH GUIDE FOR WESTERN STREAMS
Jim Schollmeyer

Successful fishing on Western streams requires preparation—you need to know what insects are emerging, when and where, and which patterns best match them. *Hatch Guide for Western Streams* is the third in Jim's successful "Hatch Guide" series. Jim covers all you need for a productive trip on Western streams: water types you'll encounter; successful fishing techniques; identifying the major hatches, providing basic background information about these insects. A full-color photograph of the natural is shown on the left-hand page, complete with its characteristics, habits and habitat; the right-hand page shows three flies to match the natural, including effective fishing techniques. 4 x 5 inches; full-color; 196 pages; fantastic photographs of naturals and flies.
SB: $19.95   ISBN: 1-57188-109-3

KAMLOOPS
Steve Raymond

This is a completely NEW EDITION done in full color and coffee table printing quality and size. Raymond has updated the entire book. Information about: the fish, lakes, insects, hatches, trout feeding habits, watercraft, personalities, history, fly tackle needs, fly selection, seasons, plus area maps, and fly plates and fly tying recipes. This is truly a great book that will inspire your next trip. 8 1/2 x 11 inches, 148 pages.
SB: $19.95   ISBN: 1-878175-73-4
HB: $25.95   ISBN: 1-878175-74-2

HAIR-HACKLE TYING TECHNIQUES & FLY PATTERNS
By Gordon Mackenzie

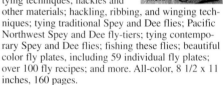

Very seldom, nowadays, is a new fly-tying technique evolved or a revolutionary fly pattern invented, but in this book Gordon Mackenzie utilizes and simplifies many aspects of using hair on a hackle to create durable flies. Hair hackles create a whole new look for flies, and they are far more durable. There are a vast variety of applications for using hair hackles.
Softbound ISBN:1-57188-252-9 $22.00
Softbound UPC:0-66066-00457-4
Spiral HB ISBN:1-57188-229-4 $35.00
Spiral HB UPC:0-66066-00483-3

STEELHEAD DREAMS
The Theory, Method, Science and Madness of Great Lakes Steelhead Fly Fishing
Matt Supinski

In *Steelhead Dreams*, Matt shares all you need to become a better steelhead fly fisherman, including: steelhead biology and habitat; reading and mastering the waters where they thrive; steelhead habits; techniques for all four seasons; effective presentations; tackle; plus best fly styles, casting tips, Great Lakes steelhead fisheries, tying tips, and so much more. Full color, 8 1/2 x 11 inches, 144 pages.
SB: $29.95   ISBN: 1-57188-219-7
HB: $39.95   ISBN: 1-57188-258-8

FLY PATTERNS FOR STILLWATERS
Philip Rowley

Phil has spent countless hours at lakes studying the food sources that make up the diet of trout; then set up home aquariums to more closely observe the movement, development, and emergence of the aquatic insects. In this book he explains the link between understanding the food base within lakes to designing effective fly patterns for these environs. Phil covers all major trout food sources for the whole year. He gives detailed information on each, plus how to tie a representative pattern and fish it effectively.
SB: $29.95   ISBN: 1-57188-195-6

SPEY FLIES & DEE FLIES
Their History & Construction
John Shewey

Spey Flies & Dee Flies is the most thorough and up-to-date book on these traditional flies and the methods and materials with which they are tied. Includes: in-depth historical information cited straight from the letters, books, and other writings of the first tiers; step-by-step photos and instructions for flies and useful tying techniques; hackles and other materials; hackling, ribbing, and winging techniques; tying traditional Spey and Dee flies; Pacific Northwest Spey and Dee fly-tiers; tying contemporary Spey and Dee flies; fishing these flies; beautiful color fly plates, including 59 individual fly plates; over 100 fly recipes; and more. All-color, 8 1/2 x 11 inches, 160 pages.
SB: $29.95   ISBN: 1-57188-232-4
HB: $45.00   ISBN: 1-57188-233-2

READING WATER
Darrell Mulch

Understanding water currents and how different flies react to them is at the heart of fly fishing. In this very thoughtful book, Darrell Mulch presents his ideas concerning fly types and water dynamics and how you should approach the stream. His drawings are extremely helpful for anglers wanting to know more about recognizing and approaching the different lies fish prefer. 8 1/2 x 11 inches, 64 pages all-color.
SB: $15.00   ISBN: 1-57188-256-1

FEDERATION OF FLY FISHERS FLY PATTERN ENCYCLOPEDIA

Over 1600 of the Best Fly Patterns
Edited by Al & Gretchen Beatty

Simply stated, this book is a Federation of Fly Fishers' conclave taken to the next level, a level that allows the reader to enjoy the learning and sharing in the comfort of their own home. The flies, ideas, and techniques shared herein are from the "best of the best" demonstration fly tiers North America has to offer. The tiers are the famous as well as the unknown with one simple characteristic in common; they freely share their knowledge. Many of the unpublished patterns in this book contain materials, tips, tricks, or gems of information never before seen.

As you leaf through these pages, you will get from them just what you would if you spent time in the fly tying area at any FFF function. At such a show, if you dedicate time to observing the individual tiers, you can learn the information, tips, or tricks they are demonstrating. All of this knowledge can be found in *Federation of Fly Fishers Fly Pattern Encyclopedia* so get comfortable and get ready to improve upon your fly tying technique with the help of some of North America's best fly tiers. Full color, 8 1/2 x 11 inches, 232 pages.
SB: $39.95   ISBN: 1-57188-208-1
SPIRAL HB: $49.95   ISBN: 1-57188-209-X

Ask for these books at your local fishing or book store or order from:
1-800-541-9498 (8 to 5 P.S.T.) • www.amatobooks.com
Frank Amato Publications, Inc. • P.O. Box 82112 • Portland, Oregon 97282